The DELAWARE FINNS

OR

THE FIRST PERMANENT SETTLEMENTS IN PENNSYLVANIA, DELAWARE, WEST NEW JERSEY AND EASTERN PART OF MARYLAND

BY

E. A. LOUHI

D1232346

CLEARFIELD

Originally published
New York, 1925

Reprinted for
Clearfield Company, Inc. by
Genealogical Publishing Co., Inc.
Baltimore, Maryland
2001

International Standard Book Number: 0-8063-5103-9

Made in the United States of America

To the Venerable Memory of the

Forefathers of the American Nation

CONTENTS

Page

Introduction 7

Chapter

I. The Finnish emigration to Sweden, from where their
path led to the American shores.. 17

II. Motives and inducements that led Sweden to establish
a colony on the Delaware River... 23

III. A colony established on the Delaware River................. 27

IV. The second expedition. The Dutch withdraw from
the company. Dutch colonists coming to the Dela-
ware 31

V. The third expedition. Finnish colonists brought to
the Delaware River 35

VI. The fourth and the fifth expeditions. More Finnish
colonists brought to America.. 45

VII. The sixth, seventh and eighth expeditions. The Finns
beseeching the queen to be permitted to go to America 51

VIII. The ninth and tenth expeditions. The Finns flocking
to get passage for America.. 57

IX. The Delaware settlements under the Swedish admin-
istration 65

Chapter   Page

X.   The Delaware colony conquered by the Dutch............ 73

XI.   New expeditions of Finns arriving at the Delaware
        River 81

XII.   The first period of the Finnish settlements under the
        Dutch rule.. 89

XIII.   England replacing Holland as the ruler of the South
        River 123

XIV.   The first period of the Finnish settlements under the
        English rule.. 129

XV.   The second period of the Finnish settlements under
        the Dutch rule... 153

XVI.   The second period of the Finnish settlements under
        the English rule.. 161

XVII.   The third period of the Finnish settlements under the
        English rule.. 207

XVIII. The last stages of the Finnish settlements on the
        Delaware 269

INTRODUCTION.

THE Finns or the Ural-Altaic peoples are a very ancient race, who were at their height of supremacy at about the sixth and fifth millenniums before the beginning of the Christian era. They dominated then a great area in the Eurasian continent, including the vast steppe region from Mongolia to the rivers Pruth and the Danube, and to the eastern Baltic shores in the west. In the south it embraced the Iranian plateau, Mesopotamia, Asia Minor and Egypt. The islands of the eastern part of the Mediterranean Sea also were included in the domain. In the east and in the southeast the boundaries of this domain are most clearly traceable today for the radical difference of the Ural-Altaic and the Mongol languages. Where the lake names in the map end with "kul," "kal," or "gol," that is ancient Ural-Altaic territory and where they end with "nor," it denotes that the territory was originally occupied by the Mongol peoples. All these words mean "lake."

The Iranian plateau was the center of the Ural-Altaic civilization during the seventh and the sixth millenniums B. C. It was in these regions, and further to the north, where the soil was first cultivated and animals domesticated by man. In these regions likewise metalurgy was invented and man's earliest picture inscription was developed into a syllabic cuneiform writing.

Mesopotamia became occupied by the Ural-Altaic peoples before the seventh millennium B. C., and it was in the valley of the Euphrates and the Tigris that the Ural-Altaic civilization rose to its zenith. Here in the lower valley, a nation of city states, Sumer, developed. The Uralic or Finno-Ugrian name "Sumer" indicates a marshy region, just as was the original aspect of the

7

country before it was traversed by a drainage canal system. The Erythrean Sea, (the Sea of Separation), or the modern Persian Gulf reached much higher up the valley at this period, so that the rivers Euphrates and the Tigris emptied to the gulf in separate outlets.

Egypt, although being not occupied by great numbers of the Ural-Altaic peoples, owes its civilization solely to this race. The Egyptian civilization was founded and carried on to its highest development by the Ural-Altaic peoples. When they emigrated to the valley of the Nile, they have not left a dated monument, but they have left an imperishable testimony of their presence in Egypt, in the old Egyptian language, in the Hieroglyphic writing and in the early Egyptian pottery.

The author of this book, at the time of the discovery of the Tutankhamen tomb, inquired into the Egyptian Hieroglyphs and to a great surprise found several hundred derivations and words of the same root as the respective words used today in the Finnish language. Besides that the old Egyptian language contained many grammatical forms analogous and typical to those of the Finno-Ugrian languages. Among these is the prodigious use of suffixes by the people who initiated the Hieroglyphic writing in Egypt. The early Egyptian scribes likewise had in their language three numbers,—singular, dual and plural. This existed in the Finno-Ugrian languages up to 2500 B.C., and is still retained in the Finnish dialects spoken by the Ostiaks and the Voguls in the northwestern Siberia and by the Lapps in the northern Europe. The plural of nouns in the Old Egyptian was generally formed by adding "t" like in Finnish. The conjugation of the verbs was likewise similar to Finnish. Besides no articles were used and the possessive pronouns were represented by suffixes, all of which make the Ancient Egyptian nothing less than a Finno-Ugrian language.

Modern discoveries in the sites of ancient Sumer and Elam, whose people were Ural-Altaian, have established as a fact that the early picture writing of Elam, Sumer and Egypt was originally the same and that the early pottery of these three countries was likewise identical. The early home of the ceramic art may have been Elam.

The earliest known name for Egypt was Kemi. This is a Finno-Ugrian name which simply means "a stream." There is a river of that name today in the Northern Finland and another in the Eastern Karelia. Later the country as well as the river began to be known as Nile or Niile. This is likewise Finno-Ugrian name which means "to creep" and undoubtedly refers to the annual creeping of waters of the river over the country. The aboriginal Negroid Egyptians had several names of their own for the country and the river, according to locality. Egypt is the name applied to the country by the Greeks and is a comparatively new name which may have been derived from Hakeptah, which is the Egyptian name for Memphis, the ancient capital of Egypt.

By the time of the emigration into Egypt the islands of the eastern part of the Mediterranean Sea also fell to the dominance of the Ural-Altaic peoples. Of these Crete became the most important, and like Egypt it developed a civilization of its own pattern. Some of the blond, blue-eyed descendants of the Uralic colonists still exist in that Island today.

At the close of the fourth millennium B.C., the purely Ural-Altaic culture production had passed its zenith in Mesopotamia. The Sumerian civilization had exhausted itself, but it had developed a new people of vigor, to carry on the achievements of the parent civilization and in its turn to suckle and guide new civilizations, that were going to sprout up along the Mediterranean coast and among the barbarian intruders from Europe to the Iranian plateau and the Caucasus regions. There had been going on a Semitic immigration to Akkad, a neighbor of Sumer in the Tigris Euphrates valley, whose people also were Sumerians. These immigrants, coming from the wilds of Arabia, absorbed the Sumerian culture, the religion, the art of building and the cuneiform writing. The Semites finally became so dominant in numbers that a new speech, the Babylonian language was born for commercial and everyday use. The Sumerian however remained the language of learning and the sacred language of religion. It was cultivated in the sanctuaries throughout the whole endurance of the Babylonian empire, that was later born and continued so even after Babylonia had passed to history, almost to the birth of Christ. The mysterious inscription, as told in the story of the Book of Daniel, that appeared on the wall of the royal palace in Babylon when Belsharusur or the Biblical Belshazzar was feasting with his lords and ladies of the court, while Cyrus was preparing outside of the walls of the city for his sanguinary night attack, was plain Finno-Sumerian language which then was the language of learning and religion of Babylonia, like Latin in Europe during the middle ages. The inscription "Mene mene, tekel, upharsin," of which the Book of Daniel gives a complicated interpretation and which has been baffling modern scholars who have made many ridiculous translations of it, simply means word by word "go, go, on way a disaster," or in better English "wake up, wake up, a disaster is coming." The words "mene" and "tekel" still today retain their daily use in the language of the Finns.

Of all the ancient Ural-Altaic nations, Elam had the greatest endurance and the most eventful history. Situated in the mountainous country northeast of Babylonia, it could be easily defended against foreign attacks. The Elamites were a warlike people and in several periods they held the Mesopotamian countries under their suzerainty. It was as late as 645 B.C., when Ashurbanipal with the Assyrian army succeeded to enter Susa, the capital of Elam. The temples and palaces of Susa were then destroyed and the enormous riches in precious metals, that had been collected during millenniums, were carried to Assyria. Elam did not have energy thereafter to rise into a dominant position.

Among the Ural-Altaic nations in the Asia Minor, the Hittites played the part of a world power, which was in its height of greatness at about 1400 B. C. The Hittites were the first ones who worked iron and also invented the art of making steel. They supplied Egypt of most of her needs in metals and metal products.

Of the smaller Ural-Altaic nations in the Asia Minor, Lydia deserves to be noted for her contribution to commerce of the uniform minted money. While the Etruscans, who emigrated from the Asia Minor to Italy and were the true founders of the Roman civilization, deserve an honorable mention. During the four millenniums B. C., the forefathers of the people of Finland lived in the central Russia, where their kinsmen still in part survive. As they lived peripheral to the centres of Ural-Altaic civilization and were surrounded in the north by Mongol nomads and in the west by Indo-European savages, they were not able to develop a monumental civilization of their own. Their main occupation was agriculture and cattle raising. Metal working arts were also highly developed and through the Russian Finns these arts, as well as the knowledge of cultivating soil and keeping domestic animals, spread among the Germanic hunting and fishing folks in the central Europe and in the Baltic regions.

The southern coast of the Gulf of Finland became more tightly occupied by the Finnish peoples during the last centuries before the birth of Christ, by the advance of emigrants from central Russia. While at the middle of the first millennium of our era, a slow emigration of Finns took place over the gulf to the southwestern parts of Finland and overland to the eastern part of the country. Before the emigration of Finns to Finland, the country was sparcely occupied by the Lapps and by few Scandinavian settlers in the southwest. The new immigrants who became dominant in the country in course of time, were known by their national names. Those that came oversea to western Finland were known as Taueesti or "further Esthonians" and those who settled by land to the eastern part of the country were known as Karjalaiset or "cattlemen." Finally the Germanic peoples started to call the new occupiers of the land as Finns, after Germanic name of the land. The Finns themselves had an ancient name Suomaa, for the country, which means "marshland," and of this the present national name of the country, Suomi, has been derived. In their national language the Finns call themselves Suomalaiset or "people of the marshland." Finland formerly was full of marshes, left by the glacial epoch which ended about 6000 years ago.

Writers generally quote the ancient Roman historian Tacitus when they write about the Finns. This is an error, as Tacitus wrote in the latter part of the first century A. D., while the present people of Finland were not then known as Finns and Tacitus therefore could not have meaned them by his Fenni.

The Laplanders, who belong to the brave Mongol race, have been the neighbors of the Finnish peoples so long that they even have lost much of their original language and acquired the Finnish. Their kinsmen were the earliest inhabitants of the Scandinavian peninsula, although long since assimilated to the present inhabitants and it is interesting in this connection to note how Norway received her name. The Mongols called the lake "nor" and applied the same name to the long narrow strips of water that penetrate the country from the ocean. As the "nors" were the only feasible ways of communication in the highly mountainous land, the country became known as "Norvegr," "Nordvegr," "Northweg" and "Northvegia," which all mean "lake-way" and hence the "country of lake ways" or the "country of fjord ways." In comparison we may note that the Irish earlier called the Norsemen as Lochlannac or "Lakeland men," and Norway as Lochlann or "Lakenand." Of this original Mongol word "nor" as the basis, have been derived a great number of words in several languages, as "north," "Nordic," etc. In the Finnish language the north is anciently called "pohja," which means the "bottom of the world" and all words referring to the north are derived of that name.

In Finland the Lapps had given names to the principal lakes before the arrival of the Finns. In their Mongol tongue, which under the Finnish influences had become corrupted, they called the lake "jaur," from the original Mongol name "nor." The Finns adopted the Lapponic name for lake, only changing it to "järvi" to harmonize it with the Finnish language. The original Finnish name "kulju" for lake is applied today in the Finnish language only to a small lake or to a pond.

While the Ural-Altaic peoples in the Southern Russia had been constantly disturbed by the aggressiveness of Indo-Germanic peoples, the Finns lived alone in the Central and Northern Russia in peace and tranquillity. It was only after 375 A. D., when the Ural-Altaic Huns retaliated against the Germans and Slavs, and some Slavs were forced to seek peace among the Finns in the north that some trouble could be expected. For a long time however the people lived together in peace and two Slavic nations developed in the midst of the Finns, about the Lake Ilmen. These were called by the Finns as Slavjanit and Krivitsit. The Slavs adopted the democratic form of the government of the Finns, there were no kings nor princes, but the nations and government units were headed by elected elders or presidents. In the middle of the ninth century, the Scandinavian Vikings did no longer satisfy themselves by robbing expeditions but began to linger in the land and levy taxes upon the peaceful Finns and Slavs. After three years the people however succeeded to unite and drive the foreign bandits out of the country. But the former peaceful life did not return, the people had learned violence from the expelled parasites and internal disturbances ensued. Finally the nations became into an agreement to install foreign princes as their rulers and a commission was elected in 862 A. D., to go to Sweden, where a great number of pirate chiefs were known to exist, of which to elect suitable men and fetch them to Russia. The Finns, occupying the seashore, had the ships and took the commission to Sweden. There they elected as their princes three Viking brothers, Rurik, Sineus and Truvor, among which the Finno-Slavic country was divided. These princes with their families settled in the Finnish towns as the capital of their respective domains, which indicate that the empire was in the beginning more Finnish than Slavic. As the Finns call Sweden Ruotsi, from the word "ruotsaa" or "to row," which was the occupation of the Viking sea rovers before they learned to use the sail, the new federation became known among the Slavs after the nationality of the rulers and retains it in the present Russian national name Rossiya. The Finns however called the country Wenäjä, which name they apply to Russia today. This comes from Wäinäjoki or the Dwina river, whose upper course was the Finnish territory that received the earliest Slavic immigration.

After two years of the establishment of the triad government, two of the princes died, leaving Rurik, the elder brother alone to rule. He now deemed it advisable to move from his capital, Laatukanlinna, a Finnish town on the southern coast of Lake Ladoga, to Novgorod, a Slavic town, which was situated more in the centre of his domain. As Novgorod now became the seat of government and the chief military depot, the commerce likewise concentrated there, which all worked for the advancement of the Slavic element of the country. In 882, Oleg, the successor to the throne after Rurik, marched with his Finns and Slavs against Kief, which was conquered and made the capital of Russia. This conquest made the Finns to cease to be the backbone of the new Russian power and the Slavs gained the dominant position in it. The vast Finnish territories in the central and the northern Russia became thereafter the prey of the aggressive descendants of Rurik. About the headwaters of the Volga river old agricultural Finnish nations existed, with numerous cities and "lins" or forts. Here the descendants of Rurik made themselves, one way or other as princes of the cities. One of these princes, Yuri, had married a daughter of an elder of Merja, a Finnish country, which centered in the fork of Volga and its tributary Oka, including Moskva or Moscow and Kremlin, both of which retain their Finnish name today.

Yuri's sons having been born in Susdal, an ancient city of Merja, and being Finns from their mother's side, were so much more acceptable to the "ancient and high inhabitants" of Merja. After Yuri's death in 1157, Kief fell into decadancy for internal strifes between the Slavs and Vladimir in Merja then rose as the capital and its half Finnish rulers thereafter were regarded as the supreme rulers of all Russia. Merja with its Finnish inhabitants became the nucleus of the nationality who called themselves the Great Russian, who made Russia what she once was and ruled her as well.

As to the physical characteristics of the Finns, they are light complexioned, with very white hair when children, but in the later years the hair turns to tow-color or reddish. Black hair or black and brown eyes scarcely exist among the Finns. Blondness is the original characteristic of the entire Finnish race, although for climatic environment and assimilation with other races is nowhere so striking today as among the Finns of Finland, Esthonia, northern and central Russia and in parts of Siberia. The eyes of the Finns are dominantly blue, but often also light gray. The stature approaches tallness. The head form is dominantly round-skulled and the brain capacity, according to existing data, the largest of all men. Writers, who have not seen Finns, generally attribute "high cheek bones" to them. This is an error, as the smallest percentage of prominent cheek bones can be found among the Finns than among any other people of mankind.

The Finnish language, being the oldest tongue spoken by man, has not failed to acquire a development consistent to its great age. During the last twenty-five years attention has been paid to utilize the natural beauty of the language and as a consequence in the National Theatre in Helsingfors one may today listen to the most harmonious and sonorous speech of man.

CHAPTER I.

The Finnish Emigration to Sweden, from Where Their Path Led to the American Shores.

AT the beginning of the second millennium of our era, Christianity had won much following in Europe and the people were enthusiastically spreading the idea among the infidels and pagans. The Scandinavian sea rovers, after hard opposition, had adopted this new religion and as newly converted always, became the most enthusiastic supporters and propagators of the "true religion." In this high spirit of enthusiasm, and also for the reason that some of the Finns had acquired the habits of the Vikings and were beating them in their own game by robbing the very homes of the Vikings, Erick Jedwardson, king of Svea, made in 1157 a crusade to the city of Turku, in the southwestern Finland and at the point of sword Bishop Henry, a Scotchman, baptized the inhabitants into Christianity. With the aid of these newly converted Christians, new crusades were made in Finland and during the following couple of centuries all the Finns became baptized and at the same time subjects to Sweden.

At the first half of the sixteenth century, Sweden and Finland became the supporters of the Lutheran doctrines, as students from these countries had become acquainted with them in the University of Wittenberg in Germany. This change went on without opposition from the people, as Christianity in its Catholic form had remained rather external among them. The Catholic church domains in Sweden and Finland were confiscated by the state. Also king Gustaf Vasa of Sweden acquired some 2000 land estates for his own benefit. As Gustaf Vasa was a man who appreciated wealth, he endeavored to have these lands cultivated for his benefit, therefore the Finns were welcomed for this, which caused a migration of people from Finland to Sweden. After the death of Gustaf Vasa, a Catholic reaction set in. Prince Juhana, his youngest son, had been given a part of Finland as his dukedom. Juhana married a Catholic princess Katherine of Poland and became influenced by her. Juhana's son Sigismund, who had been raised as Catholic, inherited the crown of Poland and Sweden and had his abode in the Polish capital Vilna. Another son of Gustaf Vasa, Carl, who had his dukedom in Sweden, became the opponent of Sigismund and endeavoring to increase the man power of his own domain, influenced many Finns to settle as pioneers in the uninhabited forest lands of his territory. This again caused more migration of Finns to Sweden. Most of the Finnish nobility sided with Sigismund in his controversy with Prince Carl and one of them, Klaus Fleming, who held the highest office after the king in Sweden, that of State Marsk, besides being the Governor-General of Finland and Esthonia and the commander-in-chief of the Swedish-Finnish armies and the navy, halted the army and the navy in Finland as they were returning from a war with Russia. During the time preparations were made of an expedition against Prince Carl in behalf of Sigismund and while negotiations were going on to separate Finland from Sweden and make her a principality under Poland, Admiral Fleming as the prince, the soldiers were billeted with the peasants, who were required to house and feed them without compensation, as was the custom in those days. A part of the army was mercenaries of all nations, who did not sympathize with the peasants and even the own men were brutalized by continuous warfare. The soldiers assumed mastery in the peasant houses and committed atrocities, becoming a pestilence to the country. The peasants were complaining that, "We have no peace in our homes, some of us have been killed, other so badly beaten that they never will recover." The peasants of Northern Finland were especially dissatisfied against the billeting as they had been exempted of it by Juhana, in return of guarding the northern borders of Finland against Russian invasions. As petitions directed to Fleming, by the peasants, did not bring release, the peasants sent their delegation to Prince Carl in Sweden, who, while expressing his sympathy, could not do anything else but advised the peasants to take the law into their own hands. This the peasants did and at the end of 1596 two armies of the peasants of Northern Finland started a movement toward the south, clearing the country of the billeted soldiers. Simultaneously there were peasant uprisings in the Central Finland. However, as the peasants were poorly armed and untrained the peasant movement was crushed by Fleming's trained and well armed troops, in the course of fourteen months. Retaliations followed and the position became worse than ever for the peasants. Many of the peasants were forced to escape for their lives to Sweden, where they were welcomed by Prince Carl, were given land and enjoyed his special favors when Carl soon became the king of Sweden.

By the Finnish migrations and colonizations in Sweden, purely Finnish communities were born, called by the Swedes as "Finnmarker," or Finlands. Between 1600 and 1650, Finnish pioneer settlements were found all over in the state forest lands, in the provinces of Angermanland, Medelpad, Helsingland, Gestrikland, Dalarna, Westmanland and Vermland, in the south-central Sweden. The Finnish colonists in these provinces amounted to 13,000 souls. Also in other provinces, as in Sodermanland, Nerike and Upland were found a number of Finnmarker, and in the East Gothland and West Gothland were found likewise few Finnish settlers.

The Finns retained their own language and in the larger settlements built their own churches. For some time everything went well with the Finns in Sweden. They had got their farms cultivated and became the envy of the Swedish peasants, who did not look favorably on these foreigners. Then there was going on the Thirty Years' War in the Central Europe at the first half of the seventeenth century, Sweden taking the leading part in the war. This war required much copper and iron in the armaments, and by exporting copper king Gustavus Adolphus of Sweden endeavored to realize money to conduct the war. And it so happened that these metals were found in the mountainous forest lands where the Finnish pioneers had settled. As the mining industry was in the hands of the nobility, government officials and men of influence in the kingdom, whose habit it was not to buy land that they might have use of, but to apply means to get it vacated for them. A strong weapon in their hands to force the Finns to vacate their lands was the pioneers' method of putting land under cultivation by burnbeating. By this method the forest is cut down in the autumn, the timber, suitable for building and for firewood, is taken away and in the spring the branches were burned and grain sown into the ashes, which gave a good crop for three years. After that the land was left for reforestation or put under cultivation permanently. This method of cultivation was considered destructive to the forest and had been prohibited by law, but the Finns in the mountain lands and marshes hardly suitable for cultivation, used this method as their privilege for pioneering and which had been so understood and even granted to them.

As the metal industries consumed much charcoal, for Sweden has no coal, much forest was used for the production of charcoal. The wartime shipbuilding industry also figured in the consumption of forests. The forests in the central Sweden became fast consumed and this was all more or less credited to the Finns and their method of cultivation by burnbeating. It is logical that the Finns could not open their farm plots in the forests where they were assigned to pioneer and to let the forest grow over the plot too. This the mine owners used for their own benefit with the government. The Finns therefore fell in disfavor with the government and the Swedish peasants took advantage of it by setting up to drive away the Finns, burning their homes and massacring the peoples. In the province of Vermland where was a great Finnish population, the Finns endeavored to protect their homes and a regular war was fought between the Finnish pioneers and the Swedes. There were suggestions among the Swedes to kill the Finns off entirely and in some instances this was carried to the letter. As the homes and fields of the Finnish pioneers were destroyed, many of these families were hiding in the forests and mountains, seeking their living by hunting. But the hunting being subject to restrictions, these refugees became chased for game pouching. Others in their destitute were seeking employment at the mines and farms and became branded as vagrants. On September 4, 1636 an order was issued commanding all Finnish vagrants to leave Sweden and to return to Finland before the Walpurgis night of 1637, on pain of being put in irons and kept to work on the government's castles and estates.

These persecutions and massacres of the Finns in Sweden were going on while their more fortunate brethren were shedding their blood in the Central Europe for the glory of Sweden. In exchange of their blood the Swedish flag had been raised over almost all territories around the Baltic Sea. In the Thirty Years' War they won to Sweden the eternally glorious name of the Liberator of Religions. The Finnish cavalrymen swam their ponies over the Vistula the Danube and the Rhine like to a fiest, in going to meet their opponents. And under the heavy sabres of these brawny, broad shouldered bears of the North, nothing could stand. "Hakkaa päälle," (strike on), was the Finnish command for a charge and in the churches of their opponents were prayed "God deliver us from Hakkaa päälles." The Finnish infantry troops considered themselves favored by the Swedish kings, when they were drawn up to stand for the greatest burden of the battles. The incomparable soldiery of the Finns had just then made Sweden one of the great powers of Europe.

Sweden as a great power was then planning a colony on the Delaware River, and when colonists were needed it was found a good way to get rid of the Finns in Sweden by prevailing upon them to go to America, or by sending them forcefully to the colony.

CHAPTER II.

Motives and Inducements that Led Sweden to Establish a Colony on the Delaware River.

BEFORE the advent of the seventeenth century, Swedish foreign commerce and navigation had been during several centuries entirely in the hands of the Hanseatic League. This commercial power had now collapsed, but during the first half of the seventeenth century two-thirds of the Swedish foreign commerce was carried on Dutch vessels. Sweden had made good in the fields of war and her national pride and self respect had been awakened by the growing political importance. She was now endeavoring to develop everything in her own nationalistic lines. The Swedish language had displaced Latin as the language of religion and learning and now many Swedish commercial enterprises, to take the foreign commerce and navigation into their own hands, were established under the government's patronage and endowment.

In the autumn of 1624, a Dutchman, William Usselinx, founder of the Dutch West India Company, went to Sweden as king Gustavus Adolphus was then visiting home from the battle fields. Usselinx had an audience with the king, in which he interested Gustavus Adolphus for colonial trade. The king was a willing supporter to the ideas of Usselinx and offered him freedom to establish a company in Sweden to carry out these plans. A few days later Usselinx had his draft of the charter for "The South Company" ready and issued a prospect in which he had encouraging words of praise to the Swedes and hints to the fabulous riches to be had in the lands behind the oceans. The governors, mayors and counsellors of the cities and other officials were commanded to aid and assist the founder in raising subscriptions for the company's capital stock. A charter of privileges was also issued to the company. In the name of the king the charter says: "We have maturely considered it, and as far as is in our power we have sought to bring about that the advantages, profits and welfare of our kingdom and our faithful subjects, as well as the propagation of the Holy Gospel, might be in the highest improved and increased by the discovery of additional commercial relations and navigation."

Usselinx was very successful in receiving subscriptions for the company's capital, the king himself subscribed 450,000 dalers. He sold the stock to bishops, to the members of the council of state, generals, admirals, to the nobility and to the cities. He made a trip to Finland and to the Baltic provinces and was everywhere well received on account of his royal recommendations. But to collect the money from the subscribers proved to be a difficult task. The field had been badly exploited by enterprises that ended in failure, besides there was a great stringency of money on account of the heavy expenses of the war that was then going on, and furthermore, most of the subscriptions were from the aristocracy to whom to apply law would not have been advisable. Even old man Gustavus Adolphus never paid a penny on his subscription. Usselinx collected money enough for his salary and expenses and did not get discouraged, but, while years passed by, he enlarged the scope of the company, drafted new charters and gave from time to time to the company a bigger name. In one of his prospects, issued in 1626, he says that: "His Majesty's dominions would be enlarged, his treasury enriched, and the people's burdens at home diminished, if every good subject would contribute to put this plan into execution, without waiting to see what others would do. Then there would be no want of money to carry it into effect, and the kingdom, through the Lord's mercy, would have another eye, and its prosperity and riches would increase beyond what it had never done before. The public taxes would be lessened, and would be afterwards very light; and in process of time, every industrious man would thrive. And lastly it would greatly tend to the honor of God, to man's eternal welfare, to his majesty's service, and the good of the kingdom; in short, it would be highly beneficial to the whole nation."

In the beginning of 1629, Usselinx left Sweden and traveled in France, Spain, Portugal and Holland interesting the crowned heads and governments to his commercial schemes. But in 1632 we meet him again in the headquarters of the Swedish armies in Germany where an extension to the old charter was drawn up with the sanction and approval of Gustavus Adolphus. The territorial restrictions of the old charter were removed and the entire world was to be its field of activity. The king took interest in the prospect, but on November 6, 1632, he fell in the battle of Lutzen. The chancellor of state, Axel Oxentierna, who became the head of the government of Sweden during the minority of the king's daughter Christina, endeavored to carry out the wishes of the king and on May 1, 1633, signed a commission for William Usselinx as general director of the "General Commercial Company." In the following month Usselinx published at Frankfort-on-the-Main a general summary of his prospects in two books, the "Argonautica Gustaviana" and "Mercurius Germanica." In the Argonautica he says that the company would increase the prosperity of all Europe and the participants especially, it would spread the gospel among heathen peoples, redound to the honor of God and it was sure to become a noble jewel of Sweden and the German land.

During a convention of the Protestant League at Heilbronn, Germany, in the spring of 1633, Usselinx's projects were laid before the assembled nobles of Protestant Germany. And in each convention of the league Usselinx was busy in distributing his prospects and in interesting the members of the conventions to his scheme. In the convention at Frankfort in 1634 it seemed that his great idea was going to be carried into operation, but on the next day bad news arrived from the battle field. The Swedish-Finnish and Protestant German armies, under the Finnish field

25

marshal Kustaa Horn and Prince Bernhard of Weimar, for the latter's engaging into a decisive battle contrary to previous decisions, had suffered a defeat and the war was thereafter continued with varying fortunes for a time. All attentions were now drawn strictly to the war and Usselinx was left to oblivion, but he had paved the way for others to carry their plans in the same line into operation.

CHAPTER III.

A Colony Established on the Delaware River.

IN the course of the Thirty Years' War, Sweden had developed to be one of the greatest producers of copper, but the copper market was now flooded and new consumers for copper were sought. As much Swedish copper was lying in the warehouses in Amsterdam, a Dutch merchant Samuel Blommaert interested the Swedish commissioner in Holland, Falkenberg, in the copper trade in the West Indies. Blommaert was a director of the Dutch West India Company and knew well the trade conditions in America. The Dutch merchant interested in the matter also another business man of Holland, Peter Minuit, who had been governor of the Dutch West India Company's colony, the New Netherland, in America, but had become in disagreement with the Dutch company and was looking for new employment. Minuit was desirous to establish a company in the pattern of the Dutch enterprise, but could not do it in Holland, as the charter of the Dutch West India Company prevented all competition in that country. Both gentlemen knew well the statutes of the Delaware River, Blommaert having even been interested in some land there. Minuit proposed a trading expedition to the Delaware under the Swedish flag and drew an outline for a colony on the west side of the river, which was to be called "New Sweden." A dozen of soldiers were to be taken there to guard the occupied places and suitable persons to trade with the Indians and to cultivate tobacco. Of the expenses of the expedition the Dutch promoters were to furnish one-half and the Swedes were requested to furnish the other half. Minuit sent his proposition to Oxentierna at Stralsund, Germany, in June 1636, and in the meeting of the Council

27

of State at Stockholm on the following September 27, these plans were discussed.

While these negotiations were going on, another promoter, Joachim Stumpff of Hamburg, Germany, was interesting the Swedish government in the same lines, giving new impetus to the matter. In one of his letters to the Swedish government Stumpff says: "The Spaniards have sailed to America 144 years and have gained immence riches, for it is well known what Spain was before she began to sail to these regions. It would bring to Sweden eventually a larger income than the entire revenues of the state; it would supply means for carrying on the war against the Papists, and it would give a base for attacking the enemy in their weakest spot, for the King of Spain is nowhere so easily attacked as in the West Indies. That is his heart."

Minuit was sent to Sweden to carry out his plans for the expedition and arrived at Stockholm in the beginning of March 1637, while Blommaert was to manage the company's affairs in Holland. Admiral Klaus Fleming, one of the before mentioned Finnish noble family of Flemings, who was one of the five men assigned to rule Sweden during the minority of Queen Christina, was appointed as the general director of the company. No salary was attached to this office, Fleming was to do this as one of his duties in the government, and had already transacted the correspondence with the Dutch promoters. The Swedish share of the company's capital had been subscribed by the members of the Swedish government, Fleming having subscribed a part of it.

Preparations were now made by Fleming and Minuit for an expedition to the Delaware River. A charter of privileges was granted to the company, including the sole right in Sweden to trade in America from Florida to Newfoundland, and all articles brought from America were to be free from duty. Supplies were bought in Holland and merchandise for trade, as duffels and other cloth, axes, hatchets, knives, pipes, mirrors and looking-glasses, gilded chains and finger-rings, combs, ear-rings and other trinkets for the Indian trade. Also wines and distilled liquors for trading in the West Indies. Two ships, the Kalmar Nyckel and the Fogel Grip had been prepared by Fleming for the voyage, and after many delays the expedition left Gothenburg in the beginning of November 1637, Minuit as commander and all the officers, except one, and most of the sailors, soldiers and servants were Dutch. On the North Sea the ships met a heavy storm, were separated from each other and arrived in Texel, Holland, both badly leaking and Kalmar Nyckel having lost her main mast. The ships had to go through heavy repairs and new provisions had to be secured, which all tended to raise the cost of the expedition much higher than were the estimations. But Blommaert confronted the Swedish stockholders in his letter with the hope that "a good, rich Spanish prize will be able to pay it all." The relations of Sweden and Spain were not very friendly at this time. Spain had attacked and confiscated Swedish ships, and in order to retaliate, the Swedish ships were heavily armed with guns by the admiralty and orders were given to attack Spanish ships where ever seen.

The voyage over the Atlantic was successful and the ships sailed up the Delaware about the middle of March 1638, where Minuit bought some land from the Indians, on the west side of the river, sailed up the Minquas Kill about two miles and chose for a site of a trading post the peninsula where the city of Wilmington now stands. At the point of this peninsula he built a fort, which he named Christina, after the girl-queen of Sweden, while the Minquas Kill he called "the Elbe," now known as Christiana Creek.

Soon after the arrival, Minuit sent the Grip to Jamestown, Virginia, to exchange some merchandise to a cargo of tobacco, but was denied the freedom of trade there without the permission of the King of England. Therefore the ship returned to Christina, where her cargo was unloaded, after which she left for the West Indies, on May 20, 1638, and in conjunction with a fleet of pirates was praying upon the Spanish silver fleet. Meanwhile Minuit after having made necessary arrangement and leaving his brother-in-law Henrick Huygen as commander of the trading post, proceeded on board Kalmar Nyckel, about the middle of June, to the Island of St. Christopher, where some wines and distilled liquors were exchanged to a cargo of tobacco. While at the island, Minuit with his skipper were invited as guests on board a Dutch ship when a sudden storm arose driving the ships out to the sea. Kalmar Nyckel returned to the harbor after the storm was over and having waited many days for the return of Minuit, she set sail for Sweden and Minuit was never heard again. On her home voyage, the Kalmar Nyckel again met a storm in the North Sea, near the coast of Holland. The main mast had to be cut and the vessel suffered other damages, making it necessary to put into Vlie for repairs. On arrival at Medemblik the ship was put under arrest by the officials of the Dutch West India Company, who claimed the sole right to trade on the Delaware River. She later however was released and arrived happily to Gothenburg in the beginning of the year 1639.

The Grip returned to the Delaware River in the spring of 1639, after having cruised the West Indies about ten months. Her skipper was afterwards accused of having done the pirating all to his own benefit. A Negro slave, that he brought to the colony, was all that he left for the company's profit. The ship left the Delaware at the end of April with a cargo of skins obtained from the Indians and arrived at Gothenburg about the beginning of June. The cost of the expeditions had now reached the sum of 46,000 florins and the undertaking had ended in a loss, but the stockholders hoped that the second voyage would bring larger returns.

CHAPTER IV.

The Second Expedition. The Dutch Withdraw from the Company.
Dutch Colonists Coming to the Delaware.

ADMIRAL FLEMING, who became the principal supporter of the colonial enterprise, had made preparations already in summer of 1638, for a new large expedition, but all the resources of the Swedish realm were required to the prosecution of the war, and the preparations to continue the colonial trade met countless obstacles. Furthermore the Dutch stockholders of the company showed unwillingness to continue the expeditions, as they were members in the Dutch West India Company and their membership in the rival company was made unpleasant for them. However after many delays the ship Kalmar Nyckel was again assigned for an expedition. Supplies for the voyage and merchandise for the trade were bought by Blommaert in Holland. Captain Cornelius van Vliet, a Dutchman, who was appointed commander of the expedition, was sent to Holland to hire officers and sailors that could be used for the journey. And Johan Hindricksson, governor of the province of Elfsborg was instructed to hire some soldiers, to replace the Dutch soldiers in the colony, as the Dutch and Swedes did not get along well together. However, in his letter of July 24, 1639 to the government, the governor informs that he had tried his best but had been unsuccessful to secure soldiers. But he had a proposition to make, he had learned that there were some soldiers who had deserted the army and returned home. Hindricksson thought that it would be a proper punishment to such soldiers and other criminals to send them to New Sweden. Accordingly the government instructed Hindricksson on August 7, and on the following day Olof Stake, governor of Vermland and Dal, to capture any such soldiers that were found in their districts and send them immediately to Gothenburg to be in readiness for departure.

In the letter to Governor Stake, the royal government says that, "The company's ship, which in June, last, returned from New Sweden to Gothenburg, shall again immediately go back there, and we have deemed it advisable to permit the married soldiers and others who from your province as well as from the province of Elfsborg without delay can be gathered, who have either deserted or otherwise forfeited their lives, to be sent on the ship to New Sweden with their wives and children. For this we present them with their lives as well as give to each soldier a suit and ten dollars in copper. Therefore if any such offenders are found in Vermland and in a hurry can be gathered such a way that no tumult will arise, we graciously order you that you at once let them be captured and immediately, without delay to be sent, well guarded, with their wives and children to Gothenburg. Correspond without neglect about the matter with Governor Johan Hindricksson, to whom we have likewise written. The offenders who have well deserved their punishment, must be made known by you that in return of this voyage we have permitted them to keep their lives and that they will be pardoned and be free to return to their homes after one or two years, if they do not desire to stay longer in New Sweden. As there is no doubt that such a journey shall cause among the wives and children, who are innocent for their men's crimes, a great crying, and lamentation among their friends and relatives, so you must the most carefully and with discretion handle this case, and while you use the power of your office, you shall try to prevail upon them with gentle and good manner for this journey, so that no new tumult and riot will rise for us in that district."

The ship Kalmar Nyckel left Gothenburg for the colony in the beginning of September 1639, having on board Joost van Langdonk, a Dutchman who was sent out as factor, and Peter Hollander Ridder, another Dutchman, who had lived some time in Finland, was sent as commander of the colony on the Delaware. In the North Sea the ship sprang a leak and had to be taken to Medemblik, Holland, for repairs. After they had gone to the sea, they soon found the ship leaking again and were compelled to return. The ship had to be unloaded and new repairs were made. A second time they left the harbor, but before long the ship was leaking as before and had to be taken to Amsterdam for new repairs. The company's agents in Amsterdam found that the captain had charged the company for goods that were not found on board. He had to be removed from service and Pouwel Jansen was engaged in his place. New sailors also had to be hired as the old sailors refused to go neither with the ship nor the captain. On December 27, the ship was ready to sail, but a great storm swept over the coast and she was prevented to leave until February 7, 1640. The skipper and factor were accused by Gregorius van Dyck, a Dutchman who also went to the colony, in his letter to Admiral Fleming on May 23, 1640, of having spent their time on the voyage in smoking and drinking and damning the Swedes. They hated especially the Swedish priest the Rev. Reorus Torkillus and refused the pastor a little drink of fire water when he was feeling bad, although there were barrels of liquor on board. The journey was rather rough and many people were sick, but the ship arrived safely in the colony on the seventeenth of April, 1640. About the middle of May she set sail for the return voyage, with a large cargo of skins, and arrived happily to Gothenburg about the beginning of July. Several soldiers and people returned with her from the colony, among them Henrick Huygen the factor and Mans Kling the only Swedish officer in the colony.

The future of the commercial venture did not look very bright, the expeditions had brought a considerable deficit, as the expenses of the expeditions for the long delays and many mishaps on the sea had risen very high. The Dutch stockholders became dissatisfied and wanted to withdraw from the company, but the Swedish government was desirous to continue the enterprise and decided in February 1641 to buy out the Dutch stockholders.

The Dutch founders of the company had intended to bring over colonists to the Delaware from Holland, and there were some families in Utrecht who had prepared to go to the colony. Samuel Blommaert wrote on their behalf to the Swedish government in 1639, and at the end of the year they sent their agent Joost van Bogaert to Stockholm on the same mission. A charter was issued to their patron Henrik Hooghkamer on January 24, 1640, allowing him to establish a colony about twenty miles above Fort Christina, on the west side of the Delaware River, with their own government but under the suzerainty of the Swedish crown. They left Holland on board the ship Freedenburgh about the end of July 1640 and arrived to the colony on the second of November, being about twenty families and fifty souls in all. Joost van Bogaert was their director. The ship Freedenburgh left the colony for Holland about December 3, with a quantity of skins belonging to the New Sweden Company.

CHAPTER V.

The Third Expedition. Finnish Colonists Brought
to the Delaware River.

HEN the Kalmar Nyckel arrived from the second expedition in the beginning of July 1640, it brought letters and reports to Admiral Fleming and Chancellor Oxenstierna from Ridder the new commander of the colony, and from Van Dyck who also went with the second expedition as an employe of the company. In their letters they request for colonists, and skilled workmen. Ridder complained that he did not have a man who could build a common peasant's house, or saw a board, adding that it would be impossible to find more stupid people in all Sweden, than those in the colony. It is true that those people that were brought to the colony before the third expedition were mostly adventurous city dwellers, who had not been brought up to any creative work but to parasitical ideals, who cherished in their minds of obtaining the peltries from the Indians in exchange of trinkets and of guarding the trading post. The letters arrived in Stockholm on July 12, 1640, and when discussed about in the meeting of the Council of State, it was ordered that a letter should be written to Johan Hindricksson, governor of the province of Elfsborg and Gothenburg, to the effect that since the crown's ship had returned from America with safe voyage and her royal majesty intended further to continue the same trade to America, the governor was to be commanded to gather people with horses and all their belongings and to prevail upon them to go to that country. The letter to the governor was written on July 13, 1640.

Preparations for a new expedition were now revived and

Hendrick Huygen, who returned from the colony with the second expedition, was sent to Holland to buy supplies for the voyage, and to hire sailors. Also other Swedish government agents in Holland were instructed to buy merchandise for the colonial trade. The Kalmar Nyckel and another ship the Charitas were assigned for the voyage and Fleming ordered them repaired.

But no success had been attained in securing colonists, when a letter arrived from Gustaf Leijonhufvud, governor of the province of Nerike and of Bergslagen or the mining districts of south-central Sweden. Governor Leijonhufvud had previously in a letter of July 27, 1639, to the government, complained that the Finns in the Finnmarks of his province were destroying much forest. He petitions for new courts and law readers for the Finnish districts of Linne and New Kopperberg. He also proposes that something more drastic than money fines must be laid upon the Finns as, he says, they care a little about fines. About these he desired the government's advice. Another letter from the Governor Leijonhufvud arrived to the government while colonists were much wanted for New Sweden. In this letter he tells of having a multitude of Finns in the mining districts of his province. To some of these he is disposed to allow to occupy abandoned farms (from which the Finns had been driven away) and asks what to do with the rest of the "vagrant Finns."

On July 30, 1640 the government replies to Leijonhufvud's letter and says, "In gracious answer it satisfies us if some good men among the Finns, who will take up abandoned farms and practice no burnbeating, may use them. The unsettled cannot be trusted with the abandoned farms, but you may prevail upon them to go with their wives and children to New Sweden, to where we are sending Kalmar Nyckel (which lately returned from there and is now in Gothenburg), with a multitude of people. You make them understand that there is a choice and fruitful land, overgrown with all kinds of beautiful forests and there are all kinds of wild animals in plenty, and that they can go there with confidence as a great multitude already have gone there with the Swedes and are now living there. Here are now also some Finns who are desirous to go on this ship. You would make us a great service if you could manage to get these or other families there, but if they cannot be persuaded, then you take advantage of the patent which we have published for such unsettled Finns."

By the patent is referred to the order issued on September 4, 1636, commanding all "Finnish vagrants," whose homesteads had been burned and destroyed and who had been driven to destitute and to seek for employment at the mines, to leave Sweden and return to Finland before the Walpurgis night of 1637 on pain of being put in irons and kept to work on the government's castles and farms. To a man thus driven to destitute with a great family, there was a slight chance to travel back to Finland. That had required a considerable capital.

Four Finnish peasants in the parish of Sund, in southwestern Sweden, near the Norwegian boundary line, had been found in 1640 guilty of burnbeating on their farms. These men, Eskil Larsson, Klement Joransson, Jons Pafvelsson and Bertil Eskilsson, were therefore ordered to the army and their property confiscated to the crown. They applied to the government for permission to go to New Sweden, which was granted and Governor Olof Stake of Vermland and Dal was instructed on July 9, 1640 to hold them on bonds for appearance at Gothenburg as soon as the government called them there. Eskil Larsson however had escaped from the army and was now held in Smedjegard prison at Stockholm.

Some Finns in Stockholm had presented themselves voluntarily to go to New Sweden, but still the number of colonists was not sufficient. Mans Kling, who returned from the colony with the second expedition and who knew about the new country, was therefore commissioned on September 26, 1640 to go to Bergslagen or the mining districts in the province of Dalarne, northwest of Stockholm, where the population was mostly Finns. He was instructed to collect and hire unsettled Finns in these districts, and to instruct them to proceed to Stockholm before the sailing of the ship. The governors in the districts that he was expected to visit were requested by the government to aid him in his work. He visited the Finnish settlement of Kopparberget and other places and some colonists came from there.

On February 8, 1641, the government again wrote to Governor Leijonhufvud ordering him, in case he could not prevail upon people to go to New Sweden, to capture all the "forest destroying" Finns found in his district, about whom he had made complaints. They were to be kept in readiness for the sailing of the ship.

In the spring of 1641, Kling was again sent out to gather soldiers and servants and he hired fourteen men, many of which were Finns.

Johan Printz, who later was appointed as governor of New Sweden was likewise requested to look for skilled workmen and young people in Finland, who would be willing to go to America. Johan Printz had acquaintances in Finland, as in the Polish war in 1625, and in the ensuing campaigns he had become identified with the Finnish cavalry. When Sweden entered to the Thirty Years' War in 1630, Printz was appointed as captain in the Finnish cavalry regiment of the province of Pohjanmaa (Osterbotten), Finland. After the death of king Gustavus Adolphus, Printz retired from the army for a while and rented a government land estate, Korsholm, in the province of Pohjanmaa. In 1634 he was in trouble with his Finnish peasant neighbors of Mustasaari, but before that had been advanced to the rank of major in the Pohjanmaa regiment and had again a short visit to the scene of war in Central Europe. In 1638, Printz was again back in the province of Pohjanmaa, recruiting men to his regiment. During the latter year he was appointed as lieutenant-colonel in the Swedish West Gothland regiment and in April 1640 was forced to capitulate the city of Chemnitz in Germany to the Papist forces, whereafter he without leave went to Sweden and became expelled from the army, although freed of further punishment. A letter of Printz to Chancellor Oxenstierna, from Korsholm, in the province of Pohjanmaa, in the winter of 1641, reveals that he was there recruiting emigrants for the Delaware colony among the people at that province who were known of being capable carpenters, shipbuilders, blacksmiths, farmers and sailors. The recruiting of Printz in the province of Pohjanmaa did not have great results immediately, but from this province came to the Delaware colony such colonists as Knut Martinson, Marten Martinsson, Hindrich Jacobson, Jacob Clemetsson, Matz Erichsson, Hendrich Larsson, Martin Thomasson, Brita Mattson and her husband Petter Gunnarsson Rambo, who already was in the colony. With this expedition came from Southern Finland, Karl Johnsson from the town of Käkisalmi (Kexholm) and Mats Hansson from Admiral Fleming's family estate near the town of Porvoo (Borgo). Both of these latter once were sent for punishment of some misdemeanor. One immigrant Mickel Jonsson came from Reval, Esthonia.

Emigrants who would voluntarily depart for the colony were still hard to be secured. On April 13, 1641, the government wrote to Governor Carl Siggesson of the province of Skaraborg to allow a trooper, Hans Mansson, who had destroyed some fruit trees at the royal estate of Warnhem, to choose being hanged or to go to New Sweden with his wife and children. He was to be allowed to return home after six years. The sentence was to be kept secret from the public until executed.

On April 16, 1641, a royal letter was sent to Governor Olof Stake of Vermland and Dal, in which it is said, "We can understand of your humble letter, Mr. Governor, how you have according to our order made your best to prevail upon the forest destroyers and Finns who are in your province, that they would go voluntarily with their wives and children to New Sweden. And as the same Finns now have moved to Norway and but occasionally visit in your province and also are uncertain to secure, you have, subject to our further orders let a multiude of them be captured and to be taken to Carlstad prison, and you humbly ask us what to do with them.

In gracious answer it delights us that you have been busy to get such destructive and forest destroying Finns and drifters alive. And we graciously order you that if the same who have been so captured would not go to New Sweden, you detain them to secure dependable bondsmen to guarantee that they would take up abandoned farms or new homesteads and use them as law provides. But if they cannot secure dependable bondsmen, then there is no other way but they have to go either to New Sweden or to be put in irons and to work in our or crown's castles and estates. If they allow to be prevailed upon to go to New Sweden, then you may correspond about it with our Lord Mayer Klaus Fleming and wait for information from him, when and to what place they will be taken to board a ship for New Sweden. We graciously do not require your answer."

The ship Charitas left Stockholm for Gothenburg on May 3, 1641, having on board eight hired soldiers, two soldier prisoners and two misdemeanants who were sent for punishment, and twenty-three others, among which were some hired servants for the company, a nobleman and a priest who both took a trip to the colony for adventure, and several other adventurers, besides few regular colonists. But in Gothenburg, where the ship Kalmar Nyckel was prepared for the voyage, were gathered the imprisoned and many other Finns with their families, who all were born pioneers and colonists. Both of the ships left Gothenburg in July 1641. The officers on the ships and for the trading post were Dutch, with one exception and the majority of the soldiers and some of the sailors were Swedes and Finns. The actual colonists were nearly all Finns, most of whom had their families with them. Among the Finns that arrived to the Delaware River with this - expedition were:

Anders Andersson, involuntary emigrant, served the company until 1648, then became freeman. Had a farm in the neighborhood of Finland. Has numerous descendants in Pennsylvania.

Mans Andersson, was employed as servant for the company until 1648, thereafter became freeman and began a farm at Finland which the company in 1654 acquired.

Anders Hansson, hired as soldier by Kling, began later farm at Finland.

Matts Hansson, brother of the former, was hired as constable (gunner), brought his wife with him to the colony. Became freeman in 1646. Was one of the commissaries of the Finnish colony during the Dutch rule.

Matts Hansson, from Admiral Fleming's family estate near the town of Porvoo, Finland. Was sent as punishment for the colony and in 1653 received permission to return home.

Israel Helme, involuntary emigrant, from Mora, Central Sweden. Brought his family with him. During the Dutch rule he became a prominent business man and was one of the most influential men in the Finnish colony and on the Delaware River before the establishment of William Penn's colony.

Ivar Hendricksson (also spelled Ivert and Evert), was hired as soldier by Kling. In the colony he was later known as a turbulent fellow. Had a farm first time at Finland and later at Crane Hook, where he was captain of the Finnish militia during the rule of the Duke of York.

Karl Johansson, bookkeeper from Kakisalmi, a town on the Lake Ladoga, in Finland. Was sent for punishment for some misdemeanor. Worked in the colony as commissary of provisions and auditor of accounts. Returned to Finland in 1648.

Clement Joransson, sent for burnbeating. Was planting tobacco at Upland in 1644. Served also as a soldier and later became freeman.

Jons Pafvelsson, sent for burnbeating. Died on July 9, 1643, at Upland.

Mans Jurrensson (also Joransson), involuntary emigrant. Worked as laborer and later became freeman.

Peter Larsson Cock (Kock), involuntary emigrant. Was held in Smedjegard prison at Stockholm waiting for the sailing of the ship Charitas. Planting tobacco at the Schuylkill River in 1644. Later became freeman. Married Margaret Helme, daughter of Israel Helme. Peter Cock became one of the leaders in the Finnish colony after the downfall of the Swedish rule and was the most influential man on the Delaware River at the arrival of William Penn. He had six sons and six daughters and his family had branched in 1693 into forty-seven persons, bearing the name of Cock, besides the children of her daughters. Peter Cock died in 1688, in great prosperity. His descendants bear mostly the name of Cox.

Eskil Larsson, involuntary emigrant. Had been condemned to serve in the army and his property confiscated for burnbeating.

He had escaped from the army and was held in Smedjegard prison at Stockholm from where he was placed on board the ship Charitas. Was planting tobacco for the company at Upland in 1644.

Bertil Eskilsson, the former's son. He had been condemned to the army and his property confiscated for burnbeating. Later he requested to be sent to the Delaware Colony, which was permitted. He had a farm at Kalkeon hook in 1677.

Hendrick Mattson, a boy hired by Kling, his salary was to be 10 R.D. a year and received 10 D. in copper money on departure. Was planting tobacco for the company at the Schuylkill River in 1644. Became a soldier on October 1, 1646, and served until March 1, 1648, when he became a freeman.

Knut Martensson from Vasa Finland, came over as a sailor on the ship Charitas. Was planting tobacco for the company at Christina in 1644. Had a farm at Finland in 1677.

Anders Classon Mink, involuntary emigrant. Was herding the company's hogs in 1644 and became freeman in 1646.

Clas Andersson Mink, the former's son. Was herding hogs with his father in 1644.

Paul Mink, another son of Anders Classon Mink, also born in Sweden. Lived yet in 1693 as a farmer.

Mans Mansson, came over voluntarily and worked four years for the company to pay for the passage over the ocean. In 1654 he rented land from the company at Finland, the company was to furnish a pair of oxen and give half of the seed and in return the company was to receive half of the product of his land.

Martin Thomasson, from Pohjanmaa, Finland. Served as soldier and was killed by the Indians on March 4, 1643, between Fort Christina and Elfsborg.

Johan, a boy hired by Kling. Was drowned at Upland on March 1, 1644.

Olle Tossa (Tossawa), came over as a sailor on the Kalmar Nyckel. During the Swedish rule he went under the name of Olof Toorsson. One of his descendants has a two century old gravestone standing at the Trinity Church in Wilmington, Delaware.

The voyage over the ocean was stormy and two colonists and some cattle died and had to be thrown overboard. They arrived to the settlement on November 7, 1641. The ships left the Delaware at the end of November, and taking cargoes of salt in Rochelle, France, they arrived at Stockholm about the first of June 1642. Many of the old employees of the trading post returned to Sweden, among them the commissioner Langdonk. The sum of 11,172 florins was paid in salaries for the returning servants, soldiers and sailors, as money was not sent to the colony.

On the arrival of the new colonists, they found the trading post in rather sad condition. Only six beaver skins, and a number of fishhooks and axes were in the storehouse, and the traders were eagerly waiting provisions to arrive from Sweden. The merchants from New England and Virginia came with their sloops, loaded with provisions to the Delaware settlements, but the traders did no longer have anything with which to buy the provisions, the merchandise and the peltry were all gone. However large supplies arrived now with the expedition, and a majority of the newcomers were people who despised above everything the idea of living upon the fruits of other peoples' labor. Productive labor, according to their ideal, was the highest and noblest occupation of man. The Finnish colonists immediately felt at home in the silence of the vast forests and at once saw their opportunity. Plots were selected for farms, and verdant knolls, shadowed by majestic elm trees, were occupied for log cabins. The woods were thick with game, and the fish were playing hide and seek, jumping in the November sunshine on the placid waters of the noble River Delaware. Ripe, wild fruit was abundant in the forests on their arrival, and the falling leaves were departing a fragrant scent into the atmosphere. The scenery, rich in the gorgeous hues of autumnal foliage, was filling the hearts of the settlers of wonder and hope, infinite and sublime. When the spring came, the monotony of the stately forest on the Delaware was broken by farm clearings and smoke pillars ascending from the log cabins at the New Finnish settlements of Finland and Upland. The grain was sprouting from the furrows in the fields and the Delaware colony had then been founded on the basis that was going to be the foundation of American civilization, and of all civilizations in the past, today and forever.

CHAPTER VI.

The Fourth and the Fifth Expedition.

More Finnish Colonists Brought to America.

EARLY in 1642, preparations were begun for a new expedition, and the government assumed all the expenses connected with the journeys, except the board and salary of the company's servants and the voyage of the colonists. The colonists were required to pay a fare for their voyage, by working for the company in the colony. Later on this fare was fixed to be 16 riksdalers a head, or about equal to 144 American dollars of present day money value. For a man with a big family it took years to work this out, while starting a farm and supporting his family.

As the New Sweden colony had become mostly a Finnish settlement, John Printz, who had lived many years in Finland and had belonged to the Finnish cavalry in the wars and therefore was acquainted with the language and manners of the Finns, was requested in the spring of 1642 to become the governor of the colony on the Delaware. This he accepted and was commissioned accordingly on the fifteenth of August 1642.

Goods and provisions for an expedition had been again bought in Holland by the Swedish agents and new efforts were made to secure colonists, as Ridder, the governor in the colony had made earnest requests for more people to secure the land against the attempts of the English to settle there. An agent was therefore sent to the Finnish settlements in Vermland in June to hire laborers. Letters were also written to several governors asking them to prevail upon people to emigrate with their families to the colony, but few were willing to go and force again had to be employed.

In the summer of 1642 the council decided that game poachers and deserted soldiers should be condemned to serve in New Sweden for a number of years. However even then the number found was insufficient and in August the governors Carl Bonde, Peter Kruse of Dalarne, Johan Berndes of Kopparberget and Olof Stake of Vermland and Dal were requested to capture forest destroying Finns in their territories. These people with their families were to be kept in readiness for transportation to Gothenburg within three weeks after the first of August.

Among the Finns that came with this expedition were:

Anders Andersson, involuntary emigrant. Served as soldier at Elfsborg in 1644. Returned home in 1653.

Christer Boije, a Finnish nobleman, who came for adventure. In the summer of 1643 he was sent to New Amsterdam to bring back deserted colonists and to purchase oxen. On July 10, 1643 he acted as judge in case against Lamberton who attempted to establish English settlements on the Delaware and was a member of the jury on January 16, 1644 examining Isaac Allerton in the same matter. Acted as commander at Upland. Returned to home in 1644.

Johan Fransson, bookkeeper from Viipuri (Viborg), Finland. Was sent to the colony for some misdemeanor.

Anders Andersson Homman from Sollentuna near Stockholm, Sweden. Served as soldier until March 1, 1648, then trumpeter until 1653. He lived in 1693, having then nine people in his family. His descendants belonged to the Trinity Church in Wilmington.

Lars Andersson from Sollentuna, Sweden. Was employed as soldier at Tinicum in 1644. Returned to Sweden in 1653.

Peter Mickelson, a peasant from Finland. Was sent to the colony for punishment. Died on July 31, 1643 at Elfsborg from an epidemic.

Marten Martensson from the province of Pohjanmaa, Finland. Served as laborer for the company and later became freeman. He is claimed of being the forefather of John Morton, one of the signers of the Declaration of Independence of the United States.

The ships Fama and Swan had been prepared for this expedition and they left Gothenburg on September 12, 1642. The expedition arrived to the island of Antigua at the Christmas time and the colonists spent their holidays there. On the arrival at the Delaware Bay, about the end of Janaury, 1643, they met a fearful snow storm. The Fama ran ashore and lost her main mast, sprit sail and three anchors. After more than two weeks' delay in the bay, the ships arrived at Fort Christina on the fifteenth of February 1643. In the middle of April the ships left the colony with Governor Ridder, who returned to Finland, where he permanently settled in the province of Viipuri. And at least eleven other employees of the company returned to Sweden as their places were filled by the new arrivals. Large cargoes of beaver and otter skins were taken to Sweden. They arrived safely at Gothenburg in the end of July 1643.

Preparations for a new expedition were again going on and on October 16, 1643, the question of collecting emigrants was considered at the meeting of the Council of State. Since the Finnish pioneers in the back forests were suspected of game poaching by the Swedes, it was decided later on that the game poachers should be sent to the colony. But the number of colonists was very small with this expedition, indicating that the game poachers existed largely in the minds of their Swedish brethren. One colonist came from Finland, a soldier from the town of Kajaani in the Northern Finland, who was sent for punishment.

Among the Finnish colonists who arrived with the fifth expedition, were:

Wolle Lohe, engaged by Papegoja as soldier on December 1, 1643.

Swen Swensson, a youth whose father Swen Gunnarrson arrived at the colony with the first or the senond expedition. He was one of the Swensson brothers from whom William Penn exchanged land for the site of Philadelphia.

Hindrick Olufsson, who became a soldier on December 1, 1646. Returned to Sweden in 1653 and came back to the colony as a Finnish-Swedish interpreter in 1655.

As usual the merchandise for trade was bought in Holland, as the manufacturing of articles useful in trading with the Indians had not been developed in Sweden on account of the war industries continually keeping all hands busy.

Two ships, the Fama and the Kalmar Nyckel were prepared for the voyage, but only Fama was going to the colony, while the Kalmar Nyckel was assigned to go to the Caribbean Islands for trading. All kinds of wooden utensils were brought from Finland for the West India trade, also tar, pitch and lumber. The ships left Gothenburg on December 29, 1643, and the Fama arrived at Christina on March 11, 1644. About July 20, she set sail for Europe with a large cargo of tobacco, much of which had been raised by the colonists, also skins, part of which had been brought in by the settlers.

At the departure of the ship Fama from the colony, the total of male inhabitants in New Sweden was ninety-three, as the adventurers returned as fast as they came and twenty-six had died from disease within a year. Fama took back four adventurers again to Sweden. However, as many of the Finns brought their families with them the total population was considerably larger than the above figure. There were also seven Englishmen living at Varkens Kill, on the east side of the Delaware River, who had submitted to Swedish rule, but later on they moved away. The Dutch, who established a settlement on the Delaware, within the Swedish territory, under Joost van Bogaert, had all moved to Manhattan and some perhaps had returned to Holland.

The Fama arrived in Holland about the first of October 1644 and the Kalmar Nyckel soon afterwards with a cargo of tobacco. There had broken a war between Sweden and Denmark, therefore the cargoes had to be sold in Holland. The returning servants and soldiers were transported to Sweden, but the ships arrived to Sweden only in the summer of 1645, and were fitted for participation in the naval war.

The war between Sweden and Denmark had bearance on the colony's future, as Admiral Klaus Fleming, the director of the New Sweden Company and the staunchest supporter of the colony, fell during the struggle. In the war Fleming was commanding the Swedish navy, created by him, against the Danish navy under the command of King Christian IV. Admiral Fleming, who was born of a prominent and ancient Finnish family in Finland, held many high positions in Sweden, such as being one of the five counsellors appointed to rule Sweden during the minority of Queen Christina, he was also State Admiral and Lord Mayor of the city of Stockholm. He had used his great energy in building a Swedish navy to secure from Denmark the mastery of the straits connecting the Baltic to the North Sea, which was the last link at the time in making the Baltic a Swedish inland sea.

CHAPTER VII.

The Sixth, Seventh and Eighth Expeditions.

The Finns Beseeching the Queen to be Permitted to go to America.

AFTER Admiral Fleming's death, Axel Oxenstierna, State Chancellor of Sweden, was the logical successor as head of the colonial enterprise. But he was not a business man and also found little time for the colonial affair, consequently the colony suffered neglect. John Printz, who now was the governor of the colony, requested in his letter sent with the Fama in 1644, for a large number of soldiers and colonists, but it was not before in May 1646, that the ship Gyllene Haj sailed from Gothenburg to the Delaware. No special efforts had been made to secure colonists, although John Papegoja, who acted in the colony in the capacity of a commander, also requested in his letter of July 15, 1644, to Per Brahe, at times governor-general of Finland, that a lot of Finns should be sent to the colony under the command of an industrious and thrifty man. A soldier, Peter Olofsson, who had been condemned to death was the only recorded passenger on the Gyllene Haj bound to New Sweden.

After a stormy voyage the ship arrived to the destination on October 1, 1646, after she had lost her sails and topmasts. Almost all the crew were sick at the arrival and for the sickness and ice in the Delaware River, the ship could depart for Europe only in the beginning of March 1647. The return trip was safe as usual and the ship arrived to Gothenburg in June, with returning soldiers, servants and officers and having 24,177 lbs. of tobacco as her cargo.

The seventh expedition did not either have many colonists,

51

with this expedition came however, the Rev. Laurentius Caroli Lokenius, a native of Finland, who preached in the colony for forty years. The ship Swan sailed on September 25, 1647, arriving to the colony safely in the beginning of 1648, and set the sails for the return voyage on May 16, arriving to Stockholm on July 3, 1648, with a valuable cargo of skins. Ten or more of the employees of the company and one freeman returned with the vessel to Sweden, leaving the total number of male inhabitants to 83, besides the women and children.

The Finnish colonists on the Delaware had become prosperous by this time and letters sent to their relatives and friends in Sweden, were full of praise of the country to which they had been brought to. As a result, there are found two letters in the Royal Archives at Stockholm, written by a Finn, Mats Erickson from the province of Vermland in Sweden, on behalf of two hundred Finns in that province, beseeching for permission to be allowed to go to America. In the records of the Council of State it is said that 300 Finns had applied permission to go to America. The writer adds that if they were not allowed to go to the colony, they would then move to Denmark. When the matter was discussed in the Royal Council on June 12, 1649, the queen thought it strange that they should ask for such permission as there was enough land to be had in Sweden.

New Sweden was looked as an undesirable place by the Swedes however and especially by the soldiers, as can be seen of a letter of General Lars Kagg. On July 1, 1648 he writes from Kalmar in the Southern Sweden, complaining to the government that soldiers in his province deserted the army despite during some years the deserters have been hanged. He says from the regiment of Colonel Skytte alone 300 men had deserted. He wished to know what kind of punishment they should have to make it an example for others and adds that as it is known that they have a great dread of New Sweden, it would be profitable that when a ship sails over, some of them be taken there.

The ship Kattan was preparing in Gothenburg for the expedition and some colonists were sent there from Stockholm on the ship Gasen, but most of the Finns had gathered in Gothenburg. Merchandise for the expedition was brought in from Holland as usual. On July 3, 1649 the Kattan set sail for the colony, she had on board more than seventy colonists of which two came from Finland as punishment for shooting elks. These were Israel Petersson from Odkarby and Anders Mickelsson from Aland. The ship had besides twenty-four sailors and six officers, some of the latter to remain in the colony. In her cargo were 4,948 yards of cloth, 224 copper kettles, 160 pairs of shoes, 300 axes and various amounts of other articles. Besides several cannon and a large quantity of ammunition, intended for new forts in the colony. Also provisions estimated for twelve months. It was a pleasant voyage over the ocean, and when they reached the Caribbean Islands they stopped at Antigua, St. Christopher and St. Martin for refreshment. Everybody had money, many of the Finnish colonists had sold their properties in Sweden and had their moneys with them as they were coming to the colony to stay. The salaries of the soldiers, sailors and the officers were paid for months in advance, as there was plenty of money now in Sweden for big war indemnities were coming then in. Even forty-one of the colonists were handed 10 riksdalers each for traveling expenses, on their work in the colony.

On Saturday evening, August 26, they were ready to leave the Island of St. Martin, but one of the men, employed as servant for the company's plantations, had fallen so much in keeping good time in the town that the ship had to leave him on the island after having waited for him late to the night. All night and the next day they were sailing with a favorable wind, all sails set, but about two o'clock the next night the ship received a shock from a cliff, then another one. A third shock and a cliff had penetrated the prow and the ship remained there. As day approached they could see at the distance of about thirteen miles a small uninhabited island, about 80 miles from Porto Rico. The women and children were brought to the island in the life boats, but the sailors remained on board the ship until the next day, when a storm arose, and to prevent the ship breaking up, the masts were cut down and thrown into the sea. The provisions were brought to the island, but their water supply had been thrown to the sea in the attempt to refloat the ship, and fresh water could not be obtained in the island. After five days a small bark passed within a mile or two of the island and the victims fired two distress signals for help, however the skipper of the bark thought them to be a shipwrecked pirate party and did not dare to come to their rescue, but proceeded to Porto Rico to notify about the prize. Soon after two Spanish ships were sent to the wreck and on their arrival the Spaniards asked what people they were, and when the Swedish pass was delivered, they declared never having heard of such country before. The victims were challenged to fight or surrender, after which the Spaniards robbed the cargo and searched the victims for money and valuables. The ship was burned and the victims were brought on the third of September to Porto Rico, where they were led to the market place of the town with drums and great noise. A bonfire was built and all the books the victim carried were burned as heretical. When the victims protested against the treatment accorded to them, the Governor de la Riva promised that they should be set free, but their goods could not be restored. Thereafter the people were compelled to make their living by working in great misery. Shortly after their arrival, they were permitted to dispatch letters and two representatives, the Rev. Nertunius and Joachim Lycke, to Sweden to report their condition and to request the government to send a vessel for their aid. After some time a Dutch captain Didrick Didricksen arrived at Porto Rico with his ship, the Prophet Daniel, loaded with slaves. The shipwreck victims implored him to release them from their misery. He agreed to take them either to America or Holland, but as he was about to leave, the governor made a prize of him, took his money and sent his ship to the King of Spain as a gift. A Finnish captain, Hans Asmundson Besk, who had served in the Swedish navy and was sent to the colony in the capacity of commander, had proved troublesome for the authorities in Porto Rico, he was therefore put on board the Dutchman's ship and sent to Spain.

The monks in Porto Rico were trying to convert the victims into the Catholic religion, by promising them money, new clothes and other good things. Many also became "converted," but the monks proved to be liars, the promises of worldly remunerations were not kept.

In the course of time many of the sailors, soldiers and some colonists, among the victims, found means for leaving the island, but the colonists with wives and children had to stay there. However in April 1650, the city captured a little bark and with the permission of the governor some of the victims bought it. The governor supplied some provisions and issued a passport and about the first of May the remnants of the shipwrecked people, twenty-four souls in all, left Porto Rico, their object being St. Christopher, where they hoped to get on board some Dutch ship going either to America or Europe. After sailing that day and the following night, a French bark met them near the island of St. Cruz and captured the ship of the victims, brought the people to the island where they again were robbed of what they had. On the island the victims were submitted to the most cruel torture at the hands of the French. First they were conducted to the governor, who searched their clothes for money and valuables and then for his amusement caused some of the men to be bound to posts and commanded his soldiers to discharge four shots by their sides. Later the governor caused four men, Johan Rudberus, Joran Dufva, a colonist called Andreas and the mate of the ship Kattan, to be bound with their hands on their back and suspended on hooks about a yard from the ground, for two days and two nights. Others had their fingers screwed off with pistol locks and the feet of the women were burned with red hot iron plates. A certain woman, with whom the governor had forced relations, was killed by the command of the governor.

At this time a Dutch bark arrived to St. Cruz to get a supply of fresh water. The bark was made a prize by the French, but later it was returned to the skipper, who set sail for St. Christopher. At the time two brothers, Johan and Anders Classon from Holland, were trading with tobacco at the latter island and the skipper related them the sufferings of the victims. The brothers were touched by the story and requested permission to go to St. Cruz to bring away the victims. The governor granted their request and gave them a passport together with an order for the release of the prisoners. One of the brothers provided the ship and the other supplied the provisions and the sailors. When they arrived at St. Cruz only five of the victims were still alive, a man, two women and two children. The two women and the children were put at once on board the ship, but the man, Johan Rudberus, had been sold to a captain for 500 lbs. of tobacco. He managed to make his escape, however, and was brought on board the ship at night, but he was discovered by his master, who demanded and received his 500 lbs. of tobacco for the claim of his slave. They left the island on the same day and on the following day the two women and the oldest child died of exhaustion and the other child soon afterwards. Rudberus was taken to Holland from St. Christopher by Captain Johan Classon and arrived at Stockholm in the autumn of 1651 to tell the sad story.

In all nineteen of the colonists, besides some soldiers and sailors, who had been able to escape from Porto Rico, returned to Sweden. About fifty colonists, in great part Finnish women and children, had found their graves in the islands of the West Indies.

CHAPTER VIII.

The Ninth and the Tenth Expedition.

The Finns Flocking to Get Passage for America.

ON March 16, 1652, the colonial business was discussed in the presence of the queen in the meeting of the Council of State at Stockholm. Three years had passed since the last expedition was sent, which did not arrive to the colony, and in more than four years they had not received in the colony merchandise for trade. There were ships that had been riding years at anchor in the harbors of Gothenburg and Stockholm and in 1651, merchandise for a new expedition had been brought from Holland and was decaying in the cellars at Gothenburg. While the question of obtaining colonists no longer was a problem as the Finns in Sweden were beseeching the government to be taken to the colony. Several people acquainted with the colony were questioned in the council meeting, and the general complaint was that since Admiral Fleming's death there had not been anyone to manage the company's business. It was known however that the land supported the people without help from Sweden, but the Dutch and English were getting all the peltry from the Indians, as the Swedish traders in the colony did not have merchandise. The management of the New Sweden Company was then assigned to the care of the department of commerce which lately had been organized, but another year passed and no new expedition had been sent. The government of Sweden was then in state of chaos. Queen Christina, who received the reign of the realm into her hands in 1644, while eighteen years of age, had since begun to neglect the affairs of the state entirely and was spending her time in continuous array of pageants in the company of wicked admirers and adventurers, who gathered to her court from the centers of corruption and decadency in Europe. During her short reign, the lower nobility increased one hundred per cent and the counts and barons five hundred per cent. The indemnities received after the Thirty Years' War were soon gone, and the country sunk under the heaviest debt in its history. The resources of the state were depleted by donations of territories to grabbing nobility. Three-fifths of the entire Finland had thus been given to the mercy of social parasites, who by their agents plundered the peasants to pay for their revelries at the court. Men who held offices far from the capital, were hanging about the court, among them was Per Brahe, Governor-General of Finland, who enjoyed more than princely income from his enormous land donations in Finland. Even the little money belonging to the New Sweden Company had been used in the maintenance of the royal palace.

News from the colony, that the Dutch had built a fort there, however caused the attention of the Swedish government to the colony and in August 13, 1653, the queen instructed the admiralty to fit out a ship for a voyage to America. The ships Orn and Gyllene Haj, lying at anchor in the harbor of Stockholm were assigned for the expedition. Many Finns had from time to time applied to be taken to the Delaware colony, so Sven Schute was instructed on August 25, 1653 to hire fifty soldiers and to collect two hundred and fifty colonists. Schute was sent to the Finnish territories, first he was to go to Westmanland sending the people from there to Stockholm, from there he was to proceed to Vermland and Dal as hundreds of Finns in these territories were awaiting opportunity to get passage to America. The governors in these provinces were requested to assist Schute in gathering the people. When the colonists at these places were all enlisted they were to be kept in readiness to proceed to Gothenburg as soon as Schute heard from Mayor Broman of Gothenburg that the Orn had passed through the Danish Sound. The Orn left Stockholm on October 8, 1653, having on board sixteen hired men and twelve young boys sent from an institute in Stockholm. In Gothenburg had gathered more than 350 people from the Finmarks of Vermland and Dal, who had sold their properties at any price in the hope that they found room in the ship to go over to America.

The Orn arrived at Gothenburg on November 8, but was delayed there as she was waiting for the other ship, the Gyllene Haj to arrive from Stockholm. After extensive repairs the Haj finally left Stockholm for Gothenburg on November 23, 1653, having on board forty-one people, including the sailors and officers of the ship. This also included captain Hans Asmundson Besk, who was coming to the colony with his family of eleven persons, having received from Queen Christina a donation of land on the Delaware. The Haj arrived at Ohresund on the 30th of December, where six sailors, a servant and a prisoner, destined to the colony, deserted. To be able to proceed, four new sailors had to be hired here. The Haj finally arrived to Gothenburg on January 17, 1654, leaking and with a broken mast and anchor, having run on banks in the Sound. The colonists at Gothenburg had been waiting eleven weeks for the ship to sail and on February 2, the Orn set sail alone, but about one hundred colonists had to be left behind for lack of room in the ship. On March 20 they arrived to the Canary Islands, having had a stormy voyage and the passengers as well as the crew were sick, many having died on the voyage and been thrown overboard. The governor of the islands, Don Philipo Disalogo, offered them every kindness and banqueted the officers. He had also the news for them that Queen Christina had abdicated her throne, had forsaken the religion for which her father died and become a Catholic. The people of the town were not however quite friendly to these strange white haired creatures, as when the colonists landed, a noisy crowd gathered and threw stones on them. A complaint about this was made to the governor, who at once sent an officer with several drummers all around the town to proclaim on the street corners that if any person would attack the passengers in any manner whatever, he should forfeit his life. The refreshments on the island revived the people and the majority recuperated from their sickness, but many died in the harbor. After five days' rest at the Canaries, they left the islands, taking few canary birds with them to the colony. The passengers used their time in fishing and quantities of fish were caught during the journey. However the heat became unbearable when they came nearer the tropic and a violent disease broke out among the people, causing great suffering. On April 10th one hundred and thirty persons were sick with dysentary and intermittent fever, some jumping into the ocean. On April 16th the ship arrived at St. Christopher, where Governor Everet sent them several boats of refreshments. As they had a salmon net on board for the colony, the men were making use of it while two of the officers went to inquire of the French governor about the ship-wreck victims at St. Cruz. The governor told that the people had left long before. A large ox was also bought with some cloth at St. Christopher to strengthen the people with fresh meat. After two days' rest they left the island and arrived on the first of May to the Virginia Bay, where they met a severe thunder storm. After some sailing towards the north in cloudy weather they thought that they had passed the Delaware Bay and on the ninth of May turned back arriving again to the Virginia Bay on May 12th. They supposed this to be the mouth of the Delaware River and again met a storm, losing a sail and some riggings and the people were very sick, some dying daily. On May 16th they sailed towards north in company of two English vessels and reached the Delaware Bay on the 18th. On Saturday night May 20th they anchored in the river before Fort Elfsborg, built by Printz, which they found deserted. On the next morning, which was Trinity Sunday, they moved up the river while religious services were conducted on board. At the arrival before Fort Casimir, that the Dutch of New Amsterdam had built in the summer of 1652, soldiers were landed and the fort occupied without fight. The name of the fort was changed to that of Trinity Fort. On May 22, the ship was anchored in the harbor of Christina and the new arrivals were at once distributed to the homes of the old settlers, who used all means they had at their disposal to revive the sick people, but many still died. Many of the old settlers likewise became infected with the sickness and the epidemic spread to the Indians, who believed that evil spirit had arrived in the ship and offered their medicine men to chase it out.

The passage from Europe to America in those days when sails were used, was by the tropic regions where the air current as well as the ocean current is, on account of the rotation of earth, prevailingly towards the west. The homeward passage from America to Europe was through more northern latitudes, where the currents are prevailingly towards Europe. The passage from Europe to America in those days was therefore, on account of the heat, a torture especially for the northern peoples. The food supplies likewise during the long journey turned bad, causing weakness and therefore less resistance against sickness.

The population of the colony greatly increased on the arrival of the Orn, as it had dwindled to seventy people in all. The servants of the company, such as farm hands, carpenters, millwrights, blacksmiths, sailmakers, and others who were employed with monthly or yearly salaries by the company, on the company's board, went back to Sweden with each expedition, if not for other reason than to receive their pay, as salaries were paid on their arrival back to Sweden. Money was not sent to the colony, although the servants received part of their salary here, in clothes and other necessities. While soldiers, officers, ministers, barber-surgeons and the factors were on the goverment's budget and were paid in Sweden. Besides many of the soldiers, servants and prisoners had been sent to the colony for certain years as punishment and when their time was up, most of these people went back to Sweden. Each ship returning from the colony took a number of these people back to Sweden. Many colonists had also died and others had deserted to the English colonies in the south for the harsh rule of Governor Printz. With the departure of Governor Printz, who left for Sweden in the beginning of October 1653, the population decreased by thirty-two people, who returned to Sweden with the governor. Although among the returning soldiers and servants were many Finns who went to get their pay, the Finnish freemen did not cherish in their minds of going back to Sweden, as the persecutions that they had gone through there were too fresh in their minds. Many of the Finnish soldiers and servants bought supplies and land from the company for their accrued salaries and also became permanent settlers, while some of those who had returned to Sweden, came back to the colony to stay, bringing their families and friends with them. The Finns who had come to the colony as freemen, never returned to Sweden, although some migrated to Maryland and New Netherland. Those seventy people, that were in New Sweden on the arrival of the Orn, were mostly Finns. About 350 people, nearly all Finns, were on the Orn as the ship set sail from Gothenburg, almost a hundred died during the voyage and in the colony after their arrival. On the middle of July 1654, the population was 370 people, including some Hollanders of the twenty-six families that had settled around the Dutch Fort which was captured on the arrival of Orn, twenty-two of whom became Swedish citizens, although they all later moved to New Amsterdam. Besides there were few English families, who were included in the total population.

The ship Orn left the colony on July 15, 1654, with a cargo of tobacco, arriving to Gothenburg on September 24th. Some old people returned with the ship to Sweden.

After the new colonists who came with the ill fated Orn had revived somewhat from their sickness, the first task was to build new houses. As a large number of new Finnish freemen arrived with the ship, much new land was cleared for cultivation. During the rule of Governor Printz the progress of the colony had been very slight, on account of uncertainty, as property rights, except his own, were not respected by the governor. At the departure of Printz in the autumn of 1653, there were 158 morgens or about 300 acres ready for cultivation in the colony, including what the English and the Dutch had improved. The crop of 1654 was good, but the yield of the little fields was not enough for the greatly increased population, so that much corn had to be bought from the Indians and other provisions from the neighboring colonies. The Indians predicted the winter to be cold, so the colonists prepared their houses accordingly. The Indians were right, the winter being as cold that the Delaware River froze all over, but early spring followed.

The Gyllene Haj had got repaired in Gothenburg and set sail for the colony on April 15, 1654, having on board some of the Finnish families who could not get room on the Orn. On June 30, the ship arrived to Porto Rico with bills and demands for the ship Kattan and its cargo. They also had a letter from the King of Spain, but did not succeed to collect anything. Many of the people were sick and Captain Besk died at the island on July 22, and was buried on the same day outside of the town. While at the island, the mate of the ship attempted to escape and had to be put in irons, until the ship sailed. They left Porto Rico on August 15 and passed, by mistake or malice of the mate, the Delaware Bay. Seeking it further in the north, they sailed behind Staten Island and the ship was captured on September 15, by Peter Stuyvesant, Governor of New Netherland, in retaliation of the capture of Fort Casimir on the arrival of the Orn. The colonists were induced by Stuyvesant to settle in New Netherland and many of them did so, as a number of Finns were already living there.

CHAPTER IX.

The Delaware Settlements under the Swedish Administration.

ALTHOUGH the Finnish colonists' letters to their families and friends in Sweden were full of praise of the country where they were settled and where they could make their living with the utmost ease, everything in the colony was not ideal. But in comparison of massacres and hiding in the woods for their lives in cold and hunger in Sweden, they were ready to forget their hardships here when they wrote to their people. When Johan Printz was sent to the Delaware Colony as governor, he was invested with practically unlimited power to rule the colony in the name of the Queen of Sweden. Besides being a governor, his instructions of August 15, 1642, appointed him to be the judge and prosecutor, and was empowered to impose punishment in fines, imprisonment and death according to Swedish usages. A harsh man invested with such power could not resist of becoming a tyrant. Printz came to the colony with the fourth expedition, arriving at the end of January 1643, and already in the spring of the same year several colonists deserted the Delaware settlement and went to New Netherland. Printz sent his agents however there to bring them back, as there was an understanding between the governors of New Sweden and New Netherland that deserters should be returned. The runaways were captured with the aid of Dutch soldiers about twenty-four miles from New Amsterdam, where they had settled and had been discovered by the Indians, who against reward informed the Swedish agents about their whereabouts. The prisoners were put in irons and taken in a bark back to New Sweden.

The colonists were prohibited to trade with the Dutch and with the Indians, the New Sweden Company having the sole right for trade. Thus the colonists had to sell their products to the company at the company's price and buy their necessities from the company likewise. Although in few cases some merchantmen who came to trade with the company obtained, against duty, permission to sell to the colonists. The sale of fire arms and ammunition to the Indians were strictly prohibited, but nevertheless governor Printz himself sold these things to the Indians. Besides he transacted business privately in a large scale for his own profit and to the company's loss, with the Dutch and English merchants, in skins, tobacco and provisions. A list made after a fire at his place on the Tinicum Island in December 1645, shows that his stock in provisions was larger than that of the company's, besides a wealth in precious stones, pearls, gold, silver and other valuables, after having been less than two years in the colony and having not raised his salary as it was paid on his return to Sweden. According to the records in the account books Printz had used also 11,288 riks dalers from his own means to the company's need on May 25, 1648, and according to his report had fifty heads of cattle at his estate on the Tinicum Island in 1653.

But if a colonist made a sale to other party than the company, he was severly punished by the governor. A colonist Knut Persson was sick and in distress and to get money for necessities he left his gun with Peter Cock, requesting him to sell it to the Indians. Cock was afraid to do it and said to Persson that he did not dare to sell the gun. But Persson answered "when the governor sells so many guns to the Indians, why should I not dare to sell mine." Later on the gun was stolen from Cock's house by the Indians and the news reached to governor, who summoned Peter Cock to answer at court, since Persson had died in the meantime. The jurors in the court desired Cock freed, but Printz told them that he would do not what seems right to them but what he wished and Peter Cock was condemned to work for the company for three months on his own board. Another Finn, Peter Gunnarsson Rambo was summoned to the court, being accused of having sold grain to the Dutch and was similarly sentenced without regard to the opinion of the jury or hearing of witnesses.

Governor Printz was enriching himself at the expense of the colonists' labor. The Tinicum Island had been granted to him as a gift from Queen Christina of Sweden. On the island he built a palace for himself, called Printz Hall, but the building materials had to be brought in and the work performed by the colonists, without pay. Likewise when the colonists had prepared planks and building materials or farming implements for their own use, the governor confiscated them for the use of his plantations. In 1645, the Printz Hall burned and the colonists had to build it over again and more sumptuous. The colonists also had to do the farm work on the governor's plantations, before their own work, as a tax to the governor.

Governor Printz also confiscated a farm from a colonist. A freeman, called Lasse the Finn, and his wife had been industrious and had put a farm under cultivation in Finland, at the present Chester Creek. The governor accused them of witchery and as they were in arrears with their payment of some merchandise bought from Printz, he confiscated their farm for the debt. The value of the farm, according to the governor's statement did not counterbalance with the debt, but he professed to be kind enough to call it even. However in his report at the autumn of 1653, he places the value of the farm, which he calls Printz Torp, 2,000 riks dalers.

Of a letter written by Governor Printz to Sweden in 1644, one can judge his inhumanity towards the Indians. In the letter he proposes to the Swedish government to send 200 soldiers to the colony, with which he would be able to exterminate the Delaware Indians. "It would be no loss to the beaver trade" he says, as the skins come from the territory of the Black and the White Minquas.

In 1653, the conditions in the colony were becoming unbearable and many colonists deserted to the English colonies of Maryland and Virginia, where they were heartily welcomed and protected. In the summer the situation reached a crisis and a mutiny arose against Governor Printz. On July 27, 1653, a written supplication signed by twenty-two colonists was presented to the governor. In it they say that they were at no hour or time secure as to life and property. They complained that they were all prohibited from trading with either Indians or Christians, although the governor never failed to grasp an opportunity to trade with these parties. They accused the governor of brutality and avarice and of passing judgment in his own favor against the opinions of the jury. They further accused the governor of forbidding the colonists from grinding the flour at the mill and forbidding them the use of the fish waters, the trees in the woods, the grass on the ground and the land to plant on, from which they had their nourishment. They then prayed that Anders the Finn might be released from his fine, in order that his wife and children should not starve to death. (The rye crop of a freeman called Anders the Finn had been confiscated by Printz and other fines imposed, unjustly, as was the opinion of the colonists.) On account of these and other troubles, they said, they were compelled to send two men to her royal majesty and the New Sweden Company in Sweden, to ascertain what they should do, since they were not allowed to seek their subsistence in America.

The petition turned the governor into a rage and Anders Jonsson, who presented it, was arrested and became executed on August 1, 1653. The Rev. Lokenius, the Finnish minister, was also involved in the opposition, but for some reasons his freedom was not interfered with, as Printz was a religiously bent man.

Governor Printz however in his turn started to feel his position unsecure and without waiting for a ship from Sweden to arrive he left his position to his son-in-law Johan Papegoja and in the beginning of October he went to New Amsterdam with his wife and four daughters, followed by the commissioner and twenty-five servants and soldiers of the company. From there they sailed on a Dutch ship back to the old country, but in the colony for many generations traditions lived about Printz as the Tyrant of the Delaware.

During the time of Governor Printz some colonists had been able to escape to the English colonies of Maryland and Virginia, but entry to New Netherland had been discouraged in accordance to agreement with Printz. On November 4, 1653, the directors of the Dutch West India Company in Holland however informed Stuyvesant that there were no objections of receiving such settlers but on the contrary they would be valuable to the colony. After Printz had left the colony, some deserted colonists returned, but fifteen again went to Maryland. When Papegoja, whom Printz had left in charge of the colony, became aware of their going, he hired a bunch of Indians to bring them back, but the colonists resisted and in the battle that ensued two colonists were struck down and their heads brought to Papegoja.

With the ninth expedition, arriving in May 1654, came from Sweden a new director, Johan Rising to the colony. As Printz had left the country, Rising assumed the command, afterwards receiving appointment as governor of the colony. Director Rising's first acts were to get the deserters back from the English colonies. Two commissaries were sent to Maryland in May 1654, they were instructed to demand from the officials the return of the deserters. But the efforts did not materialize, the deserters were brought before the council in Severn which found that they were not under obligation or contract to go back to New Sweden, since they had committed no crime and had been refused a passport. In the following month two agents were again sent to the same mission and an open letter dated June 8, 1654 was also sent to the deserters, in which it was promised that "if they came and explained their affairs, however they were, they could then go wherever they pleased." But no colonist returned. Several new attempts to desert were made from time to time during the governorship of Rising, giving rise to trials, law suits and punishments. Some were put in irons, and others had to secure bonds against desertion.

At this period the Swedish crown had made donations of land to the men who came to the colony in some official capacity. This was done without consideration of the colonists who had settled on the lands, built their houses and put the land under cultivation. Thus Marcus Hook and Finland were given away to Captain Besk, who however died in Porto Rico on his way to the colony and Rising refused to ratify the donation to his heirs. Just the same the colonists did not profit much of it as Rising in his report of 1654 says that he was acquiring to the company all land of Marcus Hook and Finland, where five or six freemen were living, "the improvement only being compensated for."

On June 26, 1654, a council convened at Tinicum to examine into the charges against the Rev. Lokenius and Olof Stille for inciting a mutiny against Governor Printz. No evidences could be established against the minister, but in a letter sent to Sweden on July 13, 1654, Rising says that he was going to send the Rev. Lokenius to Sweden to answer to the authorities there the charges, but as Lokenius had contracted the epidemic that came to the colony in the Orn, he could not be sent. Olof Stille was required to secure bondsmen. The great majority of the people had complaints against Printz and Rising requested them to present their complaints in writing, which they did and grave charges were made. The colonists were forbidden, they say, on pain of death to trade with the Dutch freemen, but the governor sold them himself provisions, flour, beer, pork and other things and sold large quantities of beavers to the English for gold and sent heaps of beaver skins to Holland. Governor Printz was accused of ill treating several of the colonists, among which is the following case. A freeman called Clement the Finn had a hand-mill together with Anders, Johan and Mans the Finn. Later Clement bought the mill from the other Finns, and when he then got the mill he went after it and fetched it to himself and his house. As this had happened he immediately made it known to the governor. Then when Clement came to the church on a common day of prayer, the governor called Clement to himself before the sermon and asked him why he had taken the mill. Clement answer that "the mill is mine." Then said the governor, "you rascal, shall you take the mill without asking me." With this he seized Clement, struck him firstly in the hall and followed him with blows and strikes until he fell down and yet further he struck him on the ground, so that he lost his health through it. In addition he threw him into the church and the day after he let him be brought to Christina into the prison, where he lay for eight days. When he recovered somewhat, the governor took him out and let him do work for some weeks.

The written complaint against governor Printz was sent to Sweden but together with it Rising in his report of July 13, 1654, writes: "I would desire that full authority might as soon as possible be given here in judicial matters, in higher and lower trials and that for this purpose an executioner (with sword) be sent here. Through this, much disorder would be prevented, which otherwise might hereafter break out through secret plots." The documents were taken to Sweden by Papegoja who was sent to "explain" the affairs, that his father-in-law might not get in trouble.

On January 11, 1655 a constitution for the colony was issued by Rising. In the fourth article of the document the fare for the voyage from Sweden to the colony was fixed to be sixteen riks dalers ($144 in present money value) per head over three years of age. In the article six it is said that "Whoever desires to take into his service a laborer or a freeman, his children, his male servant or maid servant, he must pay the above transportation money after the lapse of a year and these engaged servants shall serve him for three years for board and necessary clothes." In the article eight he says: "Whoever hires from the company an intended servant over fourteen years of age, shall give beside the said transportation money, additional twenty-four riks dalers and then the servant shall serve him in six consecutive years. The servant shall annually be given board, shoes and shirts. After six years of service an indentured servant shall be entirely free. The tenth article says: "Whatever a servant may gain through work, handicraft or manual labor, hunting or fishing, commerce or trade or with anything else, that shall all belong to his employer, unless the latter grants it to him." In article thirteen it is said: "If anyone's servant or a hired man runs away from his master out of spite, then no one shall knowingly conceal the same in his house over twenty-four hours on penalty of twenty-four riks daler's fine, but shall make it known at once to the master."

The above quoted constitution which aimed to establish slavery however did not endure long. The Swedish rule on the Delaware was soon drawing to a close and better days were dawning upon the pioneer colonists.

CHAPTER X.

The Delaware Colony Conquered by the Dutch.

THE Dutch had always claimed the Delaware valley as their territory and they actually were the first ones who explored the river and attempted settlements there. In spring of 1616, Cornelius Hendricksen from Holland was exploring the country about the Delaware Bay. He ascended the river and made the first map of the Delaware. In 1620, Cornelius Mey of Hoorn sailed up the river and after him the mouth of the Delaware was called New Port May by the Dutch. When the Dutch West India Company was organized in 1621, it was invested with the monopoly to trade in the territories in America claimed by Holland. And in the same year a ship was sent by the company's permission from Holland to trade at the "South River," as the Dutch called the Delaware as distinguished from the "North River," the Hudson. Besides the Dutch, the English and French also carried on beaver trade at the river at this time. Captain Mey was again sent to the Delaware in 1623 with orders to build a fort there to acertain Dutch occupation, and a dominant position on the Big Timber Creek at Gloucester Point, (as these places are called today), on the east side of the river was selected by him as the place for block-house which he called Fort Nassau. Four couples and eight seamen were left by him to settle there. In a few years however the fort was deserted. In 1629, Samuel Godyn, an officer of the Dutch West India Company applied for privilege from his company to found a colony on the South River. Godyn was later joined by Samuel Blommaert, the founder of New Sweden Company, who also was a member of the Dutch company. They

bought from the Indians land on the south side of the Delaware
Bay, extending northward about thirty miles from Cape Henlopen
to the mouth of the Delaware River, and inland about two miles.
The patent for the territory was signed at New Amsterdam by
Governor Peter Minuit on July 16, 1630, the Indians appearing to
ratify the purchase. At the end of the same year Godyn, Blommaert and their associates sent two vessels for expedition to their
acquired territory. One of the ships became captured by the
pirates, but the other vessel, the Walvis, commanded by Captain
Peter Heyes, with provisions and cattle and twenty-eight colonists arrived in the Delaware in April 1631. Heyes landed on the
creek near present Lewes, which he called Hoornkill or Hoorn
Creek and planted a colony on the bank of the creek, calling it
Swanendael (Valley of Swans). A little fort called the Oplandt
was built where the colonists lived in security against the attacks
of the Indians. In the summer the colonists had their lands
seeded and covered with a fine crop, their cows had calved and
five more colonists had arrived, when the commander of the colony
fell in trouble with the Indians. An Indian chieftain had stolen
from a boundary mark a piece of tin stamped with the coat of
arms of Holland and had made pipes out of it, for which he was
shot. In revenge, the Indians attacked the colonists when they
were working in the field and slaughtered all the people and animals, except one man Theunis Willemsen managed to escape.
When the second expedition for Swanendael left from Holland,
under command of Captain De Vries, the faith of the colony was
known. And on their arrival to Hoornkill on December 6, 1632,
they found the ground strewed with the bones of the murdered settlers and their fort burned. De Vries remained in the river about
three months, trading with the Indians. He visited also Fort
Nassau in January 1633, which he found occupied by the Indians.
During the summer of 1633 the fort was again taken possession of
by the Dutch traders, who also built a blockhouse on the Schuylkill in that summer. In 1635, some fifteen or sixteen Englishmen from Virginia took possession of Fort Nassau, which they
had found deserted, but a Dutch bark soon recaptured the fort and

the Englishmen were sent back to Virginia. The Dutch hereafter kept the fort garrisoned permanently in order to keep the English away. Difficulties had arisen between the Dutch West India Company and the patrons of the Swanendael Company about trade at the Delaware, the matter was in the court in Amsterdam and the West India Company bought the rights of the patrons in February 1635.

When Peter Minuit with his expedition in 1638 arrived to the Delaware River under the Swedish flag, the Dutch commissary at Fort Nassau, Jan Jansen, was visiting in New Amsterdam, but the assistant commissary, Peter Mey, protested against Minuit's landing at the river and sent a report about it to Governor Kieft at Manhattan. The governor then ordered commissary Jansen to return to his post and in due form to protest against Minuit's occupancies. Minuit however claimed that the Swedish queen had as much rights on the Delaware as the Dutch and went on with the building of his fort and trading with the Indians. Governor Kieft then protested himself in a letter of May 6, 1638, against the landing and settling of Minuit, reminding that the whole South River of New Netherland had been many years in their possession.

The things however went on without a serious event for the one reason that the English had similar claims on the Delaware River district. But in 1652, Governor Stuyvesant of New Netherland by order of the Dutch West India Company, built a fort in the site of present town of New Castle, which he called Fort Casimir, without paying attention to the protests of the Swedish Governor Printz, who had order from his government to keep the Dutch out of the Delaware. This fort was manned by nine Dutch soldiers, who happened to be out of ammunition when Johan Rising arrived to the Swedish colony in the spring of 1654. Rising forced the Dutch garrison to vacate the fort and occupied it with the Swedish forces and changed the name to Trefaldighets Fort or Fort Trinity, as it was occupied on the Trinity Sunday. Governor Stuyvesant had been informed about the arrival of the Swedish ship Orn on the Delaware and a messenger was sent by him across the country with a letter addressed to the Swedish commander, in which he congratulated the newcomers for their arrival and offered his friendship. However when he heard of the capture of Fort Casimir, he became furious and made up his mind to retaliate when an opportunity presented itself. The directors of the Dutch West India Company in Holland did not either take kindly the capture of their fort, and on November 6, 1654, Stuyvesant was commanded to prepare for driving away the Swedes entirely from the Delaware River. At the end of May 1655, a warship the Waag was sent from Amsterdam with 200 men on board to New Netherland, arriving to New Amsterdam on August 3. Immediately preparations for an expedition to the Delaware were begun and a proclamation was issued, appointing the fifteenth of August a day of prayer and fasting to invoke God's blessing on the expedition. Volunteers were called and towards the end of August all preparations were ready. On Sunday, August 26, a fleet consisting of two warships and five armed merchant vessels set sail for the expedition of conquest, having 317 soldiers on board.

While Stuyvesant was preparing in New Amsterdam for the conquest of Delaware, the Finnish Field Marshal Arvid Wittenberg had reduced Great Poland under the obedience of the Swedish king and on the very day that Governor Stuyvesant left for his expedition, the victorious armies conducted the Swedish king Charles X. into Warsaw the capital of Poland.

The Indians having informed the Delaware people about the approaching danger, two men were sent to Staten Island as spies and they returned confirming the report. The forts were then repaired and preparations were made for defense. The powder supply that they had and most of the soldiers were placed to Fort Trinity and Sven Schute the commander of the Fort had orders not to allow the Dutch fleet pass that point. On August 31, the Dutch ships sailed up the river but Schute seeing the hopelessness of the situation, withheld orders to fire. Stuyvesant then demanded the surrender of the fort and as the garrison was mutinous, refusing to fight, the fort capitulated on September 1, without a shot being fired. The soldiers were taken as prisoners to New Amsterdam and the officers were held in the fort. The name of the fort was changed again to Fort Casimir.

Governor Rising was thereafter persuading Stuyvesant to be satisfied with what he had, but Stuyvesant declared that he had come to occupy the whole Delaware River and would not return before he had accomplished his object. Colonists were now collected from Upland, Finland and Tinicum regions to defend Fort Christina, but there was powder only enough for one round. On September 5, the fort was completely surrounded by Dutch forces, building batteries, on which twenty cannon were placed. Governor Stuyvesant now demanded the surrender of the fort and the entire river after which all the Swedes had to leave the river or take the oath of allegiance to the Dutch masters. Negotiations between the Dutch and Swedish commanders were begun and finally the articles of capitulation were drafted and signed by the two governors on September 15, 1655. In the sixth article of the capitulation it is said that "to those Swedish officers and freemen who are not able to depart from the colony with the governor and his party, the time of one year and six weeks is allowed in which to sell their land and goods, provided they do not take the oath of allegiance for the period that they remain." In the seventh article it is said that: "If any of the Swedes or Finns are not disposed to go away, Governor Rising may take measures to admonish them to do so; and if they are so persuaded, they shall not be forcibly detained." The tenth article says: "Governor Rising has full freedom to make himself acquainted with the conduct of commandant Schute and that of his officers and soldiers in regard to the surrender of Fort Trinity."

Fort Christina was evacuated the same day as the capitulation was signed, the volunteers were thereafter held as prisoners on the Timber Island near the fort and the officers in their own quarters in the fort. Half an hour after the Swedish forces had left the fort, Governor Stuyvesant with his officers and council appeared in Fort Christina, shook hands with the Swedish officers and offered to hand over the fort to the Swedes on the conditions that the Dutch be allowed to dwell undisturbed in possession of the land below Christina River and that the past troubles be forgotten and forgiven. The Swedes were to remain in possession of all the land north of the fort along the Delaware, the country being large enough for both of them.

Governor Rising was greatly surprised at this kind of proposition. A descendant of Vikings, whose traditions were to take theirs by force, could not apprehend benefits derived of mutual understanding. His answer to the Dutch governor was that the proposition seemed somewhat strange to him, but requested Stuyvesant to present the offer in writing, and a reply would be given as soon as the Swedish council had considered the matter. The matter was taken up on the following day and the unanimous opinion of the Swedish council was, that Stuyvesant's proposition was unacceptable, whereupon the Dutch governor was notified to that effect. Arrangements were therefore made by the Dutch to carry out the articles of surrender, and preparations were started for the departure of the Swedes for New Amsterdam. As nearly all the freemen were Finns, only few of the actual colonists desired to go back to Sweden. Those Swedes who were obliged to remain to sell their property were given a letter of excuse or permission by Rising. Several of these are found today in the royal archives at Stockholm, one reads as follows:

"His Royal Majesty, my Most Gracious King's most humble and faithful servant and Director of New Sweden:

"Hereby witnesseth, that inasmuch as the upright and intelligent Nils Matsson, freeman, of Herring Island, in the troubles of these times here in New Sweden, wherein we Swedes have been unexpectedly involved by the hostility of the Hollanders, cannot remove from this country so hastily, but on account of his property must remain here until more convenient season, and therefore desires a testimonial from me which I cannot justly withhold from him; I therefore herewith testify that during the whole period of my residence in this country, he has conducted himself as an honorable and faithful subject of the Crown, and willingly assisted in the repairs and building of the fort, as well as in other service of the Crown, and now lately in the war for the defense of the country voluntarily went down to Fort Trinity, but was taken prisoner on the way and conveyed on shipboard where, during the space of three weeks, he encountered much contumely and reproach. (Meanwhile the enemy robbing his house and stripping his wife of everything at their home.) Through all this he conducted himself as a good subject ought to do. The truth of all this I confirm with my own hand and seal.

"Done at Fort Christina, September 24, 1655.

Johan Rising."

On September 24, a court martial was held by Rising on the Timber Island, at which examinations were made into the conduct of Commander Schute, who was blamed for not giving orders to fire on the Dutch ships as they passed Fort Trinity. The commander was accused by Rising of disobeying orders and other grave charges were made against him, namely, that he had persuaded two Swedes to stay in the colony. During the examination it was brought out that a great part of the soldiers were mutinous and refused to fight. In the circumstances Schute did not think of going to Sweden to be court martialed, but remained in the colony with the Finns.

The baggage of the Swedes were now loaded on the Dutch ships and on the first day of October the vessels set sail for New Amsterdam, where they arrived nine days later. The Swedes were held on board the warship Waag and Rising was sending bitter notes to Stuyvesant about the occupation of the Delaware River and on matters connected with it. He requested in all justice that the troops should not be influenced to remain in New Amsterdam, but according to the capitulation they should go with him in the same ship. The Finnish soldiers of the garrison of Fort Trinity were accused in court martial on the Timber Island on September 24, for refusing to fight the Dutch. Stuyvesant persuaded them to stay in New Amsterdam and naturally they did so. Finally there were thirty-seven people left in Rising's party, who were placed on board three vessels and on October 23, they left for the old country.

CHAPTER XI.

New Expeditions of Finns Arriving to the Delaware River.

WHILE grave events were going on at the Delaware River, preparations were made in Sweden for a new expedition. In the middle of October 1655, about 200 Finns, mostly from Vermland had arrived to Gothenburg, desirous to go to America. However, as the epidemic that broke out in the crowded ship Orn was now known in Sweden, all of the colonists could not be taken on board the small ship Mercurius, that was going on this expedition. Of the prospective colonists ninety-six of the most suitable were finally selected, of which Hendrick Huygen, the commander of the expedition in his passenger list, made at the sailing of the ship, classifies as follows:

Swedish women	2
" maidens	2
Finnish men	33
" women	16
" maidens	11
" children under twelve years	32
	—
Total	**96**

Besides his list includes nine officers and some servants who had been in the colony before. Among the officers were the maker of the list, Hendrick Huygen, who went to the colony as head commissary, Johan Papegoja, who also returned to the colony and a clergyman, barber-surgeon and a Swedish speaking Finn as Swedish-Finnish interpreter. The servants also were Finns. There were 130 souls in all on the ship, including the sailors and officers of the ship.

Johan Papegoja who had charge of the colonists during the voyage, hired a Swedish speaking Finn Hendrick Olsson as his assistant as he could not speak Finnish and the colonists who came mostly from the Finnish settlements in Vermland knew no Swedish.

Admiral Anckarhjelm in his list of 110 colonists, including the servants, made on October 17, 1655, gives also the names of the colonists, but five of those who already had been admitted had to be left out on account of limited space in the ship, as warnings had arrived from Stockholm not to crowd the ship. More than a hundred prospective Finnish colonists had to be left behind, who had sold their property at any price and traveled a long distance in the hopes of getting passage to America. Papegoja writes that there was a great lamentation and weeping among them.

The roll list of the colonists made by Admiral Anckarhjelm is interesting on account of the Finns not knowing the Swedish language, still every one of them had a Swedish name. This is because the Finnish names were difficult to the Swedes to spell, they used to make their family names out of their fathers' Christian names by adding "son." Thus, if the father's name of Anders Halttunen was Matti, then Anders Halttunen became Anders Matson. During the Swedish rule in Finland most of the population thus received Swedish names and have remained so to the very present times, only during the last twenty-five years the Finns had started to prefer Finnish names and there has been a movement to discard the Swedish names, as many as hundred thousand Swedish names have thus been legally changed into Finnish names within one year.

The passenger list of Admiral Anckarhjelm reads:

"The Roll List of the Colonists, about to go to New Sweden, who have been examined and written down to the seventeenth of October 1655.

"From Frijisdalen (Fryksdal in Vermland).

Johan Grelson with wife and three children	5
Martin Pafvelsson with wife only	2
Nils Nilsson with wife and four children	6
Anders Larsson with wife and five children	7

Mats Matsson with wife and one child	3
Olof Olofsson, a servant	1
Gerdrud, a servant	1
Joen Staffeson, the blacksmith	1
Karin Andersdotter, a widow with one child	2
Marcus Sigfriedhsson, a servant	1
Joran Joransson, a servant	1
Nils Simonsson with wife and three children	5
Joran Sigfriedsson with wife	2
Hindrick Jacobsson with four almost grown sons	5
Grels Grelsson, a servant	1
Eric Matsson, a servant	1
Lars Larsson, a servant	1
Olof Clemètsson, a servant	1
Jons Hindricksson, a servant	1
Elissabeth Esekelsdotter, a servant	1
Oluf Olufsson, a servant	1
From Lijtestegen (Letstigen, Vermland)	
Thomas Jacobsson with wife, maid-servant and three children	6
Pafvell Persson with wife, maid-servant and three children	6
Oluf Philipson with wife and five children	7
Pavel Nilson with wife and two children	4
Oluf Nilson with wife only	2
Lars Bengtsson with wife, man-servant and four children	7
Jons Jonson with wife and six children	8
Carol Jonson with wife, maid-servant and three children	6
Eric Martensson with wife and two children	4
Johan Simonsson with wife and three children	5
From Brunskogh (Brunskog in Vermland)	
Anders Jacobsson with wife, maid-servant and three children	6

110"

The ship had been held up a month in Gothenburg, on account of contrary winds, but on November 25 the wind was at last favorable and the expedition left for its long journey. On March 14, 1656, they sailed up the Delaware to find Fort Trinity in the hands of the Dutch, who refused them permission to pass the fort. But as the colonists wanted to land, Huygen and Papegoja, who were both Dutchmen, went ashore and requested from the Dutch governor Jacquet permission to land the people somewhere at the river until further orders were received from Sweden. This was denied and Huygen was arrested as an enemy of the state. Papegoja then appealed to Governor-General Stuyvesant in a letter, dated March 14, requesting permission to revictual and return unmolested to Europe. The council in Manhattan decided not to allow the colonists to land but they should be free to return unmolested. It was likewise decided that some Swedes in the colony who had not taken the oath of allegiance be deported. A pass was issued for the ship to come to Manhattan where necessary supplies could be obtained for the return voyage. When these instructions were received, Huygen, who was released, went to Manhattan to present the colonists' case in person, but he received the reply that if the ship would not leave the river, it would be expelled by force, for this a warship was ordered to prepare for the South River. Huygen then agreed to send an order to Mercurius to come to New Amsterdam. But after more than two weeks of waiting no ship had arrived. Rumors now came in of an Indian uprising on the Delaware, therefore some soldiers were despatched overland there. The old Finnish colonists on the Delaware wanted their friends and relatives landed among them and the Indians, hearing of the Dutch refusal, gathered in great numbers around Fort Casimir and threatened to wipe off the entire colony if the newcomers were not allowed to land. Thereafter some of the old Finnish colonists with Indian chiefs boarded the ship and it was ordered to lift the anchor and it passed the Dutch fort without being fired upon. When the Dutch soldiers arrived at the Delaware, the colonists were already landed, but as the Indians were very agitated it was necessary to send a warship from New Amsterdam with troops to the river and the Indians were finally pacified with gifts bought by the Dutch from the cargo of Mercurius. The Swedish ship was later brought to New Amsterdam where the cargo was traded to tobacco and arrived to Gothenburg on September 6, 1656. Papegoja returned to Sweden already before, on a Dutch ship, and a Swedish-Lutheran minister who came with the Mercurius returned with the same ship, but Huygen remained with the Finns in the colony.

The Dutch were very nervous for the great number of the Finns at the Delaware and for their amicable relations with the Indians, as to what side they would take in case Sweden would try to recapture the colony, and if they some day would themselves expel the Dutch from the river. After the Swedes had been expelled by the Dutch, an autonomous government had been granted to the Finns in order to secure their friendship and finally the Finns were found by the Dutch to be very desirable colonists, and were persuaded to write to their people in Sweden to come to the colony. As the result of this new Finnish settlers arrived from time to time from Sweden. On July 28, 1663, the Dutch skipper Peter Lucassen brought about sixty farmers to the Delaware river, which were nearly all Finns, and December of the same year Governor Alexander d'Hinoyossa arrived with at least thirty-two Finns. In the beginning of 1664, a number of Finnish families from Sweden landed in Holland on their way to the Finnish settlements on the Delaware. A Swedish commissary, Trotzig, in Amsterdam, informed his government of this in a letter on January 17, suggesting that such immigration should be stopped unless Sweden could regain the colony. The Swedish chancellor requested Trotzig to investigate further about the Finnish migration. Accordingly Trotzig went to a suburb of Amsterdam, where the Finnish families were housed and boarded by the City of Amsterdam. He found that there were about 140 souls in all and only few of the men could understand Swedish. Friends in the Delaware colony had written to them and invited them to come over. One colonist showed a letter from his brother dated on the Delaware River in 1657. The Finns had made their way from Sweden to Christiania, Norway and had hired there a Dutch vessel to take them to Amsterdam.

It was suspected that the colonists had been enticed by special agents. Accordingly letters were sent by the Swedish government on May 27, 1664, to governors of various provinces stating that several hundred families had been enticed to leave their country and go across the mountains to Norway, in companies of five or six persons at the time. This could not be tolerated and the governors were ordered to keep close watch that it did not occur again. If the instigators of the migration could be captured they were to be kept in arrest.

An order was sent to Trotzig on May 27, 1664, to present the matters to the government of Holland and to demand that the fugitives be returned to Sweden at the expense of those who had induced them to migrate. A Swedish ambassador was also sent to Holland who in the middle of June delivered his credentials and immediately started presentations of memorials and demands in behalf of his government about the colonists and the return of the colony to Sweden. The Dutch however proceeded slowly with the negotiations and on June 26 Trotzig wrote again to Sweden that expedition to take the Finns to the Delaware River was going to leave within fourteen days. In the same letter Trotzig also writes that he had heard that a large number of families from Finland has during the last winter left for the colony, "through the direction and large promises of evil persons."

While the negotiations were going on, England captured the colony in the autumn of 1664 and the negotiations then started with England. On June 1672 a letter was sent to Swedish ambassador Leijonberg in London, requesting him to try in a polite way to prevail upon the English government to return the Delaware colony to Sweden. If they would not want to give back the land then they should allow Sweden to bring the Finns away from there. Sweden never refrained to hope to regain the colony until the War of American Independence finally frustrated her from all hopes.

When the English conquered the Delaware, there were large number of Finns coming to the colony, but this event and the measures taken in Sweden against the Finnish emigration finally closed the migration. Hereafter only few sailors and adventurers reached the settlements.

We have thus followed the early Finnish emigration to America, of which a large and vital part of the population of the states of Delaware, Pennsylvania and New Jersey comes from. Were these Finns a destructive element, as they were characterized by the Swedes? To this is Finland today, after she has been allowed to progress only little more than a century or since she became separated from Sweden in 1809, an eloquent denial. Finland is not only a country of the best homes ,as far as the peasants and the working men concern, but she has the best kept forests in the world and Europe is much dependent upon the extensive forests of Finland today. Were the Finns a people of criminals as they were preferred to be called by the Swedes? To this are the crime statistics of the world an eloquent denial. When we consult the crime statistics we will find the Finns the most decent nation of mankind today, although they used to be better people before. Were the Finns physically an inferior race? To those who do not know by history that the Finns come from a race of renowned warriors, the statistics of modern international athletics may serve as an answer. For man to man the Finns do not have their near-equal in athletics. Were the Finns a mentally inferior race? To this one may find an answer when inquiring where the intellectuals of Sweden come from. It is one interesting thing that the intellectually prominent Swedes have come mostly from Vermland, whose population was given to Sweden by Finland, and where some of the original Finns still today retain their own language. In Vermland was born Esaias Tegner, the greatest poet of Sweden. (The greatest poet in the Swedish lainguage, Runeberg was born and lived in Finland.) The very estate where Tegner wrote the best part of his work, bears a Finnish name. In Vermland were born also Geijer, Lagerlof, Dahlgren, Froding and a long line of men of science and inventors, among which was John Ericsson the builder of Monitor and American Civil War fame.

The comparison of the character of peoples does not need to be a guess work today, as one can follow black on white in the international statistics and daily papers of the different nations. Upon these measures it is safe to say that no higher type of emigrants, than the Finns, ever landed on the American shores.

CHAPTER XII.

The First Period of the Finnish Settlements Under the Dutch Rule.

AFTER the conquest of the Delaware, Governor Stuyvesant arranged a government in the South River colony. The country was now divided into two administrative and court districts, the Fort Casimir and the Finnish Colony. Captain Dirck Smidt was appointed as the Dutch commander, while the Finns were called to form an autonomous government under the Dutch rule. They elected as their magistrates Peter Cock, Peter Rambo, Olof Stille and Matts Hansson and for their commissary or sheriff Gregory van Dyck who was of Dutch origin and familiar with the Dutch language. The Finnish colony had also its own militia and their own military commander and officers. Sven Schute was elected as captain or commander of the Finnish militia, by the Finns.

Governor Stuyvesant was not however satisfied with the deportment of Dirck Smidt and as there was then in the Manhattan a man, Jean Paul Jacquet, who had been in the service of the Dutch West India Company in Brazil,Smidt was recalled and Jacquet appointed as vice-director on the South River. Instructions about his duties were given to Jacquet on November 29, 1655, in which he was especially warned to look after the Swedes who still were at the South River, that they be not allowed in the fort, and if any of them might be found who are not well affected towards the Dutch West India Company and Holland, he shall with all possible politeness make them leave, and if possible to send them to Manhattan. On December 20, 1655, Sven Schute was questioned in court at New Amstel for alleged unloyal utterances, and on March 29, 1656, Governor Stuyvesant and his council passed an order directing Schute and Jacob Svensk arrested and deported. However the order did not become executed on account of the difficulties that arose at the arrival of Mercurius with the new Finnish colonists.

A daughter of Governor Printz, Madame Papegoja, who remained in the colony to sell her father's estate, the Tinicum Island, had hard time because nobody would work for her, as she had been accustomed during the time Printz was the governor at the South River, to see the work done on her father's plantations by the colonists without wages. She preferred to be called Miss Printz since her husband Johan Papegoja, who returned from Sweden with Mercurius, immediately went back to Sweden, leaving his wife and children here for unexplained reasons. One of her father's estates was Printz Torp, which originally had been confiscated by Governor Printz from a freeman, called Lasse the Finn. Governor Jacquet refused to recognize Printz Torp as the property of Governor Printz, because the estate had been acquired in 1654 by Governor Rising to New Sweden Company and therefore became now the property of the Dutch West India Company. Therefore Miss Printz writes to Governor-General Stuyvesant the following petition:

"Tinicum, August 3, 1656.

"Noble, honorable Director-General of New Netherland.

"It is doubtless well known to the Honorable General that our late Governor, my highly respected Lord and Father, had conveyed to him a piece of land for a bouwery, partly made by freemen, who have returned to Sweden, partly cleared of the brush by his own orders and that, after he had cultivated the same for several years, it was granted to him by the King and also confirmed by Her present Royal Majesty. It has however, not been cultivated for nearly three years and is overrun with young underwood, while the house standing on it has been still more ruined by the Indians; therefore I have been induced, to have the same repaired and the land cultivated by three Finns. Now whereas against my expectation I have been forbidden by the Honorable Commandant to continue in it, therefore I am compelled, to inform hereof the Honorable General with the humble prayer, that he will please in his gracious and good will, as well as for the great friendship, which he had for my Lord and Father, to let me enjoy the same, upon which I firmly trust. Thus I pray once more, that my people at Printz Torp may remain unmolested and continue cultivating the soil and for greater security I may be granted by the Honorable General letters-patent for this place as well as for Tinicum. I hope, that this will be acknowledged by my Lord and Father as an act of great friendship and be gratefully requited as far as possible, wherewith I commend the Honorable General to the protection and grace of the Almighty.

Armgard Printz."

The petitioner was permitted by Stuyvesant to take in possession the Printz Torp plantation, but she had made many statements in her petition that were not true at all. As the freeman Lasse the Finn from whom the farm, which afterwards was called the Printz Torp, was robbed, never went back to Sweden but still lived in the country. The land never was granted to Governor Printz by any king, there was not even any king in Sweden, while Printz was at the Delaware nor during more than ten years before. At present there was no queen in Sweden but a king, as Queen Christina abdicated in the spring of 1654, which was known at the Delaware on the arrival of the ship Orn on May 22 of the same year. On the contrary the land had been donated by the queen to a Finnish captain in the Swedish navy, the document, in which Finland where the Printz Torp was situated is referred to as Marcus Hook, reads as follows:

"We, Christina, by the Grace of God, Queen of the Sveans, Goths and Vandals, Grandduchess of Finland, Dutchess of Esthonia, Karelia, etc. hereby make known that we, out of our grace and favor, as for the zealous and faithful service which our faithful servant and captain Hans Asmundson Besk, has honorably and manfully shown and performed for us and our Crown, and which hereafter, so long as he lives and is able, he binds himself to show and perform for our sake, have given and granted, as we herewith and in these our Letters Patent do confirm, grant, and give to him, his wife, and heirs forever, a piece of land situated in New Sweden called Marcus Hook, which extends into Upland Kill, that, together with all things pertaining and belonging to it on land and water, by whatever name they may be called, without any exception of those now therewith connected and formerly so connected which rightly belong thereto, or may hereafter fall to or be gained by legal decision to enjoy, use and retain as an indisputable property forever. All herewith concerned shall conduct themselves in a manner thereto concordant; not doing to the said Besk, his wife, or heirs, any hindrance hereto, nor any manner of wrong or injury, either now or in time to come. For further confirmation, etc.

Stockholm, August 20, 1653,

Christina."

Captain Besk to whom the land had thus been donated in disregard of those who had established their homesteads on it, died on his way to the colony and Governor Rising in his report to Sweden in 1654 says that he intends to buy these farms, including Printz Torp, to the company, "the improvements only being compensated for," he says. The heirs of Captain Besk, although they permanently remained in the colony, never profited by the donation.

The Fort Casimir became the center of the Dutch administration on the Delaware. In a letter of March 13, 1656, Stuyvesant is instructed by the directors of the Dutch West India Company to keep the above mentioned fort in good state of defence but not to mind of Fort Christina, only to keep three or four men there. Governor Jacquet was ordered in his instructions to lay out streets and lots at Fort Casimir, and he endeavored to make the outlying people to built their homes in the town.

The government of the Finnish colony had petitioned from Governor-general Stuyvesant some rules and instructions about the limits of their administrative power, and on August 14, 1656, their commissaries or magistrates and the sheriff appeared upon summons in Fort Casimir where Governor Jacquet delivered them their commissions and instructions. At the same time an ordinance in regard to the sale of strong drinks was read and then handed over to the sheriff to be published in the Finnish colony. There was also a murder case in discussion. The Indians had killed at Fort Casimir a daughter of Captain Besk. The matter was left to the hands of the sheriff of the Finnish colony, although he was to report it at the court of Fort Casimir, as the crime had been committed within the jurisdiction of the said court.

Since the close of the Swedish rule, when trade became free for every inhabitant, there had been rivalry in obtaining, the skins from the Indians. Dirck Smidt, whom Stuyvesant left in command of the river after its conquest from the Swedes, was strongly reprimanded for having paid too much wampum for the furs. The price of a beaverskin had become established to two fathoms of wampum, and each fathom was to be three ells long. An ell was measured from the corner of the mouth to the thumb of the opposite arm extended. But the Indians sent their longest armed men to dispose the skins, causing shortage in the treasury of the company. This was now to be remedied and on January 10, 1657 the traders of the whole river assembled and fixed prices were decided on all skins and fines for paying over the figures of the price list.

The conquest of the Delaware had cost very heavily to the Dutch West India Company, on account of the warship Waag that the City of Amsterdam had loaned for this purpose and for its 200 soldiers and supplies. For these the company had fallen to heavy debts to the city. There were therefore negotiations going on between the company and the city as early as in June 1656 about the surrender of a part of the South River territory to the city of Amsterdam. In a letter of December 19 of the same year the directors of the company notified Governor Stuyvesant of the surrender of Fort Casimir and the land about it to the City of Amsterdam. The fort was to be called New Amstel and Jacob Alrich was coming over to be the Director and Commissary-General of the new colony. Governor Stuyvesant was ordered to deliver and convey to Jacob Alrich the fort and the land on the westside of Minquas or Christina Kill, to the mouth of the bay or river at Bombay Hook, and so far to landward as the boundaries of the Minquas country. Director Alrich arrived to Delaware in April 1657 with 117 colonists and 50 soldiers.

The affairs of the Dutch West India Company on the Delaware and the moving of the company's property to Fort Christina, now called Fort Altena, were left to three representatives as director Jacquet was removed from his office by the letter of Stuyvesant on April 20, 1657, for misrule and was ordered before the council at Manhattan where he was arrested. Altena became now the centre of administration of the company's colony and the fort was garrisoned with 16 soldiers.

The inhabitants of the Finnish colony, being mostly engaged in farming, had not built yet any town of their own but were scattered in a wide area, mostly from Fort Altena to the Schuylkill River. However in the spring of 1657 they had decided to built a town and on the 20th of May they commissioned their sheriff to appear before the council at Manhattan with a request for permission to establish a town. This was what had been the wish of the directors of the Dutch West India Company, as they considered that it would weaken their position of resistance in case of arising difficulties, and the permission was not only granted but it was also judged necessary that the same should be done. The sheriff and the commissaries of the Finnish colony were therefore authorized and qualified, but also ordered and directed to concentrate the people in a town either at Upland, Passayunk,. Finland, Kingsessing, on the Trinity Hook, or at any such place as by them may be considered suitable, under condition that previous notice be given to the Director-General and Council at Manhattan, in case they should choose some other place, than those specified above.

The sheriff also requested in behalf of the Finns for their court a man who should attend to the duties of court-messenger and provost, for which the sheriff proposed Jurgen the Finn, who lived on the Crooked Kill. To this the Director-General and Council agreed and consented that the above named person may be employed for it, provided that he, opportunity offering, come to Manhattan to present himself to the Director-General and Council, when a salary shall be allowed to him.

In the summer of 1657, there had been carried on some smuggling in the ships of the City of Amsterdam plying between the Delaware River and Europe. The directors of the Dutch West India Company therefore urged Stuyvesant to appoint a commissary to the South River, who would have to reside on behalf of the company at Fort Amstel to be on hand and present on the arrival of ships. Governor Stuyvesant decited therefore to visit the South River to investigate the charges. But it was only on April 20, 1658, that it was finally determined at the council meeting in Manhattan that the governor go to the South River accompanied by a gentleman of the council, Pieter Tonneman, to adjudge the following matters: Frauds in customs, several inhabitants of the Colony of New Amstel have requested to be allowed to move into the Finnish colony and to establish plantations near Fort Altena, some necessary arrangements had to be made among and in regard the Finns.

The Director-General immediately arrived to the South River and the magistrates of the Finnish colony prepared at Tinicum the following petition to be presented to Stuyvesant.

"The Sheriff and the members of the Council humbly request the Noble, Honorable General, now here present, a favorable decision on the subjoined petition:

"1. That we may be provided with proper instructions to perform equitably the duties entrusted to us.

"2. That for their execution we may have a Court-messenger.

"3. When it is necessary, that we may have free access to the Commander at Fort Altena, to get assistance from the soldiers in cases of emergency.

"4. That an order be made that nobody shall leave these boundaries without knowledge of the magistrate, much less, that the servant-man or woman of one, when they leave to run away without their master's or mistress' permission, shall not be concealed by the other.

"Tinicum, May 8, 1658.

"The Honorable General's humble subjects,

> Gregorius van Dyck,
> Olof Stille,
> Mats Hanson,
> Peter Rambo,
> Peter Cock."

The foregoing written petition having been taken up, it was found to be a just demand; therefore the petitioners were promised and assured that upon the first opportunity a proper instruction shall be sent to them, to make use of in the course of their administration of justice and for the better execution of their duties, as far as possible.

On the second point it was deemed necessary, that for making summons, arrests and the carrying out of sentences, the Sheriff and Commissaries be supported and served by a provost, who as Court-messenger shall at the same time serve summons pursuant to the instruction, to be sent by the first opportunity offering.

Upon the third it was decided and at the same time orders given to the provisional Commissary at Fort Altena, that if the Commissaries of the Finnish colony should consider it necessary and the Sheriff ask it, he shall assist him in the execution of his duties and support and aid him with the Honorable Company's military.

In regard to the fourth and last point, an order was before this issued by a placat of the Director-General and Council, of which a copy shall be sent to the petitioners by the first opportunity; in the meantime it is decided and ordered that nobody shall be allowed to leave without previous knowledge of the Commissaries and further that thereto, as it is proper, the consent of the Director-General and Council shall first be asked and obtained, signed by their secretary, as it is customary in the province of New Netherland and if some one of the Swedish nation (as Stuyvesant and the Dutch usually call the Finns), should wish to leave or already have left the district, the Sheriff was ordered and directed to serve the same with an order to return and in case of refusal to proceed against him either by arrest or by detention, as it may be required and to give a written report of the proceedings to the Director-General and Council in due time.

Finally and lastly, whereas for the maintenance of the above mentioned arrangements, that is for the salaries of the Sheriff, Commissaries, Provost and other officers of higher and lower grade, as well as for other public concerns, by and by some subsidies shall be needed, it is recommended to the Sheriff and Commissaries to think and examine, where the same can be found and raised to the least burden of the "Swedish" nation, our good and faithful subjects, to whom we hereby assure and promise our favour and all possible assistance, as if they were our own nation, pursuant to the oath, made before or still to be taken by those, who may not have taken it.

The following oath was taken by the Finns on the South River.

"We promise and swear in the presence of Almighty God, that we will be and remain loyal and faithful to their Noble High Mightinesses, the Lords States General of the United Netherlands, the Noble Lords-Directors of the General Privileged West India Company, also to their Honorable Director-General, already appointed or in future to be appointed; that we will obey and respect and honor them, as it becomes honest and good subjects, as long as we continue in this province of New Netherland.

"So truly help us God Almighty."

On May 15, 1658, Stuyvesant reported on the affairs of the Delaware in the meeting of the Council at Manhattan, having arrived from the South River on the same day. He reported that he had found many things at the South River not in such a condition as they ought to be, especially regarding the smuggling and frauds in the company's customs, duties on goods, sent there from Holland, as there were many goods, not stamped with the Honorable Company's mark. He also reported that the Finns had asked after taking the oath of allegiance that they might be allowed and granted them, not to be obliged to take sides, if any troubles should arise between Sweden and Holland, which was granted to by Governor Stuyvesant.

On July 30, 1658, William Beekman, son-in-law of Governor Stuyvesant was appointed as commissary of the West India Company on the Delaware. In his instruction, besides seeing that duties will be paid on all goods, he was to have at the South River the highest authority over the company's officers and freemen and to maintain law and justice, as well in civil as in the military cases, pursuant to the instructions formerly given either to the former commissary or to the Finnish colony. His instructions were to be amplified until which time he was to employ for the administration of justice, the sheriff and commissaries of the Finnish colony. Beekman however did not arrive to the South River before in May 1659.

During the time of the Swedish rule on the Delaware, Governor Stuyvesant had learned that there were some differences between the Swedes and Finns, that they were a different nationality. This is why he was so liberal of allowing the Finns their self government, so much more to win them out of the Swedish influence. The Finns had however elected the Swedish Lieutenant Schute, who remained in exile in the colony, as the Captain of their militia, and there were some distrust against him from the side of the Dutch officials. On the other hand the directors of the West India Company did not see any difference at all between the Finns and Swedes, they were fighting together in all the battle fields of Europe. The directors did not know the statutes of these Delaware Finns, they always referred to them as Swedes, and were greatly surprised that Stuyvesant had ventured to allow them a self government. After they had received Governor Stuyvesant's report about the visit on the South River, they commented upon it in a letter of February 13, 1659, to Stuyvesant, objecting to the self-government of the "Swedes." They say: "We have no objections to the arrangements by his Honor (Stuyvesant) on the South River, except the appointment of Swedish officers for that nation, upon which no reliance whatever can be placed: this is inferable not only from their previous actions but also now from their request to the same Director, asking that upon arrival of any Swedish succor they might remain neutral, indeed an unheard of and bold proposition by subjects bound to this State and the Company by their oaths, who thereby clearly show the sentiments nursed in their hearts. We have therefore been so much more astonished, as it would have been much better to disarm the whole nation there, than to provide them in such manner with officers and hand them the weapons, which they will know well how to use against us, not only upon the arrival of the slightest Swedish succor, but also on other occasions: it is therefore necessary that, to prevent it, this mistake must be redressed and principally not only the aforesaid Swedish officers discharged and replaced by others of our nation, but also the time and opportunity taken advantage of, to disarm them altogether upon the least mark of presumption; further, their Sheriff and Commissaries, who are also of their own nation, must serve out their term and then, or in case of previous death their places must be filled again by men of our nationality, that they may be deprived so much more effectively of the means of conspiration and confederation and so much sooner be found out. It would therefore be useful for this purpose, to separate them from each other and prevent their concentrated settlements, or rather to put them scattered among our people, where they will be less to fear. Your Honors can hereby understand, how very important we consider this matter and you are consequently most earnestly recommended and ordered, to carry out and execute our above opinions and intentions with all carefulness as in our judgment the Company and this State are highly concerned."

To the above letter Governor Stuyvesant replied on July 23, 1659, as follows: "We have good reason to believe with our Noble Worships, that neither the Swedes nor the English, who live under our jurisdiction or outside of it, have a great affection for this state and the same might likewise be supposed and sustained from us, in case we should be conquered, from which the good God may save us, but how to prevent and improve it, Right Worshipful Gentlemen, hoc opus hoc labor est. We have thought the most suitable would be a lenient method of governing them and proceeding with them to win their hearts and divert their thoughts from a hard and tyrannical form of government and considering this we granted to the Swedish nation, (as Stuyvesant often calls the Finnish colony), at their request, some officers, that in time of necessity, against the savages and other enemies, in case of defense they might keep order, but we gave them no written document or commission, much less were any arms distributed among them. If your Honorable Worships should not consider this advisable, we shall according to your Hon. Worships' orders correct and abolish as far as possible agreeable to circumstances and occasions."

The affairs of the City of Amsterdam Colony of New Amstel had not run very smoothly since we left them on their arrival to the Delaware River in the spring of 1657. The first spring and summer they used in building a town, and when winter came they realised that they had nothing to eat. New expeditions of people arrived from Amsterdam without provisions and with little merchandise to obtain provisions with. The city had started the colony like everybody else, figuring on exploitation, but soon found out that the colony could not even live upon it, less to bring large profits to the masters. The Indians had converted much of their trade to the English colonies, since the prices for skins were reduced by mutual agreement among the South River people in 1657. The Indian trade on the South River was carried on at this period in the Finnish colony. The New Amstel colonists were tradesmen of Amsterdam, as weavers, tailors, shoemakers, etc., but there was no employment for them, as the Finns were men of all trades who could satisfy the needs of their families themselves from tanning a hide to the making of shoes, from cultivating flax and raising sheep to spinning, weaving and making their clothes and garments of the products. To illustrate best the conditions in the New Amstel colony we quote Alrich, the governor of the colony, from his letter to Stuyvesant on May 14, 1659. "The time in the first year was consumed with the erection of houses, . . . the summer passed without bringing much seed into the ground. Besides that the general sickness which has now (prevailed) during two consecutive years and unstable weather caused much delay in everything. (When the privilege), to draw victuals and other necessaries (on products to be shipped to Amsterdam) from the City's storehouse came to cease, a great (anxiety) . . . came over the people and they were very embarrassed and (in want) . . . One hundred souls came over with ship "Meulen," (in autumn 1658), besides those in the spring of last year, being according to the list sent about five hundred souls . . . the little grain belonging to the Swedes, (the Finns), which was not drowned by

the heavy rains and had not sprouted again through the great mois-
ture, has also been so dear, that we had to buy it at high prices,
equal to pork from a bird's nest, when they needed it themselves.
We had also arranged with the Honorable Governor of the Vir-
ginias, that we should get some provisions from there, whereupon
followed that his Noble Honor freighted his yacht with provisions
of bacon, meat, Indian corn, etc., and sent it hither, but to our
misfortune the skipper of her acted faithlessly and stole away
with the yacht, being so victualled, to go a privateering . . . it
has happened to us as is commonly said, a misfortune comes seldom
alone."

As to the sickness that Director Alrich mentions, about one
hundred people out of the six hundred sent from Amsterdam had
died in course of the two years for fever and for actual hunger, as
Stuyvesant says. Among the dead were the director's wife, the
surgeon, minister and the commissar. The people were accusing
Director Alrich for their misfortune and were deserting in great
numbers as can be seen from Governor Stuyvesant's letter to his
superiors on September 17, 1659. The letter says: "We mentioned
in our last letter the deplorable and bad state of affairs in the City's
Colony, on the South River, caused by the desertion and removal
of the colonists to Maryland, Virginia and other places, which
increase daily in such a manner, that hardly 30 families remain;
besides this the City's soldiers sent out with the colony, who num-
bered at first 50 men, have melted down to one half."

Besides the incompetency, sickness and hunger in the New
Amstel colony, there was a hysterical fear during the summer of
1659 that the English would come and capture the river. On May
23, Alrich writes to Stuyvesant that he had heard rumors that the
English were coming from Maryland to demand the South River
for Lord Baltimore. He says there are some unsatisfied people in
his colony who boast that they have seen or read letters, written
from Virginia to the Finns, that they should remain here as a
free colony under the English, which is openly spoken on the river.
At this time there was a naval alliance between Sweden and England and hostilities on the seas between Holland and Sweden were

going on, that made the directors of the Dutch West India Company in Holland nervous, they were expressing their fear in every letter to Stuyvesant at this period. On September 4, 1659, Governor Stuyvesant writes to the directors that "We are not quite without fear and suspicion, that if the alliance between Sweden and England and the difficulties with our state should continue long, something may not be done, against our state, which the good God may prevent, as under such circumstances we would be too weak to assist our people and keep this place properly garrisoned."

The English authorities in Maryland, having heard from the fugitives of the miserable condition in the New Amstel colony, thought that they could get the South River from the Dutch by asking. With this belief Colonel Utie with half a dozen men arrived to the river on September 6, 1659, from Maryland and informed that the country settled by the Dutch at the river was under Lord Baltimore's jurisdiction and therefore he ordered them to remove immediately or to declare themselves subjects of Lord Baltimore. To this the directors Alrich and Beekman and the Council of New Amstel protested and were allowed three weeks to consult Director-General Stuyvesant about it. The Dutch were scared to death by Colonel Utie's threats that the English would come with a force and both Beekman and Alrich begged Stuyvesant to come to the South River. On September 20, Beekman writes to Stuyvesant that he had asked urgently by letter the sheriff of the Finnish Colony that eight or ten men of their nation might be sent to him for the security of Fort Altena, until he had received relief from Manhattan, but had received no answer at all. On the following day Beekman again writes to Stuyvesant referring to the same matter, and expressing the belief that not much assistance could be expected from that direction.

By this time the directors of the Dutch West India Company and the burgomasters of Amsterdam had been released of their fear of immediate enemy expedition to their colonies in America, as the Dutch had defeated the Swedish navy in 1658, and in the summer of 1659 England was in turmoil by internal difficulties. It soon had its reflection also in Manhattan, as Governor Stuyvesant in his letter of September 23, 1659, to Alrich, condemns the conduct of the Dutch officers at the Delaware and boldly asserts that they should have arrested Colonel Utie and his party and sent them to Manhattan to answer before him for espionage. The directors in Manhattan felt now safe to send a military force to the South River, and on September 23, sixty men left Manhattan on board three ships, under the command of Captain Crieger, arriving to Delaware three days later. Beekman in his letter of September 30, makes excuses to Stuyvesant for not arresting Colonel Utie and makes it the fault of the other parties. He also states that "I received only yesterday morning answer from Sheriff van Dyck and the Commissary (of the Finnish Colony), upon my request made on the 16th instant to send eight or ten men for better security of our Fort; they excuse themselves from it and say, that your Honor had told them through Hendrick Huygen, that they should not stir in case of war, but only assist us against the savages."

Two commissaries were sent from Manhattan also to the Governor and Council of Maryland, in relation to the claim put forth by Colonel Nathaniel Utie to the South River. The head of this embassy, Augustine Heermans writes in his journal about their adventures during the journey to Maryland that they left New Amstel on September 30, 1659, with few soldiers and some Indian guides. On the second day of their journey they came to a stream which the Indians said emptied into the Bay of Virginia (Chesapeake), and called it Curriamus. Here the Indian guides knew of finding a boat, drawn on land, which they took into possession of, and dismissing the guides, they proceeded by water to Elk River and with the evening tide travelled on down the river. Having rowed nearly all night on Elk River, they arrived in the morning of October 2 near Sassafras River, where they found a Finnish settlement of people who had left the Delaware during the time of the Swedish governor Printz. There they met a Finnish soldier Abraham, who had run away from the Dutch service at Fort Altena. Likewise they found a Dutch servant girl. To both parties they guaranteed a pardon if they would return to New Amstel. The maiden accepted the offer but the soldier was not inclined to return. Abraham however accommodated the party by making a pair of oars, as they had only paddles in their boat. Here they tried to obtain information about the current thoughts in the English Colony, but the inhabitants had been little concerned what was going on among the English. After some rest they continued on, but had scarcely left the shore when Abraham and another Finn, Marcus (Siffersson) approached them in a canoe, having found that it was their boat that the party had taken from the Curriamus Creek. The party promised to return the boat on their home journey, but it did not satisfy the Finns. Marcus drew a pistol and threatened to fire if the party would not stop. Finally they let the party to proceed.

Meanwhile Captain Crieger and Secretary van Ruyven of Manhattan had investigated the affairs in the South River and had found much complaints in the City's Colony against Director Alrich. In his letter to Alrich he is accused of not allowing the people to move to Manhattan, wherefore they had to escape to Maryland and Virginia, which was the cause of the English aggression. To this Director Alrich and his council answered on October 16, 1659, and in part said: "And suppose, that all complaints were true and it were not the fault of the common people, then the difficulty must still lie somewhere else, than with the City or her officers, according to all appearances with the country itself, for the people have, one more, the other less, drawn from the warehouse for each family 3, 4, 5, 6 and 700 to 800 guilders in so short time, if they could not get along with that and get so far, that they now could help themselves, then the City of Amsterdam can complain, that she has been misled in such a manner, to spend so much money on a country and that she does not see any other benefit from it." They further accuse the people to be lazy and complain the winds to have been excessive, the rains super abundant and the fear of the English invasion having stopped all activities in the City's Colony.

The real reason of the failure of the Dutch colony on the Delaware was that the City of Amsterdam had sent here people who were not at all fit for pioneering and there was nothing here that they could do. They were undoubtedly good working people while they were at their trades in Holland. If the fathers of the City of Amsterdam had been thoughtful enough to send here mostly veteran farmers and only few artisans, things had run differently. But they had figured upon exploitation and quick returns, which did not materialize.

Messages of the English aggression in the South River had again made the Directors of the Dutch West India Company to worry and in their letter to Governor Stuyvesant on October 14, 1659, they say: "We cannot refute the suspicions and doubts arisen in regard to the Swedish nation (the Finns), settled on the South River, and that the English may very likely intend to undertake something against us there under the Swedish flag and name, the less so, because your Honors have (although with no bad intentions) apparently given them the weapons into their hands, not only by forming them into a militia company, but also by placing them under their own officers, whereas they rather ought to have been separated and scattered among our people, as we have explained at length to your Honors by our letter of the 13th of February of this year. We still persist in our opinion and therefore recommend to your Honors to carry it into effect without delay before they can get any advantage over us with the assistance of our neighbors."

The Directors in Holland did not have apprehension of the makeup of the so-called "Swedish nation" at the South River. They did not know that these people were Finns, many of whom had been with their families forcefully driven away from Sweden, or had chosen to come to America to escape persecutions in Sweden. The Finns at the South River acted independently, being well conscious of human rights and about the statute of the country, but they undoubtedly did not have much desire for the return of Swedish rule to the colony, as they had had it and which could not be but fresh and bitter in their memory.

The Finnish Colony on the South River had now incurred expenses and direct taxation was needed to meet the same. Therefore it was proposed at the meeting of the Finnish magistrates on November 26, 1659, that each family should be taxed five or six guilders. The tax levy required Governor Stuyvesant's approval and it took a long time before anything was done with it, which indicates that Stuyvesant was drawing back from the self government of the Finns, according to the orders from his superiors.

Amidst all the troubles in the New Amstel colony, Director Alrich died on December 30, 1659, after having appointed Alexander d'Hinoyossa his successor as director. Not only were the people dying in the City's Colony, but also the animals. Two of the horses left by the Swedish company at the capitulation of the river, died during the year of 1659. Some of the horses the Dutch had shot during the conquest of the South River. The rest of them were taken care of and worked by the Finnish farmers. As the horses had not increased in number on account of the killing and dying, although the number had not diminished, Beekman in his letter of March 15, 1660, accuses the "Swedes" (the Finns) of it and proposes that the horses be allowed to run wild or sold. The horses, seven in number were delivered to Beekman. Besides two of them had been running wild in the woods for two years. In the approach of the winter the horses were sold to the Finns in exchange of beef, pork and grain.

In the spring of 1660 there was a panic of the people at New Amstel. Three dead savages had been found by the Indians in the underbrushes near the town. They had been killed by two servants belonging to Director Alrich's farm. A dead Indian was similarly found in the forest near Fort Altena, this had died of drunkenness, the liquor having been bought of the Dutch preacher Jan Juriansen Becker. Besides two drunken Dutch soldiers had burned a little Indian canoe, whereupon the savages threatened to burn a house, and they hung the body of the man who died for drinking, on a scaffold before the house of the Bible reader who sold the liquor, suspecting poisoning. The Indians were very agitated, and there was a great fear among the Dutch at New Amstel.

Governor Stuyvesant in his letter to the directors in Holland says that one of the Alrich's servants probably was a Swede or Finn, but he surely was mistaken as can be seen of Vice-Director

Beekman's letter of February 3, 1660, to Stuyvesant. In the letter he says: "I received just now a letter from the Sheriff (of the Finnish Colony) whom I had requested to come to New Amstel with the Commissary, as the Savages are gathered there to talk over the murder, for they are better acquainted with the temper and manner of the Savages, than we newcomers. They excuse themselves, because they are not especially asked by the Director and Council of New Amstel, the Savages also (so they write) have told them, that they should not trouble themselves with this matter, whereas they of the Sandhook or New Amstel were not of their people. The answer was sent to them that if possible they should come here to-morrow, to consult together and that it would be unjustifiable if they could refuse assistance to prevent bloodshed when necessity required it and they were asked."

If among the Indian killers had been any Finn, the Dutch undoubtedly had referred the Indians to them.

On February 8, the Sheriff and Commissary of the Finnish Colony, at the request of Director d'Hinoyossa went in company of Director Beekman to New Amstel, where the accused murderers were held in prison. A trial of the murders were kept in presence of the Indians and after two days of conference, where little offences were reminded on both sides, the Indians agreed to forgive and forget the past instances and were allowed some gifts, upon which a written agreement was signed.

They did not seem to have knowledge of this settlement in Manhattan before after several weeks however and Governor Stuyvesant and the Council were worried, especially as they were in war with the Indians at Esopus. On the first of March, therefore, the Council at Manhattan appointed Fiscal Nicazius de Sille and three other officials to proceed to the South River, with orders to hang the murderers in presence of the Indians, as a good example. Sergeant Andries Lourensen followed the commission to engage some soldiers among the Finns, to fight the Indians at Esopus, or to persuade them to come and settle in Manhattan as freemen, "for reasons more plainly expressed in the resolution." He was to ask with all imaginable and kindly persuasive reason the Finnish

Commissaries' help and intercession, "as the service of the country and the company demands this peremptorily." The soldiers were to be offered 8, 10 or 12 guilders "heavy money" per month, and "if some persons, either married or unmarried, should be inclined to move here (Manhattan) and earn their living as freemen, to such he shall be empowered to promise in our name and for each family or else for every two working persons a pair of good oxen and that they will be accommodated and assisted here as much as possible as well with suitable fertile lands as otherwise."

Governor Stuyvesant's offers looked good enough, but there was the hook inside of them to scatter the Finns according to the orders from the directors in Holland. They were also desired as buffer against the constant attacks of the Indians upon the Dutch settlements at the North River, as the Indians would not harm the Finns. But the Finns at the South River had by this time mostly all become independent farmers, they had built more comfortable homes, put considerable areas under cultivation and had raised a good number of cattle. In a state of prosperity, Governor Stuyvesant's offer of a pair of oxen did not interest them. On the 6th of April (1660) Beekman writes to Stuyvesant that the sergeant was in the Finnish Colony, and "tries to persuade some to enlist or remove to Esopus, but they show no inclination whatever; it seems, they are admonished and exhorted by the principal men of their nation, not to scatter themselves but to keep about here as the Sheriff and Commissaries have stopped those who desired to go and reside in the Colony of New Amstel."

The Finnish farmers had not yet found it convenient to gather and build a town, although they were pressed hard by Stuyvesant and his vice-director Beekman to do so. The Dutch of the New Amstel Colony had shown them a discouraging example, by coming to a new country and building first of all a town, and then dying for hunger and maladies that were the result of the lack of proper nourishment. The Finnish farmers had thought it inconvenient to live in a town and cultivate their farms and take care of their domestic animals. Some of the Finns had been in the colony already more than twenty years and were undoubtedly for their

age inclined for peace rather than to start practically a new life
again. Director Beekman in his letter to Stuyvesant on April 6,
1660, says that "those living near Kinssessing wish to remove to
Arvenemeck, where there are now two or three families, while
on the other side, those of Kinssessing are opposed to it, desiring
that they shall come to them; the Sheriff and the Commissaries say
that there is no defense or retreat whatever at Kinssessing, as
they have to pass through much underwood and narrow creeks,
while they have a great stream at Arvenemeck, where they can
retreat or get assistance. At Arvenemeck they would have their
fields on the other side of the stream toward Passayongh, where
there is plenty of good land and they have sown a great deal last
fall. Some of the Commissaries, who live upon good islands,
maintain also, that they ought to be favored, by letting the scattered farmers move up to them."

As director Beekman saw that the Finns were not seriously
inclined to gather together in a town, he assumed a commanding
attitude. In the above quoted letter he says "I have ordered to
write down in a list within eight or ten days, where it suited every
one best to move to and if it could be undertaken safely pursuant
to the order of your Honorable Worship's edict, that it should be
granted or else that I would be compelled, to command them where
to move to, whereupon they immediately requested, because they
had not received notice in time as those at the Manhattan, that they
might wait a little time longer, whereas it would tend to their
great loss and to the ruin of their plantings of this spring, if they
had to break up strictly according to the edict; therefore I have
granted them, under your Honor's approbation, the time of five or
six weeks longer." In the same letter Beekman says that the
Finnish commissary had come to him at Altena, while he was
closing his letter and "requested in the name of all outlying
farmers, praying your Honor most humbly, to give them permission to remain in possession, until they have harvested their grain.
I understand that then they will make a village at Passayongh and
satisfy the savages for the land, whereto I was opposed and said
that they could not buy any land from the savages except with

the consent of your Noble Worship. They replied that they could get it from the Savages for a little and I answered again, that they had to await the orders from the Honorable General, I shall therefore expect by bearer your Noble Worship's orders."

Another letter of Director Beekman to Stuyvesant, on May 12, 1660, indicates that he had received some orders from the latter in regard to the Finnish Colony. He says: "I represented to the Sheriff and Commissaries at Tinicum last week your Noble Worship's dissatisfaction in regard to their discouraging and preventing some, who were willing to go to the Esopus and thus disappointing the sergeant in this matter, whereupon they made many excuses. I have ordered them to inquire and report to me in a list what number of families might be willing to settle at Passayonk, to consider (before any troubles or expenses for the purchase of the land were incurred), whether they could establish a proper village, the more as the people are very changeable in their minds and also as it is reported that they would rather go to Maryland, than to remove to another place here and sponge upon the others. Therefore I have not yet informed them of the prolongation until towards winter or after the harvest, as granted by your Honor; I have only recommended to them to be on their guards and make preparations for living together."

On May 25, 1660, Beekman again writes to Governor Stuyvesant, saying that: "On the 19th inst. I received a note from the Sheriff van Dyck in answer (to the orders left with him and referred to in my last to your Honor); he says, that the community had chosen deputies, to send to me with the request, that I should petition your Honor in their behalf, that they may not remove and each one remain on his own place. This request was made by Pietar Kock (Peter Cock) Pietar Andreasson and Hans Mansson. I informed the said deputies once more of your Honor's orders; they said not land enough to pasture their cattle could be got at Passayunk, therefore they could not break up, saying further, if we must break up, then we shall go away or move to where we may remain living in peace and requested besides urgently to write to your Honor of their propositions, for which they would pay me.

Sir! they desire only delay and intend altogether not to obey any order, indeed to the great disrespect of your Honor, as I have written to Gregorius van Dyck on the 21st inst., whereupon I received an answer on the next day, in which he requested, that I might defer a little writing about this matter to your Honor, as he first would speak with the most influential men and then communicate to me their opinions, but these are only pretences."

The Finnish farmers had common sense more then their Dutch harriers, to understand that towns are not for the cultivation of soil. In the circumstances they could not use the town even where to spend their nights, as domestic animals cannot be left alone, they need the presence of people in order to thrive. Besides, although the Delaware Indians were very friendly to the Finns, they could not be depended too much. By this time many of the Finns seem to have got tired of the constant bothering, and such uncertainty undoubtedly must have been very depressive to a man who had spent his best years to built a farm and had hoped to have a home for his family. There were many empty houses in New Amstel, built by the Dutch, who had since died for hunger or had escaped to the English colonies. Director d'Hinoyossa had induced the Finns to buy these properties and in the spring of 1660, some twenty Finnish families contemplated to move there, but were discouraged in this by the Finnish Commissaries. Others moved to the Finnish colony at the junction of the Elk River and the Sassafras River in Maryland, but the English were all the time in hostilities with the Indians and the Sinnecus Indian revengers kept the small isolated colony in constant anxiety, so that many Finns returned to the South River.

Amony the social events that happened in the Finnish Colony at this period, was a divorce granted to a farmer in Upland, or rather to his wife. This being the first divorce recorded at the Delaware River.

One of the Finnish Commissaries, Peter Rambo, resigned from his office. In his petition he makes the excuse that he has to take care of a very large family and therefore could not well, unless to his great disadvantage, spare the time to attend to the aforesaid office.

Beaver skins and wampum were the currency at this time on the Delaware River as well as in New Amsterdam as can be seen of a letter of July 27, 1660 from William Beekman to his father-in-law Governor Stuyvesant. Director Beekman writes: "As my wife goes to the Manhattans for some needed provisions and other necessaries for the family, therefore I respectfully request, that your Honor will please to accommodate her with 150 guilders in beavers and 200 guilders in wampum." Madame Beekman was alright, she had 350 guilders to spend, but if the ladies today along the Fifth Avenue would carry a bunch of skins under their arm, to pay their shoppings, it would look rather out of date, and the ladies undoubtedly would feel even embarrassed.

There was a young loving couple in the Finnish Colony on the Delaware, who wanted to get married but were frustrated of it by their parents. The elders of the ecclesiastical affairs of the colony however authorized the Rev. Lokenius to marry the cupid stricken youngsters. This did not please Director Beekman, or rather it gave him opportunity to act according to his oath of office on the 28th of October 1658, in which he promised that "I will maintain and as much as is in my power promote the Reformed religion." Consequently he fined the minister 50 guilders.

Director Beekman had now established his court in Fort Altena and summonses were given to the Finns in law suits to appear in court there. This did not seem to satisfy the Finns and they denied the authority of the Altena court. When a court was held on August 19, 1659, there were 12 or 15 defaults in appearance. The Rev. Lokenius also refused when he was summoned to appear on the 26th of November of the same year, on the ground that he had nothing to do with the Altena court. The case was that a turbulent member of the colony had assaulted the minister, but the case had been settled. This did not however satisfy Beekman, he wanted to have a say in the matter and the assaulter Peter Mayer and the minister were summoned to appear in the court again on May 7, 1660. This time Peter Mayer did not appear and they were summoned a third time in the autumn, then the Finnish Magistrates refused to act in the case. By this time a considerable trade was carried on in the Finnish Colony. Trade agreements had been made with the Indians and the skins were coming to the South River once more from the Minquas country. Ships arrived to the colony to buy the stocks of the traders and to trade with the inhabitants. On June 26, 1660, Beekman writes to Stuyvesant that two ships were then doing business in the Finnish Colony.

The policy of ridding the Finns out of their own officers, as was the order of the directors in Holland, took a large step when their Sheriff Gregorius van Dyck was discharged on March 21, 1661, by Stuyvesant on pretenses that he had very little to do in his office, and that his duties can be discharged by the commissary Beekman.

In the latter part of September, 1661, the South River was in turmoil and gossip by a scandal. The wife of the Finnish minister the Rev. Laurent Lokenius had eloped with a trader Jacob Jong. As the trader left debts to Director Beekman and to the West India Company, the Director immediately wrote to the Governor of Maryland and to the Magistrates at the Finnish Colony on the Elk River, requesting the arrest of the elopers. Director Beekman in one of his letters to Governor Stuyvesant says: "On the 24th of September I was at Upland to inquire after the effects of Jacob Jong; I have found some of our commodities in his trunk. I received also from his landlord a certain open letter, wherein this Jong writes me and specifies, what goods and grain he had left for us in his trunk and chamber. But according to this statements we found only about one-fourth of the value, he gave also an order for four hogs, of which only two were acknowledged, the others being reported dead. I suppose, we shall be able to find a guaranty in his landlord, who on the morning, after the said Jong had decamped during the night, had the audacity (without our knowledge and in absence of any Commissary though some of them live at Upland) to open the room of Jacob Jong with an axe and finding the key inside, to examine the chest and everything; he has apparently purloined a part of the commodities. It is said, that Jacob Jong went to New England, for he has not been heard of in Maryland, as I learn from the letter received as answer from Governor Philip Calvert."

The minister, for his position and his large family of children undoubtedly took the scandal, that befell on him, very hard. It is rather an indication of unbalanced mind, that he three weeks later asked from Director Beekman permission to marry a girl under twenty years, a member of his congregation, wanting to make the first proclamation of bans on the 16th of October. The case was referred to Stuyvesant by Beekman. On December 15, Lokenius applied in the court and received the divorce from his eloped wife and on the last Sunday of the following January he married, performing the ceremony himself, as he was the only minister at the South River, and the only Lutheran Minister in America.

The self performance of his marriage by the Rev. Lokenius did not suit Director Beekman, it was his opinion that everything should have been asked from his father-in-law Stuyvesant. Mr. Beekman saw also a chance to make the minister pay him what he and the West India Company had lost on account of the trader Jong. The minister was summoned to appear in the court at Altena on April 14, 1662, where Mr. Beekman appeared in the case as plaintiff and judge. Extracts from the minutes of the court in the case read: "Plaintiff sums up, whereas it is well known and was confessed by defendant on the 23rd of November, 1661, that on the 20th of September, 1661, he, Domine Lars, has had the impudence to break into the room and open the chest of the runaway Jacob Jong, when he, Jong, had fled the preceding night, and has inventoried the goods left behind by the same, as proved by a specification from the Defendant's own hand, to which Defendant was not authorized and whereby he remains accountable and responsible to the Court, having usurped and despised its authority, to pay the debts of the fugitive Jacob Jong, to us on behalf of the Hon. Company a balance of 200 guilders in grain and forty guilders to us on private account, besides a fine of 100 for contempt of authority.

"The Defendant replies, that at the time specified above he came to the house of Andries Andriessen, the Finn, and asked, whether his wife was with Jacob Jong in his room. The wife of Andries the Finn answered, that she did not know, that he might look, when he took up an axe, opened the chamber and inventoried the property.

"The commissaries having considered the case, direct that Dom. Lars shall pay the sum of two hundred guilders and forty guilders in beavers, as demanded, and a fine of forty guilders for his impudence.

"On the same day. The aforesaid Mr. Lars Carelsen was informed by the Hon. Vice-Director W. Beekman, that his marriage was declared illegal, because he had married himself, which is contrary to the order in matters of matrimony, that pursuant to the laws of our Fatherland he ought to have first asked and obtained a decree of divorce from the superior authority and that in case of delay he would be obliged to proceed against him.

"Agrees with the original minutes.

A. Hudde."

After this the Rev. Lokenius writes to Governor Stuyvesant, asking for remission of fines imposed upon him. He writes thus: "Noble, Honorable General.

Sir!

"My humble services and what further lies in my power are always at your disposal. It will not be unknown to your Honor, how, since the elopement of my wife, I have stumbled from one mishap into the other, because all my steps taken on that account have been given the worst explanation and I have been condemned to heavy fines, which considering my poverty I am not able to get together, for besides about 200 guilders paid already, I have now again been sentenced to a fine of 280 guilders, which has happened, because I was looking for my wife and thought she was in the room, which I opened by force. I found there nothing but some pairs of socks, which the vagabond robber of my wife had left behind him. I inventoried these and whereas it has been so interpreted as if I had abused the Court by this act of

115

mine, therefore I have been fined 280 guilders, as it is pretended, that the runaway was so much in debt and whereas I have been condemned to this fine in my innocence, having no other intention than to look for my wife, therefore it is my humble petition, that your Honor as Chief-Magistrate may please to be favorable and merciful to me and to forgive me, what in my ignorance has happened here and to remit my punishment considering my poverty. As to having married myself, I have proceeded lawfully therein and consent was given. I have followed the same custom, which others have followed here, who have not been called up on that account, I declare on my conscience, that it was not done with any bad intention; had I known, that this self-marriage would be thus interpreted, I would have willingly submitted to the usage of the Reformed church, which were not known to me.

"Therefore I pray once more the Honorable General may please to assist me with favor and mercy to attend to my poor vocation and means, so that I may enjoy my bread and livelihood without being a burden to anybody. The Lord Almighty, to whose protection I faithfully commend your Honor, may move your heart and mind to such mercy.

"Upland, April 30, 1662.

"Your Honor's humble subject,

Laurentius Carolus."

(Laurentius Carolus Lokenius)

This case again shows how dangerous may be a man who is arbitrarily imposed upon people, with powers to rule. Although Director Beekman was totally inefficient as far as doing anything constructive, he still had a gift of doing harm to others, and his whole career at the Delaware River was employed to destroy his fellow men's endeavors. This is not only true as to his connections with the Finnish colony, but when one reads his many letters to Governor Stuyvesant in which he constantly tries to undermine, hurt and destroy the good efforts of Alexander d'Hinoyossa, the Director of the New Amstel Colony, one becomes convinced that Director Beekman was the perpetual Scoundrel of the American Colonial History.

On the other hand, the life of the Rev. Laurentius Lokenius was devoted to the protection of the oppressed, as far as his feeble powers allowed. For this he had to stay in the rustic colony, instead of having a glorious career in Finland or Sweden. For forty years he was comforting his suffering fellow men, in poor circumstances and often persecuted for his religion. One may turn over and over again the countless records ;of .American colonial history, and will fail to find another career as noble and self-sacrificing as that of the Rev. Laurentius Carolus Lokenius.

There had been rumors for some time in the South River, that the City of Amsterdam was going to abandon its colonization scheme and to return the New Amstel Colony to the Dutch West India Company. In fact there were negotiations to this direction going on in Amsterdam, making those in the colony nervous about it. Director d'Hinoyossa in his letter to the commissioners of the colony in Amsterdam, tried to persuade the city to keep the colony and to send here farmers, instead of tailors, weavers and shoemakers. On June 29, 1660, there was a community meeting held at New Amstel and they resolved to send to the Lords-Patrons a remonstration for the continuance of the colony. The colonists' fear soon however abated, when in the middle of August a letter from the Lords-Burgomasters of Amsterdam arrived assuring that they were going to furnish money to vindicate the affairs of the colony. The Sheriff Gerritt van Sweeringen with a member of the council were now commissioned to Holland to make propositions concerning the condition of the New Amstel Colony. On the 23rd of December, 1660, there was a great rejoicing in New Amstel when a letter arrived from Holland informing that the Lords-Mayers had resolved to continue the colony, approving d'Hinoyossa as the director. Then the silence of the December day on the South River was broken by three shots from the cannon.

Director d'Hinoyossa tried his best to vindicate the affairs of the colony and to make the colony a success, but he was much hindered in his endeavors by Director Beekman, who constantly was interfering in the affairs of the New Amstel Colony and made everything to hamper the director and officials of that colony.

In every one of his letters to Governor Stuyvesant since Director Alrich's death, Beekman tries to undermine and damage the new director. This caused Governor Stuyvesant to write to the directors in Amsterdam against Director d'Hinoyossa, and much unpleasant correspondence was the result, finally culminating that Stuyvesant was in several letters strongly censored and commanded by his superiors to leave alone the City's Colony. Director Beekman however kept up his hideous work of breaking up the New Amstel Colony. Finally d'Hinoyossa decided to go to Holland in order to lay before the Lords-Principals the true situation of the colony and the necessity to acquire the whole South River for their honors.

Most of the troubles with the Indians at the South River were the result of drunkenness. Although there were regulations, prohibiting the sale of liquors and beer to the Indians upon a fine of 500 guilders, this law was little respected, as the Dutch Bible reader at Fort Altena, Jan Becker, sold liquors to the Indians in such an extent that one of them died for drunkenness. And Director Beekman in his letter of September 22, 1661, to Governor Stuyvesant asks for two ankers of brandy with which to trade maize from the Indians.

The Indians in this case were morally superior to the white men, and had voted a total prohibition among themselves. Their Sachems appeared in March, 1662, at the Finnish Colony, with a gift of 13 guilders' value of wampum, proposing and requesting that no more brandy or strong drink should be sold to their people. Their proposition and request were to be transferred in their behalf to the Dutch at Fort Altena and New Amstel with similar gifts. That the Indians appeared in the Finnish Colony with their petition, angered much Director Beekman. He writes to Governor Stuyvesant about it on March 22, 1662, and says: "They of Tinicum ought to have, according to my opinion, directed the chiefs to us and not make the Savages believe, that they have any authority. The request is a proper one, as it agrees with your Honorable Worship's ordinances and placards issued for this purpose. I shall go there to-morrow and have a conference about it with the Savages."

The request of the Indians through the Finns was interpreted by Director d'Hinoyossa and the Council at New Amsterdam in different light however, and on the 30th of March, 1662, an interdict was issued in the New Amstel Colony, prohibiting the sale of liquors to the Indians and it was ordered that "those who are found out, are to pay a fine of 300 guilders, at the same time the Savages are authorized to rob those who sell them liquors."

Director d'Hinoyossa had been endeavoring to get farmers to his colony from amongst the Finns and on June 21, 1662, Beekman writes to Governor Stuyvesant about it, saying that: "Sixteen or eighteen families, mostly Finns, residing in our jurisdiction, to whom great offers have been made by Mr. d'Hinoyossa intend to move into the Colony; they are to have 18 years' freedom of all taxes with their own judges and decisions up to 100 guilders, also free exercise of their religion—these families intend nevertheless to hold on to their lands in our jurisdiction and to sow grain on them, until they have cleared land in the Colony. In my opinion we may seize the deserted land and settle Dutch farmers on it, if it were possible to get them."

In the Finnish settlement of Upland the peaceful life of the farmers had been disturbed by a turbulent member of the village, Evert Hendrickson, also called Evert the Finn. He was tried for his misbehaviors in the court at Altena on April 7, 1663, and on the 16th of the same month at Upland, where he was sentenced by Director Beekman and the Finnish magistrates to be banished from the South River to Manhattan with the documents in the case to be judged there by Director-General Stuyvesant and the Council. He came back to the river however on June 20, to sell his farm and remained in the New Amstel Colony.

On the 28th of July, 1663, the Sheriff of New Amstel returned from Holland on the ship St. Jacob, with a load of merchandise and with fifty farmers and some girls, mostly Finns from Sweden which were recruited by Israel Helme who with the Sheriff went to this mission. The ship had besides forty-one Mennonites who established a colony at the Hoornkill. With the ship came a permission from the Commissioners of the City's Colony in Amsterdam to Director d'Hinoyossa, at his former request, to go to the Fatherland with the ship. Negotiations between the West India Company and the City of Amsterdam had culminated in the ceding of the whole South River to the City, about which Director Stuyvesant was informed in a letter of September 11, 1663. Of the different letters and reports it appears that the Commissioners of the City Colony were dissatisfied on account of the endeavors by the Company's officials here to suppress the City's Colony. On the other hand the West India Company hoped to hold its colony from the aggression of the English, with the powerful aid of the City of Amsterdam.

The Commissioners in Amsterdam, appointed by the Burgomasters to direct the affairs of the City's Colony, reported on August 10, 1663, on the colony. They say that 110 good farms already had been made and erected at the South River, which were stocked with about 2,000 cows and oxen, 20 horses, 80 sheep and several thousand swine. Nearly all these belonged to the Finns, as the Dutch had not built any farms at all and no other nationalities were found at this time on the South River, except few individuals. The commissioners praise the fertility of the land, but say that only such people must be sent there who are laborious and skilled in farming. They warn of sending any more Hollanders, but the Finns were said to be particularly fitted, and of whom many families or households are from time to time expected, as they have been notified by their countrymen in the aforesaid Colony of the good opportunities there. It is opportune here to notice that one of the Finnish colonists, Israel Helme, was now in Sweden to incite the Finns there to come to the Colony. And the Commissioners say that already some families of them have come from Sweden to the number of 32 souls, who only are waiting for the departure of the ship to the colony. They were to be given some cattle in the colony, by the City on half the increase. The cattle were to be restored by them, with half their increase in about 4 or 5 years. The passage money and farming implements were to be advanced to them by the City as a loan, payable in three years from the produce of the land, especially in wheat at the price of 30 stivers the skepel.

On December 3, 1663, Director d'Hinoyossa returned to New Amstel from Amsterdam on the ship "De Purmerlander Kerck," together with Israel Helme and Peter Alrich, son of the former director, as members of the High Council, and 100 colonists, mostly Finns, besides 50 negro slaves. Mr. Israel Helme was appointed to be the Commissary of Trade in the Finnish Colony, with his headquarters at Passayunk, while Peter Alrich was to have similar office at the Hoornkill.

The letters ordering the evacuation of the South River by the West India Company's officials were brought over by d'Hinoyossa. The new director of the entire South River offered Director Beekman the privilege to continue to live in Fort Altena and to take up some valleys near there for cultivation, for which purpose he would be provided with five or six laborers. Also the house where he lived was offered for him as a present. This was however refused by Mr. Beekman, who instead begged his father-in-law Governor Stuyvesant to provide him with some new position.

On the 5th of January, 1664, all the people of the Finnish Colony were invited to Fort Altena, by Director Beekman, who then resigned from his office. Four days later they appeared again to be released of their former oath at the request of Director d'Hinoyossa. But when the Finns learned of the new conditions, that no freeman will be allowed to trade with the English or the Indians, and that the trade in tobacco and peltries is reserved for the City of Amsterdam as a monopoly, twelve months being allowed to the merchants to dispose their stock, there arose a dissatisfaction. The peltry trade of the South River at this time was carried mostly all in the Finnish Colony, besides the Finns were the only exporters of grain and provisions. When the Finnish Commissaries and many other citizens appeared in New Amstel on the 10th of January at the invitation of Director d'Hinoyossa, in order to take a new oath, there were among them utterances as "now we are sold, hand us over." They refused to take any oath before a written document was handed to them, guaranteeing them the same privileges in trading and other matters, as they had had under the government of the Dutch West India

Company; without it they would be compelled to remove. Eight days were granted to them to advise with the rest of the Finns, after which they have to take the oath or remove. The farmers however had a weak case as they could not leave their farms, but after all they worried too early as can be seen of the following chapter.

New quarrels about the South River arose between Sweden and Holland for the departure of so many Finns from Sweden to the colony. Sweden demanded that the South River be returned to her and several memorials were delivered by the Swedish resident at The Hague to the States-General during June, 1664, claiming the river. The Dutch were accused of conveying inhabitants from Finland and Sweden to the Colony. One hundred and forty Finns from Sweden left Amsterdam, Holland, for the South River in the beginning of July, 1664, despite the protests of the Swedish ambassador, and arrived to the colony just before the English came and conquered it.

CHAPTER XIII.

England Replacing Holland as the Ruler of the South River.

AT the confluence of the sixteenth and the seventeenth centuries, England had emerged, from the rivalry with Spain as one of the greatest sea-power, and her eyes were turned with greater interest to the New World from where silver and gold was unceasingly flowing to her rival's treasury.

In the year 1584, Queen Elizabeth allowed her favorite courtier Sir Walter Raleigh to make an expedition to North America, which became then called Virginia, in honor of the Virgin Queen. Soon afterwards Raleigh sent out colonists with the intention to make a settlement on the Roanoke Island. But the colonists were looking for gold and failed to plant anything for their sustenance, hence when a new vessel arrived they had nearly died for starvation and had to be taken home. Two years afterwards a new expedition of colonists was sent out by Raleigh, these also settled at Roanoke Island. They too had hard times and their governor was obliged to sail back to England for relief. On his return, after a delay of three years, no trace of the colonists could be found and their whereabouts have remained a secrecy forever.

A new colonization attempt was carried on by an Englishman, Bartholomew Gosnold, who in 1602 visited with colonists the northern part of Virginia, that later became known as New England. His people however became homesick before the ship sailed back to Europe and had to be taken home. In London Mr. Cosnold met Captain John Smith, whose wild adventures in many lands were well known in England. These two adventurers then started to work together, urging the colonization of Virginia by

123

England. In their recommendations they used the usual "reasons" of the time, as the blessing derived from spreading of Christianity, the glory of extending the territory of their country and the enormous profits to be had by a small investment. Other interested parties uniting with the above mentioned promoters, there were in 1606 incorporated two companies, the London Company and the Plymouth Company to carry on colonization. The land on the Atlantic coast of North America, between the thirty-fourth and forty-fifth degrees of north latitude and extending fifty miles inland, was granted to these companies. The London Company was to plant its colony on the southern part of this territory and the Plymouth Company on the northern part.

In the beginning of 1607, the first English colonial expedition, that planted a permanent settlement in America, left England with three vessels, bearing one hundred and five colonists, and entered the Chesapeake Bay on the 26th of April. Coasting the southern shore of the bay, they entered a river which the Indians called Powhatan, and about forty miles above the mouth of said river established their colony, which they called Jamestown, after the name of their king, James I. The great illusions of quick exploitation, with which the colonists had left their homes, did not however materialize and within one year from the time of their landing their numbers were reduced to thirty-eight souls for hunger and its accompanying diseases. Among those who perished was Bartholomew Gosnold, the originator of the expedition. The population of the colony later rose to 500 by new arrivals and in a short time fell again to 60 souls, for same reasons as before. The half-starved and miserable remnants had started their voyage back to England, when they were met in the river by Lord Delaware, with well appointed ships and more than three hundred new emigrants with abundant supplies. The old settlers were prevailed upon to return to Jamestown.

On account of the Plymouth Company, three ships sailed from Plymouth, England, on May 31, 1607, with a hundred settlers. On August 8th they reached the mouth of the river called Sagadahoc, or Kennebec, in the present State of Maine, and on a peninsula proceeded to plant a colony, under the presidency of George Popham. More than half of the people however became discouraged and returned with the ships to England. Forty-five remained over the winter, in midst of which their storehouse burned down and when a new ship arrived they all yielded to their homesickness and the entire colony returned to England.

The first English colonial experiments were discouraging, but still people looked towards the great, unknown New World as an asylum where they might regulate their spiritual and temporal affairs according to their conscience and desire, in those times of religious persecutions. For religious differences a party of Englishmen had moved in 1608 to live in Holland. These Pilgrims, as they called themselves, after twelve years of residence in that country found the conditions there much the same as in their native land and therefore looked for the wilds of America as the only place of peace. An agreement was reached with the Virginia Company in England, under whose general government the earlier London and Plymouth Companies belonged, and within the territory of the company a place was selected as the site for the Pilgrim Colony. A joint-stock company was organized to which some merchant adventurers from England were admitted in order to secure the capital for the expenses of the voyage. The colonists after having come from Holland on a small vessel, left Plymouth, England, in September, 1620, on board another ship, the Mayflower, being one hundred and two in number. Their destination was the New Jersey coast near Hudson River, but for some reasons they arrived at Cape Cod and dropped anchor in the roadstead of what is now Provincetown, Massachusetts. After exploring the country one month's time, they finally landed, at a place which they had selected for their colony, on December 21, 1620. This became the first permanent English settlement in the North Virginia or New England, as the region was called by Captain John Smith in his map made in 1614. For their settlement, the Pilgrims gave the name New Plymouth from the name of the down in England, where they finally set sail for the New World.

Following the example of this first permanent settlement in

New England, new companies were organized in England and new expeditions of colonists came over. In 1634, the population of New England was between three and four thousand. Finally they became into clashes for territory with the Dutch of New Netherland, especially as the English crown claimed the territory occupied by the Dutch settlers.

In Virginia, where the colonists at this time had advanced to a comfortable living, a territory about the Chesapeake Bay was granted in 1632, by king Charles I. of England, to Cecilius Calvert, Baron of Baltimore. The said territory, which was named by the king, Maryland, in honor of his queen, had its northern boundary from the Delaware River towards the west "the fortieth degree of north latitude, where New England is terminated." This placed the entire territory west of the Delaware River, as far up as the present site of the City of Philadelphia, into the domain of Lord Baltimore. And we have seen in the preceding chapter that this grant of land produced much trouble between the Baltimores and the Dutch, who also claimed the land along the west side of the river.

In 1664, King Charles II. in anticipation of hostilities with Holland, determined to dispossess them of the settlements the Dutch had made on what the English claimed as their territory. On the 22d of March, the king granted to his brother James, Duke of York and Albany, a patent on the land then known as New England, which included the present states of New York and New Jersey. This was followed by a commission, issued in May to Colonel Richard Nicholls, Sir Robert Carr and two others, to proceed to New England and to reduce the Dutch to an entire obedience of the English government. Under the instructions, Colonel Nicholls and the other commissioners, set sail from Portsmouth. England, with four vessels, having on board 300 soldiers, besides the sailors, and arrived at the waters of New Amsterdam in the end of August, 1664. After few days of deliberations, Governor Stuyvesant gave up the town without fight to the English.

On October 3rd Sir Robert Carr was commissioned, by the three other commissioners, to go to the Delaware River "to bring that place, and all strangers thereabouts, in obedience to his majesty." On the last day of September, Carr arrived to the Delaware with two ships, passing Fort New Amstel without being fired upon, he proceeded up the river to the Finnish Colony, where he assured the people in distinct treaty and agreement, in compliance to his instructions, that they shall enjoy their farms, houses, lands, goods and chattels with the same privileges and upon the same terms which they were possessing them before. Trading to be free to all English domains under the conditions as prescribed to Englishmen. All the people were to enjoy liberty of conscience. The present magistrates were to continue in their offices for six months, until new arrangements could be made. The old laws for the administration of right and justice between parties, were to continue for some time.

After this Sir Robert Carr had a parley with Governor d'Hinoyossa and with the Dutch Burghers of New Amstel. The burghers and townsmen consented to capitulation and took an oath of allegiance to the English king, but the governor and the officers refused to surrender the fort, which had to be taken by force with the casualties of ten wounded and three killed on the Dutch side. After the conquest of the fort, the English military and sailors fell into wild plundering, of which the Dutch townsmen, despite their oath of allegiance suffered heavy damages. The properties of the Dutch officials and their supporters were all confiscated.

New Netherland thus falling into the hands of the English, many of the geographical names with which we have become familiar are now changed. The South River becomes the Delaware River, New Amstel becomes New Castle and New Amsterdam is changed to New York, etc.

CHAPTER XIV.

The First Period of the Finnish Settlements Under the English Rule.

HEN Fort New Amstel was taken by Sir Robert Carr, a considerable stock of merchandise was found in the fort. This booty was claimed by Carr as his prize. He also disposed houses, farms and stocks, confiscated from the Dutch officials, to his own benefit, therefore he was recalled to New York by the three other commissioners on October 24, and Colonel Nicholls was commissioned to go to Delaware in order to settle the affairs there.

Captain John Carr was appointed by Colonel Nicholls as commander of the garrison in Delaware and the Finnish Colony was left practically to take care of itself under its own magistrates and having its own militia. Many of the Dutch officers and colonists left in course of years back to their home country, but all the Finns stayed in the colony.

During the first years of the English rule the export trade suffered considerably, not only in the former New Netherland but in the English colonies, as the peltry and tobacco trade over the ocean had been largely in the hands of the Dutch merchantmen, who were now prevented of it for the war with England. The trade between New York and the Delaware was slackened on account of the tenths of all sorts of goods that had to be paid. This being the heritage of the Dutch system and was abolished on March 20, 1666, by order of Colonel Nicholls, who was the governor for the Duke of York's domains of the former New Netherland.

As we have seen, the west side of the Delaware River up to

the 40th degree of north latitude had been granted to Lord Baltimore, and the grant for the Duke of York did not include the said territory, however the land was held by the duke without immediate protest, he being the king's brother and later became king himself.

The territory about the Christina Creek had become one of the largest Finnish settlements on the Delaware, necessitating the building of a new church at Crane Hook, in 1667. Here the Finnish minister the Rev. Lokenius preached in the Swedish language in order to be understood by the Dutch as well as the Finns. This church was attended by the Dutch from New Castle, as they did not have their own minister. The Dutch and Swedish languages were very similar in those days and although the Finns were only partly acquainted with the Swedish language when they came to the country, they seem to have acquired it in the colony and Swedish became the language of communication between the Dutch and Finns.

At the time of the conquest of the Delaware by the Dutch from the Swedes, the River became divided into two administrative districts, the Finnish Colony and the Dutch settlement of New Amstel. Later when the whole river fell under the rule of the City of Amsterdam and a Mennonite colony was established at the Hoornkill, that became a third administrative district. Some kind of central government at the Delaware had been found necessary in 1668, and on the 21st of April, the governor and council at New York passed a series of resolutions and directions, among which were: "That the civil government in the respective plantations be continued till further order.

"That to prevent all abuses or oppositions in civil magistrates, so often as complaint is made, the commission officer Captain Carr shall call the shout with Hans Block, Israel Helme, Peter Rambo, Peter Cock, Peter Alrich or any two of them as councilors, to advise, hear and determine, by the major vote what is just, equitable and necessary in the case or cases in question.

"That the same persons also or any two or more of them be called to advise and direct what is best to be done in all cases of difficulty which may arise from the Indians and to give their counsel and orders for the arming of the several plantations and planters who must obey and attend their summons upon such occasions.

"That the commissioned officer Captain Carr in the determination of the chief civil affairs whereunto the temporary forementioned councilors are ordained shall have a casting voice where votes are equal.

"That the newly appointed councilors are to take the oath to his Royal Highness.

"That the laws of the government established by his Royal Highness be shown and frequently communicated to the said councilors and all others to the end that being therewith acquainted the practice of them may also in convenient time be established which conduces to the public welfare and common justice."

Thus there was a central government established at the Delaware. The reason why it had not been done before was the uncertainty of this territory on account of the war with Holland and the possible claim of it by Lord Baltimore. In the treaty of Breda on July 31, 1667, the Dutch territories in North America were finally ceded to England.

Three of the newly appointed councilors, Helme, Rambo and Cock were Finns, the Finns being the vast majority of the population of the Delaware River at this time.

The selling of liquors to the Indians had again become common at the Delaware and some servants having been killed by them in a plantation of an Englishman and a Dutchman, therefore the Indians again appealed in the Finnish colony for an absolute prohibition upon the whole river of selling strong liquors to them. On their behalf Peter Rambo appeared before the Governor and Council in New York, in the beginning of June 1668. As a result of this a letter was written to Captain Carr, which in part says: "You are therefore by these presents authorized to convene as many of those persons who are joined with you, in commission, for the management of the civil affairs, and with their advice, to give all necessary rules and orders for the good government both of Christians and Indians; and because both those murders and the restraining of the Indians from liquors, will fall into deliberation what you (upon discourse with the Indians) conclude to be the best for those plantations must be remitted hither and shall be confirmed, as if we had been present at the transactions.

Fort James, June 5, 1668,
Governor R. Nicholls and Col. Francis Lovelace."

To secure the English occupation, twenty soldiers under the commissioned officer, Captain Carr were held at this period at the Delaware. Towards whose support the farmers paid one bushel of wheat as quit-rent for each 100 acres of land that they had occupied. In 1666 a general order had been issued that all persons, who had old Dutch patents on lands, should bring them in to be renewed and those who had no patent should obtain it during a certain limited time. The farmers at the Delaware River had not paid much attention to the order, thinking that the grants made by their own magistrates were sufficient, and the order was not enforced because the uncertainty of the territory, as it legally belonged to Lord Baltimore. The order was however renewed on July 1, 1669, by Francis Lovelace, the new governor of New York, and the Delaware inhabitants were specially reminded that "these presents do declare and make known that the inhabitants in and about Delaware being under this government are likewise concerned as well as the rest."

The Finnish settlers at the Delaware were making good progress by putting new land under cultivation and adding to their domestic animals, building new farmhouses and churches and trading with the Indians. The shipping over the ocean had been resumed, bringing money to the country and new English settlers were arriving in the East New Jersey, creating new markets for the farm products of the Finns. They were enjoying the best time in their lives when a calamity befell upon them.

This misfortune being the outcome of the territorial claims of Sweden at the Delaware, we make a review of the Swedish efforts to regain the colony. As soon as the capture of the South River by the Dutch in 1655 became known in Stockholm, the

Swedish resident, Appelbom, at The Hague was instructed to demand the restoration of the colony with indemnities to Sweden. Upon this the States General and the Assembly of States of Holland were quick to pass resolution to examine the matter, but this was done only to beat time and ultimately to forget it. The Swedish-Finnish armies during these years were busy in many wars, the aftermaths of the Thirty Years' War, but Charles X. of Sweden had the intention to regain the colony and even granted monopolies for trade there in 1658. Time passed and nothing could be done on account of many wars. In 1663, when large numbers of Finns in Sweden on the inducements of the agents of the City of Amsterdam, were departing for the Delaware River, the question about the colony became revived in Sweden. A demand of the restitution of the colony with indemnities was presented to the Dutch Resident Heinsius in Stockholm. The question became acute in 1664, when in the spring of said year 140 Finnish colonists on their way to Delaware were discovered in Amsterdam by Trotzig, the Swedish commissioner. For this and other matters, Appelbom was again sent to The Hague as Swedish ambassador and after delivering his credentials to their High Mightinesses, started immediately to press with memorials the return of the Delaware colony to Sweden. At the same time Leijonberg, the Swedish ambassador in London was instructed to present a complaint against the Dutch occupancy of the Delaware. The negotiations were going on while England took possession of the Delaware and all, but this did not stop Sweden of pressing on Holland for the return of the colony. On account of the superior armies then at the disposal of Sweden, Holland could be made to listen. On the other hand the Dutch possessed one of the most formidable navies in the world who might be in position to recapture the colony from England. Hostilities between Holland and England were going on and the Swedes thought that Holland would now be willing to return the colony as it was no more under her control, but the Dutch were evasive. However as the Delaware in the treaty of Breda in 1667, had been finally left to England, the Dutch became more conciliatory towards the Swedes in the question and in the treaty of friendship made in the summer of 1667, between Holland and Sweden, it was promised that the matter should be settled according to justice and as soon as possible. The question about the colony was kept alive by Sweden and in the beginning of 1669 a report reached the Swedish government that the people at the Delaware had been forsaken and left by themselves. The Swedish ambassador in London was instructed to find out what England intended to do with the colony and in the summer a memorial setting forth the Swedish claims to the Delaware was handed to the English ambassador at Stockholm. The answer of England was however that the colony had been gained by conquest and treaty, and it was now too late to change the result. Four years more Sweden kept pressing England for the return of the colony.

The Swedish government seem to have felt pity for the Finns who had been left "by themselves" at the Delaware and in the summer of 1669 there appeared in the colony a man introducing himself as Konigsmark but to some Finns he had entrusted his real name to be Marcus Jacobus. He was accused of going up and down the river, from one place to another and making speeches inciting rebellion against the English rule. To him was associated a Finnish farmer Henry Coleman, who said to have left his farm with cattle and corn without any care taken for them, while running around with the said Jacobus. A warrant for their arrest had been issued by the high court at the river, but Coleman having got information about it, kept himself among the Indians. It was therefore ordered by Governor Lovelace that a proclamation in his name be set forth that if the said Henry Coleman do not come and surrender himself to the authorities at the river, within fifteen days after the date of the proclamation, to answer to what shall be objected against him then his estate will be seized and becomes the property of the king.

On September 14, 1669, there was a council meeting held in New York in which were discussed letters from Captain Carr that an insurrection was very much feared at the Delaware. It was ordered, that a letter of thanks be sent to the officers at the river for their great vigilance. The Long Finn, as Marcus Jacobus was called, who had been captured was ordered to be kept in irons until the governor or some persons commissioned from him shall go over to examine into and try the matter of fact, which is so "heinous and high nature." All other persons who had any connection with the plot, were to be held in bonds and an account was to be taken of their estates.

There were now courts held at the Delaware, before which suspected persons were questioned and held for bond. The Finns in the case were divided, as even the court was composed of the Finnish councilors. The Dutch likewise were involved in the case, among them was Peter Alrich, member of the council.

On September 15th, Governor Lovelace again writes, addressing his letter to Captain Carr, the Schout and Commissaries on the Delaware. He acknowledges the receipt of a packet containing documents and depositions concerning the insurrection, and thanks the above mentioned authorities for their "prudent and careful management" of the matters in connection of the case, promising that their services to his Royal Majesty and the country will not be buried in oblivion. He wishes he could go to the Delaware, but is expecting the arrival of some ships from England, requiring his presence. He thinks that the advice of their own countrymen is not to be despised who knowing their temper well, prescribe a method for keeping them in order, which is severity and laying such fines on them as may not give them liberty to entertain any other thought but how to discharge them.

The governor was disheartened that Madame Papegoja or Armagot Printz, (who had returned to the country to try to dispose with her father's ill famed plantations), had intermeddled in the unworthy design, despite all the indulgences and favors she had received from those in authority over her.

Governor Lovelace also suspects that the Finnish minister the Rev. Lokenius may have had hand in the intended insurrection and refers the quality of his punishment to the discretions of the Delaware authorities.

Some inhabitants of Delaware had sent a petition to the governor, in behalf of those complicated in the Long Finn's case, but he says, he will take little notice of it since it came not by the hands of the Delaware government. However if the parties were to make any further petition to the Captain and Commissaries of the said government, they were to send it to the governor with their advice. Governor Lovelace closes his letter by leaving the above case and other public affairs at the Delaware to the prudence and discretion of the captain and commissaries and thinks that it is very much relied upon.

Meanwhile the Long Finn had escaped but was recaptured, and Governor Lovelace in his letter of the 19th of October orders him to be kept safe a little longer until he will send some commissioner from New York to examine into the whole matter. The governor did not however want to have the ordinary people whom the Long Finn drew into the trouble too much frightened, since he had thought fit to excuse them by fines to be imposed upon them according to their guilt. On November 22d, the secretary Matthias Nicholls of New York was commissioned to proceed to the Delaware and preside there in the high court, to be held for the trial of the Long Finn and his associates in the attempted insurrection. The form of holding the court was minutely arranged and prescribed in writing by Governor Lovelace, in order that all the high bluff of dignity, characteristic of the English courts, would be observed and applied in order to overawe the accused parties. The indictment of the Long Finn was summed in the instructions as "that having not the fear of God before thine eyes but being instigated by the devil upon or about the 28th day of August in the 21st year of the reign of our Sovereign Lord Charles the 2d by the Grace of God of England, Scotland, France and Ireland, King, Defender of the Faith, etc. Annoque Domini 1669, at Christina and at several other times and places before thou didst most wickedly, traitorously, feloniously and maliciously conspire and attempt to invade by force of arms this Government settled under the allegiance and protection of His Majesty and also didst most traitorously solicit and entice divers and threaten others of his Majesty's good subjects to betray their allegiance to his Majesty, the King of England, persuading them to revolt and adhere to a foreign prince, that is to say, to the King of Sweden, in prosecution whereof thou didst appoint and caused to be held riotous, routous and unlawful assemblies, breaking the Peace of our Sovereign Lord the King and the laws of this Government in such cases provided."

Most of the sentences in the case had been decided in advance by Governor Lovelace and his Council in New York, The Long Finn was ordered to be publicly and severely whipt and stigmatized or branded in the face with the letter R, with an inscription written in great letters and put upon his breast, that he received that punishment for attempting rebellion, after which he will be secured until he can be sent and sold as slave to the Barbadoes or some other remote plantation. The chiefest of his accomplices were to forfeit half of their property and the rest of his followers were to be fined according to the discretion of the high court at the Delaware.

The list of the inhabitants of the Delaware, that were confederates with the Long Finn includes eighty-five persons and their fines, all combined make the sum of 26,582 guilders. The list which six years after the rebellion had been "transcribed and examined" by Secretary Matthias Nicholls on May 11, 1675, at New Castle, however had some errors, nine persons having been mentioned in the list twice, either by different orthography or by their nicknames and real names, as an example Evartt the Finn is the same as Evert Hendrickson. The correct number is 76 persons and their combined fines 23,252 guilders, which in present day money value would approach one hundred thousand dollars.

The Long Finn after his sentence was transferred to New York, where he was kept a prisoner in the State House. In January 25, 1670, his case was taken into consideration in the meeting of the council, when a warrant was ordered to be drawn to Captain Cousseau to receive him and another to the sheriff to deliver him. The warrant to Captain Cousseau reads: "Whereas Marcus Jacobson, commonly called the Long Finn, having for some great misdemeanor forfeited his liberty and life if the strictness of the law had been put in execution, but through the clemency and favor of the Governor and Council, have sentence only to receive some corporal punishment and also to be transported and sold into some of the remote plantations from the place where he committed the fact. These are to empower you when you shall have brought the said Marcus Jacobson alias the Long Finn to the Barbadoes, that you cause him to be sold for a servant to the best advantage for the space of four years or the usual time servants are there sold at, and that you make return of the produce to this Fort, deducting the charges of his passage and other necessary expenses about him. And for so doing this shall be your warrant."

After the above follows in the council minute book: "January 26, 1670. This day the Long Finn called Marcus Jacobson was by warrant put on board Mr. Cousseau's ship called the Fort Albany to be transported and sold at the Barbadoes according to the sentence of Court at Delaware for his attempting rebellion. He had been a prisoner in the State house since the 20th day of December last."

This closes the incident and in the council meeting at New York, on January 25th it was ordered that a letter of thanks be sent to the Commissioners at the Delaware for their good care of matters, and according to their desire and an order of the special court held at New Castle, there be an officer appointed amongst them to keep the peace and a commission be issued to that purpose.

Secretary Matthias Nicholls writes to Colonel Nicholls about his trip to the Delaware, in his letter of December 31, 1669, that "Here is nothing of news worthy the imparting to your honor, all things are quiet, only there was a silly intention of an insurrection amongst the Finns at Delaware, but the ringleaders being surprized by the officers there, their design was broken. They pretended an expectation of some Swedish ships to come and reduce that place. It was the Governor's pleasure to send me there to make enquiry in the matter, from whence I returned the beginning of Christmas week."

At this period, the old fort at New Castle had become antiquated, therefore a proposition was made by "the Honorable Captain Carr to the Worshipful Council," that a suitable place might be selected at New Castle, to erect some fortifications for time of need and that another suitable place might be chosen above Christina Creek, which would serve as retreat in times of need and should also be fortified. It was resolved and answered:

"1. That it was thought the market place, where the bell hangs, was the most convenient place in New Castle to erect block-houses for defensive purposes and it was resolved to give order accordingly.

"2. Concerning the fortifications above, the matter is left to the discretion of the people there, to choose the most convenient place or places for the defence.

"3. All however with this understanding, that, if no war breaks out with the Indians, which God may prevent, the said houses shall be used for the public service, as Council house, prison and for other public purposes, while they may be used as such by the whole river for a general and public account and expenses."

Finally it was decided that the resolutions will not be carried into effect without the acceptance of his Honor the Governor, but preparations may be made in secret, without arousing suspicion among the Indians.

The members in the council present, besides Captain Carr, were Israel Helme, Peter Rambo and Peter Cock, being the Finnish members of the council. Hans Block was the Dutch member and William Tom was an English member who replaced Peter Alrich for the latter falling in trouble at the Long Finn's rebellion.

There were now many pressing needs in the public affairs at the Delaware River, discharge of which required the governors orders or acceptance, therefore it had been thought advisable that Captain Carr goes to New York, personally to make proposals before the Governor and Council in order to hasten the execution of the same. His departure had been held up for some time by a threatening situation from the side of the Indians. This danger had now vanished as the result of understanding made with the

Indians through the Finns. In a letter of February 29, 1671, to the inhabitants of Delaware, through Peter Rambo, Governor Lovelace writes concerning the Indian affairs that "I recommend the affair to your vigilant and prudent managery. In which I cannot omit to mind you that not only your own safety but the house of my Royal Master and own nation is so nearly concerned in the recommending you to the protection of the Almighty, I remain your loving friend."

Captain Carr was now in New York; he appeared in Council meeting on April 15, 1671. During his absence from Delaware, letters from the Governor and Council were addressed to Peter Rambo. There were thirteen proposals, concerning the affairs of Delaware, tendered to the consideration of the Governor and his Council by the Captain. The first proposal being that the Town of New Castle, being the strength of the River and only place capable to defend itself against the sudden violence and incursion of the Indians. It is humbly left to consideration whether the inhabitants should not have some more than ordinary encouragement. As first, that a block house may be erected in some convenient place of the town, where a constant watch be kept. Answers to the proposals were given at a Council held on June 14, 1671, at Fort James in New York. The first proposal was answered, that the inhabitants of the Town of New Castle may assure themselves of all due encouragement. And what is proposed as to the erecting of a block house for their common defence, it is very well approved of.

The second proposition was that no sloop or vessel from New York or any other place coming to traffic or trade at the Delaware be permitted to go up the river above New Castle, for that would be the ruin of the said town as all trade deserts it and the inhabitants are left without the means of livelihood. Such an order had been in power before. This was granted and the former order was to be put in execution. Thirdly, it was stated that the distilling of strong liquors out of corn was the cause of a great consumption of that grain, as also much time was wasted by the inhabitants in connection of it. Therefore it was proposed that distilling be absolutely prohibited or restrained. Upon this it was ordered that no person in Delaware shall be permitted to distill liquors but such as give in their names to the officers at New Castle, from whom they shall have license to do so, and also that such distillers shall pay or cause to be paid one guilder per can for all strong liquors, that they shall distill, the which shall go towards the reparation of the new block house, or fort or some other public work.

The fourth proposition being that the number of liquor retailers be ascertained. That is to say, three only for the town of New Castle and some few in the Finnish villages up the river. This was granted. Fifthly it was proposed that constables may be appointed to keep the King's Peace, who shall have staves with the king's coat of arms upon them. It was granted. The sixth proposition was that the magistrates at the Delaware may have the king's coat of arms to be set up in their Courts of Judicature, as well as on their staves, which was granted. For the seventh it was proposed that what land the officers at the Delaware have made grants of, for new plantations, may be confirmed. To this was answered that all such grants as the officers have already made were to be valid. New patents were to be issued on the condition that each planter maintain a house lot in the nearest town to be erected for their mutual defence, and the new grants to be made by the governor. The eighth proposition contained that several orders issued by the Council of Commissaries of the Delaware, before and about the time of the trial of the Long Finn, concerning public charges, as the Hoornkill having officers subordinate to those of New Castle, as also for clearing the highways, maintaining fences and other matters relating to good government, should be reinforced by the approbation of the governor and his council. It was consented unto, that the above referred orders stand good, and the officers at the Delaware are to cause them to be put in execution.

The ninth proposition was that as the Marylanders had offered to clear for a highway half the way between their plantations on the Chesapeake Bay and the town of New Castle, if the people of Delaware clear the other half. The commissaries were empowered to enjoin the inhabitants of Delaware to clear their proportion. For the tenth it was proposed that a person be appointed and sworn at New Castle to be inspector of corn, beef and pork. To see that corn intended for export is duly measured and well cleaned and that beef and pork will be well packed and merchandable. The proposal was found very convenient and the permission given.

The eleventh proposal relates about the mill at Carcoons Hook, built during the time of Governor Printz, by the inhabitants, for the public use. Now some private parties are endeavoring to appropriate it for themselves. (Undoubtedly Miss Printz.) It was therefore recommended to be taken into the custody of his Royal Highness, to be used for the general good of the inhabitants. It was ordered that the mill be let out to some person and the profits reserved for public purposes.

In the twelfth proposal it was wished that no quantities of liquors be sold to the Indians under a quarter of an ancker, half, or a whole ancker. In this case the Englishmen did not seem to be so very strict, it was left to the discretion of the officers at the Delaware.

Lastly they say that the houses in the old fort are so decayed that they should be demolished and the materials used in the building of the new block house. This was granted.

Finally the inhabitants of the Delaware wished to know by what tenure they were holding their lands as it was not expressed in the new patents. This was explained by the governor that the lands are to be held in free and common socage as his Royal Highness by his Majesty's patent holds his territories in America, only with the proviso that they pay the quit-rent (a bushel of wheat for every 100 acres of land) as an acknowledgement to his Royal Highness.

The relations with the Indians at the Delaware again became strained as the Indians had killed two Dutchmen at the Matiniconck Island. In a meeting at Fort James on September 25, 1671, the new governor of New Jersey, Philip Carterett being present, it was decided to prepare for war with the Indians and the officers at the Delaware were ordered accordingly. Another meeting was held on November 7th at Elizabeth, New Jersey, as the murderers were living in the territory of that state. A letter had arrived from the Delaware, being an answer of the governor's order for the preparation of a war against the Indians. The letter reads:

"Right Honorable.—The Indians not bringing in the murderers to their promise I went up with Mr. Aldrichs to Pieter Cock and there called the Raedt (council) together to inform your honor what we think most for our preservation and defence of the River.

"First we think that at this time of the year it is too late to begin a war against the Indians, the hay for our beasts not being to be brought to any place of safety and so for want of hay we must see them starve before our faces; the next year we can cut it more convenient.

"Secondly our corn not being thrashed or ground we must starve for want of provisions which this winter we can grind and lay up in places of safety.

"Thirdly that there must upon necessity a war in the spring (started) and by that time we shall make so much as we can preparation but wait from your honor assistance of men, ammunition and salt.

"Fourthly we intend to make towns at Passayunk, Tinicum, Upland and Verdrieties Hook, whereto the outplantations must retire.

"Fifthly we think that your honor's advice for a frontier about Mattinacunck Island as very good and likewise another at Wiccaco for the defence whereof your honor must send men.

"For there anything else unwritten we have sent Mr. Alrichs and Mr. Helme to advise your honor what is best to be done but intend to stop Thomas Lewes until your honor's order, for we think it not convenient any corn or provisions be sent out of the river until this bruit be over for we know not the next year whether we shall have any corn or not, we have no more at present, but to inform your honor that Captain Carr is not recovered but remain,

(It is signed)
Will Tom
Peter Rambo
Peter Cock
H. Block
Hendrick Jansen
Ed. Cantwell
M. Roseman
Ole Torsen" (Tossawa)

"that if possible there be hired fifty or sixty North Indians who will do more than 200 men in such war."

Judging from the language, it is apparent that the letter was written by Will Tom, Captain Carr being sick. The murdered Dutchmen were servants of Will Tom and Peter Alrich.

Upon serious considerations of the above letter in New York, it was decided that the season was not fitting to commence a war with the Indians, so the expedition was deferred until a more convenient opportunity. Meanwhile the persons in authority in Delaware were to endeavor to have the murderers brought in either dead or alive. And if captured alive, they were to be put to death in the most public and shameful manner possible, so to strike a terror in the rest of the Indians. Some resolutions and orders had been made at Delaware showing their intentions to retire into towns for their better safety and security against the Indians in case of a war, the said resolutions were very well approved of and it was ordered, that at their best and soonest convenience they be put in execution. It was ordered, that the inhabitants at New Castle and parts adjacent upon Delaware River be digested into several companies as the towns and number of the men will permit; and upon return of the names of the officers, that shall be chosen amongst them to have the command of such companies they shall have commissions for their respective employments under his Majesty's obedience. In the mean time those officers, that shall be chosen, are to act and proceed with allowance, till they be confirmed. Further it was ordered that every person that can bear arms from 16 to 60 years of age, be always provided with

a convenient proportion of powder and bullets, for their mutual
defence, upon a penalty for their neglect herein, to be imposed
according to law by the commission officers in command. The
quantity of powder and the bullets to be adjudged competent for
each person should be at least one pound of powder and two pounds
of bullets. If the inhabitants in the River shall not be found suffi-
ciently provided with arms, his Royal Highness' Governor is
willing to furnish them out of the magazines or stores, they being
accomptable and paying what they shall receive. It was also
ordered that the places where the townships upon the river shall
be kept, be appointed and agreed upon by the Schout, Commissaries and the rest of the officers there according to their proposal
sent, as also where the block-houses and places of defence shall be
erected as well in New Castle as in the River. The selling of
powder and ammunition to the Indians was left to the discretion
of the officers, who also were to try to get allies among the Indians
to fight the murderous tribe and their allies.

Two days later Governor Lovelace addressed a letter from
New York to Captain Carr in which he expressed much displeasure
for the backwardness of the people of Delaware to start a war
against the Indians, of which he blames Captain Carr. The captain is also blamed of having allowed the fort at New Castle decay
down without letting the soldiers keep it in good shape. The
governor intends to visit the river in the spring and expects tha
by that time the murderers from amongst the Indians be brought
in dead or alive.

The Finns were not favorably inclined to start a war against
the Indians, as the Indians did not harm them, besides an alleged
murder of a woman and four children by the Indians was not true,
but the party had drowned in a storm on their way from Maryland
to Delaware on a sloop, as they had found out. Also the murderers
of the two Dutch servants were known and could be secured and
punished, for this the Indian Sachems appeared in Peter Rambo's
house, a little after the governor's letter to Captain Carr, offering
to bring the murderers in within six days, dead or alive. Their
proposition being accepted, they sent out two Indians to the stout-

est of the murderers, to bring him in, not doubting easily to take
the other, he being an Indian of little courage; but the least
Indian getting knowledge of the design of the sachems, ran to
advise his fellow, and told him to escape, or else they would both
be killed, who answered he was not ready, but in the morning
would go with him to the Maquas, and advised him to go to the
next house, for fear of suspicion, which he did, and the two cap-
tors coming to the house of the stronger Indian, one of them
being his great friend, he asked him if he would kill him, who
answered "no, but the sachems have ordered you to die"; whereupon he demanded "what his brothers said"; who answered, "they
say the like." Then the Indian, holding his hands before his eyes,
said, "kill me"; whereupon his captor shot him with two bullets
in the breast, and gave him two or three cuts with a bill on the
head, and brought his body down to the Finnish village of Wiccaco, where they were rewarded and the body was taken to New
Castle. When the other Indian heard the shot in the night, naked
as he was, he ran into the woods; but the sachems promised to
bring the other alive. A good many Indians came with the body
and their sachems promised that if any other murders were committed by the Indians, the murderers would be brought to the
white men.

The cause for the troubles with the Indians at this time was
that they were treated with violence by the Englishmen in Virginia and Maryland. Instead of buying with little presents the
land that the Indians rightfully possessed, the Indian sachems
complained that wherever the English come they drive us from
our lands, and they will do the same on the Delaware if not timely
prevented.

As many Finns became settled in New Amsterdam and other
places along the Hudson River during the time the Delaware river
was settled by them, there had been attempts to establish Lutheran Congregations, but this was suppressed by the Dutch authorities who permitted only the Dutch Reformed Religion. After the
conquest of New Netherland by the English, the Finns and probably some Dutch with them appealed to Colonel Nicholls for per-

mission to procure a Lutheran minister, which was granted on December 6, 1664. The Lutheran services were held in private houses, but they had now decided to build a church and therefore requested permission from Governor Lovelace to send a member of the congregation to the Finnish settlements on the Delaware to collect money for the building fund. The following pass was issued to Martin Hoofman, a Finn, by the governor: "Whereas the Minister and Officers of the Augustana Confession or Lutheran Congregation in this city under the protection of his Royal Highness the Duke of York, have requested by licence to build and erect a House for their Church to meet in, towards the which they do suppose all or most of their profession will in some measure contribute, and there being diverse of them in the South River at Delaware, to which place a sloop being now bound a convenience presents, so that they have pitcht upon Martin Hoofman, to negotiate there for them; these are to require all persons that they permit and suffer the said Martin Hoofman to pass out of this port in the sloop belonging to Captain Martin Creiger bound for New Castle in Delaware, and the officers there are likewise required no way to hinder or molest the said Martin Hoofman in his endeavors of collecting the benevolence of such of the Lutheran Profession in those parts, towards their intents as aforesaid. Provided it does noway hinder or tend to make division or disturbance amongst the people, nor shall occasion the breach of Peace, the which all his Majesty's good subjects are obliged to keep. Hereof they are not to fail. Given under my hand at Fort James in New York the 16th day of January, 1672."

The church that was now built by the Finns in New York, was situated at the lower end of the Manhattan Island, "under the fortification and the bulwarks," at the present Battery Park.

Governor Lovelace was now preparing to go to the Delaware, overland, "as well to conclude a peace among the mutinous Indians in those parts, as to settle affairs on that river, under his majesty's obedience." For this purpose he ordered twenty mounted soldiers to be summoned from Long Island for the body guard of himself and retinue as well as "for the reputation of his Royal

Highness." Captain Garland with three of the soldiers was dispatched about ten days earlier to make preparations for the arrival of the governor and his retinue. The governor was to start his journey on March 22, 1672, and Captain Garland was given the following instructions: "Go with the horses allotted by the captain, as speedily as you can, to Nevesink, thence to the house of Mr. Jegoe, right against Mattiniconck Island, on Delaware River, where there are some persons ready to receive you. Being arrived at the river side, you are to go to Wiccaco, or where you shall be directed, where Captain Carr and the commissaries are, to whom deliver the letter, and then follow their instructions. You are to see that all conveniences for me and my party be made ready for our accommodation, as provisions, boats, etc., and likewise a considerable guard of men at Mattiniconck Island. After all these things are in order, you are to meet me with your party, and such other volunteers as are disposed to accompany you, and meet me one day's journey, which is at the great Indian plantation where I intend to lodge that night, and purpose to be there by God's help, on the 24th instant, and perhaps on the 23d. When we are there at the general rendezvous, I shall set things into further order. You are to treat the Indians and others with all civility, and to contrive it so that the Sussink Indians may be there when I pass by. You are to assure all the Indians that the intention of my coming amongst them is out of love and friendship to them."

Governor Lovelace's intentions seemingly were to dazzle the Indians with a mighty array of troops, the expenses of which were afterwards to be borne out of the fines of the Long Finn's rebellion.

In the beginning of April the governor appears in the Delaware, making some provisions for the government of Apoqueming and Hoornkill. Larger changes, concerning the affairs at Delaware, were made after the governor's return to New York. At a council held at Fort James in New York on May 17, 1672, the Town of New Castle was erected into a corporation, to be governed by a bailiff and six assistants. The English laws were, according to the desire of the inhabitants, to be established in all plantations upon Delaware River. The office of Schout was converted into a Sheriffalty and the High Sheriff's power extended both in the town and the river. Two men were annually to be elected for the Sheriff's office, of which the Governor will nominate and confirm one. The officers and magistrates had requested that ships from Europe be allowed to enter to and from Delaware without being obliged to make an entry into New York for custom duties and that duties be paid in the Delaware. The request was left for further consideration. Captain Nicholls' charges for the horses and men commanded from Long Island for the Governor's Delaware expedition, were ordered to be borne out of the fines of the rebellion of the Long Finn.

To advance the growth of New Amstel as a commercial centre by securing the trade of the Delaware River to her, it had been proposed in behalf of her inhabitants, and on the 14th of June, 1671, ordered by the Governor and Council in New York, that no vessel shall be permitted to go up the river above New Castle to traffic. This order was prejudicial to the Finnish farmers, as the people above New Castle were Finns, but it was profitable to the Finnish merchants, among which were the Finnish commissaries. Since the order went to effect, Governor Lovelace had given special permission to vessels to trade in the upper river, especially for grain which was found only there for sale. Finally the prohibition had been found inconvenient as on January 27, 1673, it was resolved at the council held in New York that "Upon its being represented to the Governor and Council the inconvenience of debarring sloops and vessels of this place from going up the River above New Castle, although it be permitted to all vessels within the government to go up the River to Albany, as also the distaste which had been taken, that some have had licences so to do, while others are restrained; it is thought fit and hereby ordered, that the prohibition thereof shall be taken away, and it shall and may from henceforth be lawful for any sloop or vessel to go up the said River, bringing a certificate from the Governor of his coming from hence, but that no other vessel shall have the like liberty, but such as do sail from this place thither directly."

The agents of Lord Baltimore were now showing more interest in the claims of the west side of the Delaware River up to the fortieth degrees of north latitude as contained in their master's patent. They had surveyed for their people some lands in the Hoornkill district and even contrived to drive away from there the people who were holding Duke of York's patents on their lands. About this Governor Lovelace wrote on August 12, 1672, to Philip Calvert, the Governor of Maryland, as follows: "I thought it had been impossible now in these portending boisterous times, wherein all true hearted Englishmen are buckling on their armors to vindicate their Honor and to assert the imperial interests of his Sacred Majesty's Rights and Dominions, that now (without any just ground either given or pretended) such horrid outrages should be committed on his Majesty's Liege subjects, under the protection of His Royal Highness Authority, as was exercised by one Jones, who with a party as dissolute as himself, took the pains to ride to the Hoornkill, where in Derision and Contempt of the Duke's Authority bound the Magistrates, and Inhabitants, despitefully treated them, rifled and plundered them of their goods; and when it was demanded by what authority he acted, answered in no other language but a cockt pistol to his brest, which if it had spoke, had forever silenced him. I do not remember I have heard of a greater outrage and riot committed on his Majesty's Subjects in America, but once before in Maryland. Sir, you cannot but imagine his Royal Highness will not be satisfied with those violent proceedings, in which the indignity rebounds on him. Neither can you but believe, it is as easy an undertaking for me to retaliate the same affront on Jones his head and accomplices as he did to those indefencible inhabitants. But I rather choose to have first a more calm redress from you, (to whom I now appeal) and from whom may in justice expect that right in the castigation of Jones cum socys, that your nature and the law has provided for. Otherwise I must apply myself to such other remedies as the exigence of this indignity shall persuade me to. Thus leaving it to your consideration I still remain,

Your very humble servant."

While these quarrels about the territory on the west side of the Delaware River were going on between the agents of the two English noblemen, grave events were taking place in Europe. In August, 1672, a copy of the declaration of war by England against Holland was sent to the Delaware River by Governor Lovelace with orders that it be publicly read. The governor further ordered: "That the great guns be with all convenient speed sent up to the Block houses in Delaware River according to my former order; and that the greatest be disposed of according to the distance of the place." On October 7, 1672, the Governor writes to Captain Carr that the Marylanders are preparing to invade the Delaware, further adding: "My instructions and orders to you and the officers in general are, that you put yourselves into the best posture of defence possibly you can, by, fitting up the Fort in the Town, keeping your companies in arms both there and up the River, who are to provide themselves with fitting ammunition, and that all soldiers be at an hour's warning upon any alarm or orders given. That in the Town especially you make your guard as strong as you can, and keep a strict watch; and if any comes to\demand the place, that you first desire to know their authority and commission and how it comes to pass those of Maryland should now make such an invasion, after so long quiet possession of those parts by his Royal Highness' deputies under his Majesty's obedience, and by other nations before that, several years before the date of the Lord Baltimore's patent, whom they never disturbed by arms, and whose right is now devolved upon the Duke. Stand well upon your guard and do not begin with them, but if they first break the peace by firing upon your guards or any such hostile action, then use all possible means to defend yourselves and the place, and command all his Majesty's good subjects to be aiding and assisting to you, who I hope will not be wanting to their abilities. In all matters of concern you are to take the advice of the chief officers there."

The quarrels continued and although not any great invasion from Maryland took place, the Marylanders were aggressive in the Hoornkill district, where they were making their settlements and were putting the country there under their government. In the spring of 1673, Captain Carr and others proposed to Governor Lovelace that the place be reduced under the government of the Duke of York, whereupon it was decided in the Council meeting in New York, on April 14, that a commission be sent to make inquiry of all irregular proceedings in the Hoornkill "and to settle the government and officers there as formerly under his Majesty's obedience."

CHAPTER XV.

The Second Period of the Finnish Settlements Under the Dutch Rule.

S we have already seen, war between England and Holland was declared in the summer of 1672, a war which furnished one of the most interesting chapters in the history of Holland. A series of desperate naval battles were fought between the combined English and French fleets with one hundred and fifty ships and the Dutch fleet of seventy-five vessels, which resulted in the defeat of the Anglo-French squadrons.

On the 15th of December, 1672, Cornelis Evertsen, son of a renowned Dutch admiral of the same name, was promoted to the rank of commander of a squadron of fifteen ships of the line, with which he proceeded to the West Indies, where he captured seven and burned five vessels and obtained considerable booty. Afterwards he destroyed sixty-five French Newfoundland trading vessels and sailing back to Martinique he met a Dutch Captain Jacob Benckes in command of four men-of-war. Having joined forces they visited all the English and French islands in the West Indies, inflicting damage on the enemy, and afterwards sailed to Virginia. They were riding at the mouth of the Bay, when an English trading fleet from Virginia was leaving for England, convoyed by two men-of-war. The English mistook the enemy to be of their own nation and in the battle that ensued the Dutch raiders captured or destroyed eleven vessels, loaded with tobacco and other products. From parties, on a vessel coming from New York, which vessel they captured, they learned of the condition of the fort and the number of the garrison, also that Governor Lovelace was visiting then in Connecticut, whereupon they cried, forward to New York. In the last days of July, 1673, the Dutch fleet arrived to New York waters, and feasted on Governor Lovelace's sheep and cattle, captured in Staten Island. The wind turning favorable, they sailed up the Bay before Fort James and demanded the fort to surrender within half an hour. This having not been done, the Dutch fleet commenced to lay broadsides upon the fort, which was replied as long as the garrison had powder, whereafter the English flag was lowered and the gates opened without any capitulation. About 600 men of Dutch infantry, that had been landed from the Hudson River, above the fort, marched then down the Broadway and entered the fort. The English garrison of about 50 men were taken as prisoners on the Dutch ships.

The Dutch commanders now were keeping their meetings in the City Hall of the City of New Orange (formerly New York) and in the Fort Willem Hendrick (formerly Fort James and still earlier Fort New Asterdam), receiving deputies from villages and towns in New Netherland, who came to surrender their places under the Dutch rule. Only men who were "upright protectors of true Reformed Religion" were to be nominated for any offices. On the 11th of September, former Governor Lovelace, who soon after the fall of New York came to the town by invitation, was ordered to depart from New Netherland either to New England or to be taken on a ship, then expected to sail to Holland. Mr. Lovelace chosed to go to Holland. The governor's and other English military officials' property was confiscated.

On behalf of Captain John Carr, commander on the Delaware, his wife Petronella appeared before the council of war at Fort Willem Hendrick on September 4th, requesting permission for her husband to settle under the Dutch government. The petitioner's request was granted on condition that her husband previously take the oath of allegiance, when he shall be considered a faithful subject and enjoy the property lawfully belonging to him. Captain Carr had not however taken advantage of the privileges granted to him, he left the South River, whereupon his property was seized.

The local governments in the towns and villages about the North River and Long Island had been quickly settled and the Dutch commanders could have started for the South River, but the people there saved this trouble from them by sending commissaries to them like all the settlements in New York and New Jersey had done. The deputies from the South River appeared before the Commanders and the Council of War in New Orange, on September 12, 1673, and after delivering their credentials, declared the submission of the people of the South River to the sovereignty of their "High Mightinesses the Lords States-General of the United Netherlands and his Serene Highness, the Prince of Orange." After which they presented a document, made up of a series of articles containing requests for privileges. The requests were immediately taken into consideration and orders issued upon them. The people at the South River were allowed, until further order from authorities in Holland, free trade and commerce with Christians and Indians. A person was to be appointed as Commandant over the River, who shall be authorized to enlist 10 or 12 men on the account of the admirals, and furthermore, to summon every sixth man from among the inhabitants of the River, and to order a fort to be built in the most suitable place, such as the commandant shall judge necessary for the defence of said river. The commandant shall appoint a person to examine what debts were due to and by the English government, report whereof being made to the Honorable Governor, further order shall be issued thereon. The people were allowed freedom of conscience. The Honorable Governor shall, at the proper time, make a disposition of the marshy land above the town of New Amstel (New Castle). The Finns or Swedes and the English on the South River were to enjoy the same privileges as the Dutch. The English were required to take the oath of allegiance. In compensation and consideration of the excessive expenses which the inhabitants of the South River shall have to incur in erecting the fort, they were granted and allowed exemption from all rent charges and excise on wine, beer and distilled liquors which will be consumed on the South River until the month of May in the year 1676. All inhabitants of the South River were to have and hold all their houses, lands and goods lawfully belonging to them. As numerous people from Maryland had taken up lands in the South River and had obtained deeds on them, it was therefore ordered that such persons shall be permitted within the time of three months to apply to the governor and obtain confirmation of their patents, (and were obliged within the same time to settle under the Dutch government, and take oath of allegiance, on pain of forfeiting their lands.

For the maintenance of good order, three courts of justice were ordered to be established at the South River, namely in New Amstel, in Upland and at the Hoornkill. The inhabitants of each of the said districts were to nominate by plurality of votes, for their court eight persons as magistrates. The nominations were to be delivered to the Commander Peter Alrich, who shall transmit them to the Dutch Admirals and their Council of War, when four out of the eight nominated for each court, will be elected as magistrates. The area of the jurisdiction of each court was defined as follows: To the New Amstel Court shall resort the inhabitants dwelling on the west and east side of the South River, from Christina Kill to Bombay Hook, with those of Apoqueminy Kill included. To Upland Court the inhabitants on the west and east side of the South River, from Kristina Kill upwards unto the head of the River (in the Catskill Mountains) to the Hoornkill Court, the inhabitants on the west and east side of the River, from Cape Henlopen to the Bombay Hook.

Captain Anthony Colve, who had been commissioned as Governor-General of New Netherland by the Dutch Commanders, began his administration on September 19, 1673. On the same day he issued a commission to Peter Alrich as Schout and Commandant on the South River, both on the west and the east side. Commander Alrich appearing in the Fort Willem Hendrick and taking the oath for his office, promises "to maintain and help maintain the Reformed Church."

The 20th of September was a busy day to the Dutch Commanders, this being their last day in Manhattan. They returned to Holland with their prizes, two more ships having been taken in

New York waters. For the protection of New Netherland they left only one man-of-war and a sloop. The burden of the government of the New Netherland now fell on the Governor Anthony Colve. On the 25th of September he issued an order to Commander Alrich to administer the oath of allegiance to the inhabitants of the South River from Cape Henlopen to the headwaters. The commander was also requested to report what he had done and to send a list of all the inhabitants residing on the river. The former Justice of the Peace of Apoqueminy, Captain Walter Wharton, had been called to appear before the Governor-General in New Orange (New York), and on September 25th a commission was issued to him for the office of Surveyor on the South River.

On September 27th, a series of instructions were drafted by the Governor-General for Commander Alrich or Alrichs. The commander was to see that true Christian religion in conformity with the Synod of Dortrecht be taught and to maintain it by all proper means, without tolerating, that people holding another belief may make the least attempt against it. He was to keep his soldiers in good order and try to be on friendly terms with the commissaries on the South River. To each soldier he was to issue as a weekly ration six pounds of meat or three and half pounds of bacon, six pounds of bread, half a pound of butter or instead two stivers in money, half a barrel of beer for seven men and to each man one schepel of peas per month. He was to do his best, to get information of the doings and proceedings of the English in Maryland and Virginia and to report them to the Governor-General.

On October 6th, new regulations were issued concerning the soldiers' rations. One and half pecks of peas were to be issued to each man per month instead of a schepel. Beef and pork rations were made a trifle larger and a pack of salt for each man per three months was added.

On the 12th of October instructions were sent by the governor to Peter Alrich in his capacity as Schout or Sheriff and to the magistrates of the different courts in the South River. The

Sheriff and Magistrates were to support the Reformed Christian Religion. The Sheriff was to be present, as often as possible, at all the meetings and preside over the same; but should he act for himself as party, or in behalf of the rights of the Lords Patrons or of Justice, he shall, in such case, rise from his seat and leave the Bench and in that event he shall not have any advisory much less a concluding vote, but the oldest Schepen (magistrate) shall then preside in his place. All cases relating to police, security and peace of the inhabitants, also justice between man and man, shall be finally determined by the magistrates of each of the different jurisdictions, to the amount of, and under, sixty florins in beavers, without appeal. In case the sum be larger the aggrieved party may appeal to the meeting of the Sheriff and Councilors delegated from the different districts, for which purpose one person shall be annually appointed from each court jurisdiction and who shall assemble in the most convenient place to be selected by them, and who shall have power to pronounce final judgement to the amount of 240 florins in beavers and thereunder. But in all cases exceeding that sum each one shall be entitled to an appeal to the governor-general and council in New Orange. All inhabitants of the different court jurisdictions shall be citable before said sheriff and schepens or their delegated councilors who shall hold their meetings and courts as often as they shall consider requisite. All criminal offences shall be referred to the governor-general and council and the offenders to be sent before them. Smaller offences, such as quarrels, abusive words, threats, fisticuffs and such like, are left to the jurisdiction of the magistrates of each district. The Sheriff and Schepens shall have power to conclude on some ordinances for the welfare and peace of the inhabitants of their district, such as laying out highways, setting off lands and gardens and in like manner what appertains to agriculture, observance of Sabbath, erecting churches, schoolhouses or similar public works. Also to enact ordinances against fighting and wrestling and such petty offences, provided such ordinances are not contrary but as far as is possible, conformable to the laws of Holland and the statutes of New Netherland; and, therefore, all orders of any importance shall, before publication be presented to the chief magistrate, the governor-general, and his approval thereof requested. The selection of all inferior officers, and servants in the employ of the schout or sheriff and the schepens, the secretary alone excepted, shall be made and confirmed by themselves. The sheriff shall, by himself or deputies execute all the magistrates' judgments and not discharge any one except by advice of the court. Towards the time of election, the sheriff and schepens shall nominate as schepens or magistrates a double number of the best qualified, the most honest, most intelligent and wealthiest inhabitants, exclusively of the Reformed Christian Religion or at least well affected thereunto, to be presented to the governor who shall then make his election therefrom with continuation of some of the old ones in case his Honor may deem it necessary.

Governor Colve, after the departure of the Dutch commanders, fell in trouble with his English subjects in Long Island, who refused to take any oath of allegiance and the enforcement of it let the governor into more troubles with the English colonies in New England. In the South River, the Marylanders likewise resumed their aggression, driving away the Dutch as well as the English settlers in the Hoornkill district and burning their houses. Therefore a proclamation was issued by Governor Colve, on January 14, 1674, to be published on the South River, and which in part says: "And in order to prevent such cruel tyranny for the future and to deliver all good inhabitants from it, it is necessary to make proper arrangements; therefore all inhabitants of the South River of New Netherland are hereby commanded and directed to place themselves immediately under the orders of Commander Alrichs, as soon as an enemy appears, when it will be decided what is most necessary for their better protection and which is the way, to do the most harm to the enemy."

The Dutch authorities in Manhattan felt very nervous after the departure of the daring commanders with their fleet, great reparations and reinforcements were therefore made in the fortifications. It was now also found that some of the houses of the town had been built so near the fortifications that they were embarrassing the defence. Nineteen of them had to be ordered immediately moved and on October 16, 1673, an order for this was issued by the governor and council. Among these houses was the Finnish church that had been built one year earlier. The church, which was situated "under the fortification and bulwarks of the city of New Orange," at the lower end of the Manhattan Island in the present Battery Park, that now became in existence on account of the removals, was moved "to lot in Company's garden No. 5" The lot having been given to the church in return of its old lot, besides 415 florins in wampum was promised as indemnification for expense of moving. The indemnifications were to be paid out of extra custom duties and undoubtedly not much had been paid before England again became the master of the town.

The lot in the company's garden No. 5, where the Finnish church was moved, was on the Broadway, at 65 of the present street number, in the spot today stands the American Express Company Building. Above the church was the graveyard, the site being today occupied by the Empire Building, at 71 Broadway, on the southwest corner of Broadway and the Rector Street, the next block down from the Trinity Church. As there were not new Finnish emigrants coming, except few individuals, to New York, and the Finns had German and other ministers, who preached them in the Dutch language, the church is sometimes referred to as the Dutch Church and later became identified as the Old Lutheran Church. It was standing, rebuilt, in the same place in 1767 and is pictured in the old maps.

CHAPTER XVI.

The Second Period of the Finnish Settlements
under the English Rule.

THE great preparation for defence, carried on in the Manhattan, as well as at the Delaware, on the command of Governor Colve, were all in vain. A treaty of peace was concluded on February 9, 1674, at Westminster between England and Holland, the sixth article of which says, "that whatsoever countries, islands, towns, or forts, have or shall be taken on both sides, since the time the late unhappy war broke out, either in Europe or elsewhere, shall be restored to the former lord or proprietor, in the same condition they shall be in when the peace itself shall be proclaimed." Thus New York and the Delaware again fell under the English rule, which was to be the last period of foreign domination over the said territories.

The Duke of York's title to his territory in America was renewed on June 29, 1674, by the issuance of new letters-patent, in which he was to hold the territory as before "to his own proper use and behalf with power to correct, punish, pardon, govern and rule inhabitants thereof by himself or such deputies, commissaries or officers as he shall think fit to appoint." Two days later the duke commissioned Major Edmund Andros as governor over his territory of New York and the Delaware River Colonies.

In the instructions to Governor Andros, by the duke, the seventh article reads: "You shall give all manner of encouragement to planters of all nations, but especially to Englishmen, to come and settle under your government, and you shall assigne them lands, either of the unplanted or of such planted lands as shall be confiscated from time to time, by the crimes and convictions of the former possessors, or shall escheat to me; making this difference, that such as shall be settled in lands formerly planted, be obliged to certain services (gratis) for the ease of the government beyond what the others obliged to, and if you can reserve out of the confiscated lands and others, sufficient for the maintenance of the government, you shall do good service in applying the rents of them to that use."

Import and export duties were defined in the said instructions. Duties were to be paid for imported goods in New York and if the goods were taken up the river to Albany, a new duty was to be paid there. The same rule was to apply to the Delaware River. Beaver skins were to pay export duty one shilling and three pence per skin, all other skins proportionately. Tobacco also had an export duty.

At the end of October 1674, Major Andros arrived to New York and immediately started to restore the government to the state as it had been before the time of the Dutch occupation. On November 2nd, an order was issued by the new governor that the magistrates in the different court districts at the Delaware, who were in office at the time of the Dutch coming here in July 1673, be reinstated for the time of six months or further order. However Peter Alrich the former bailiff was excepted, "he having proffered himself to the Dutch at their first coming, of his own motion and acted very violently (as their chief officer) ever since." The following letter was sent to the commissaries of the three different districts at the Delaware. "Being confident of your willingness and readiness for his Majesty's and your country's service, I have sent you the enclosed order authorizing you who were commissaries at the time of the Dutch coming into these parts in July 1673, to resume your places of Magistrates in Delaware River, and will not doubt of your acquitting yourselves in all respect as becomes your trust; So desiring to hear at large of the state of things with you, by the first opportunity, I remain,

"Your very loving friend,

E. Andros."

The reinstated Magistrates and Commissaries for the Finnish Colony were Peter Cock, Peter Rambo, Israel Helme, Lars Andriesson (Lasse the Finn) and Wuolle Swain (Swenson). And the High Commissaries, who also were reinstated by the letter of the Governor on November 4th, for the central government of the whole river were Peter Cock, Peter Rambo, Israel Helme, Hans Block and William Tom. To the High Commissaries it was left to pass an order for the election of a constable in each of the court districts. Captain Edmund Cantwell, who resumed his office as Sheriff and William Tom, who continued as secretary, were commissioned on November 6th to take possession of the fort at New Castle and any properties belonging to the Dutch government, also to repossess any of his Majesty's subjects to their just rights. On November 11th, Captain Cantwell was also authorized to administer the oath of allegiance to the commissaries and other persons who had particular trust reposed in them. There were not any English garrison sent to the Delaware River, the defence there was left to the colonists themselves. Only one man was employed to take care of the fort in New Castle.

According to letters passed between Captain Cantwell and Governor Andros, the people at the Delaware were well satisfied with the change of the government, which much pleased the governor.

In April 1675, there was some fear of trouble with the Indians at the Delaware River. Two Englishmen had been killed at the Millstone River in New Jersey by the Indians and on the other side an Indian had died for drunkeness at Raritan River in New Jersey and another had died for broken ribs sustained when a Scotchman, living among the Finns in Upland, threw him out of his house. On account of offences on both sides the Indians refused to comply to demands that the murderers of the Englishmen be delivered for punishment. On the 24th of April, the Indians, friendly to the Finns, having heard that one of the sons of Peter Cock and another man Walker, who had gone overland to New York with letters, had been killed by hostile Indians. This caused a great agitation in the Finnish Colony, but afterwards the report proved to be an error.

In the beginning of May, 1675, Governor Andros, in company of Governor Carteret of New Jersey, with their retinues and with a body-guard of thirty mounted soldiers, came to the Delaware River. The governors were met at the Falls (Trenton), by Captain Cantwell with a complement of Delaware militia, on May 4th. Among the first things the governor transacted at the River, was to commission officers for the militia companies. There were now in the Finnish Colony four companies of militia, in Crane Hook, Verdrietige Hook, Upland and Passayunk. In New Castle was a company and Apoqueminy and the Hoornkill were both to establish a company. Each company had in its command a captain, lieutenant and ensign.

On the 13th day of May there was a conference held in New Castle between the governors and the Delaware magistrates on one side and the Indian sachems of New Jersey on the other. The sachems, four in number, arrived in the morning to Peter Rambo's plantation in Passayunk, from where they were escorted down the river to New Castle by Israel Helme, Lars (Lasse) Cock and Samuel Edsall. The Indian chieftains appeared in the courthouse before the governors and magistrates and were welcomed by Governor Andros with expressions of his desire to continue in friendship with them and his readiness to protect them. The governor's speech was translated into the Indian tongue by Israel Helme, who acted as interpreter. The sachems replied, through Mr. Helme, to the governor's declarations, with thanks, expressing their readiness to continue in good friendship.

The chiefs were then told that the governor is not asking help from their nations if some of the Indian tribes behaved bad, he can deal well enough with them, but is only wishing to be kind to those that will live quietly and well. They were also told that they must not harm the Christians nor their cattle and the Christians will not do them any injury, but justice shall be done as they might see today in the trial of James Sandyland, who was accused of throwing an Indian out of his house with the result that the Indian afterwards died of broken ribs.

The first sachem now rises up and walks up and down taking

notice of his old acquaintances Peter Rambo, Peter Cock, Lars Cock and Captain Cantwell, then taking a band of sewant, he measured it from his neck to the length downward and said his heart should be so long and so great to the governor and the Christians and should never forget the governor. Whereafter he presented the belt of wampum to him, throwing it at the governor's feet.

Then the second chief rises up and professing much friendship, thanks the governor for his kind expressions and presents him another belt of wampum. The belts being fifteen and twelve wampums high respectively.

In return of their presents, the governor gave each chief a coat and a lapcloth for which the Indians expressed their thanks. Whereafter they fell to a dance and singing, with expressions of their appreciation.

The accused man, James Sandyland, was then brought in to make answer to a presentment brought in against him by the sheriff, for suspicion of being the cause of the death of an Indian. The presentment was read, upon which he pleads not guilty and relates the whole manner of the Indians being at his house and his putting one out of doors. The Indians were then questioned, through Israel Helme, about the circumstances of the death of their man. Their statements were found conflicting, one said the man died five days after the accident, other again that he lived six weeks and two months. The difference between wilful murder and accidental was explained to the Indians and James Sandyland was given leave to confer with them. Whereafter the case was left to the jury, which brought in their verdict, that they find the prisoner not to be guilty, and James Sandyland is ordered to be cleared by proclamation.

Four other cases concerning affairs between the colonists were handled this day. On the following day, May 14th, the court was continued at eight o'clock in the morning. Many cases were handled in that day among them were petitions and matters of public interest. The location of the Finnish churches was taken up. The Finns living at the site of the present city of Philadelphia as in Wiccaco, Passayunk and Kingsessing, had their nearest church in the Tinicum Island, it was therefore ordered that the magistrates of Upland, do cause a church to be built at Wiccaco to the convenience of inhabitants living in Passayunk and upwards. The said court being empowered to raise a tax for the building of the church and to agree upon a competent maintenance for their minister, of all which they are to give an account to the next General Court, and they to the governor for his approbation. The church at Tinicum Island was to serve for Upland and parts adjacent. And the Crane Hook church to continue as before. The church at New Castle was to be regulated by the court in as orderly and decent manner as may be.

Thus the Finns were to have three churches, the New Castle church was then considered as a Dutch Reformed Church, which had been dominant during the second period of the Dutch rule, while the Lutheran teaching was suppressed.

The business of Highways being taken into consideration, it was ordered, that some convenient way be made passable between town and town at the river. The manner of doing it, to be ordered by the several courts in their respective areas, and likewise the charges, within three months.

A prohibition was enacted against the selling of liquors to the Indians in small quantities. No less than two gallons to be sold. Governor Carteret of New Jersey promised to give similiar order in his territory. The distillation of corn and grain was prohibited in the river. A ferry boat was to be built and maintained at the Falls (Trenton), to be stationed on the west side of the river. Lastly it was decided that the next General Court shall begin the second Tuesday in May next, unless called upon extraordinary occasion.

On May 17th Governor Andros and his party were home bound and stopped on the way at Peter Rambo's plantation in Passayunk, where a court was held. Present in the court were the governor, the Finnish magistrates Peter Cock, Peter Rambo, Israel Helme and Lars Andersson (Lasse the Finn), the sheriff Captain Cantwell and Messrs. Gab. Minvielle and Richard Cornell of New York. The matter under consideration was the "scandalous business" of Captain James Sandyland and Laurens Holst. It was ordered that James Sandyland pay for fine the sum of 300 guilders and Laurens Holst 200 guilders. One-half of the fines was to go towards the building of the new Finnish church at Wiccaco and the other half to be collected by the sheriff in the name of the king, (actually to the Duke of York). Mr. James Sandyland or Sanderlin was also impeached of his office as captain of the Finnish Militia of Upland, and the lieutenant of the same company Hans Jurriaen or Yrjanen was promoted captain, John Prince was made lieutenant and Jonas Keen or Kyyn was made the ensign.

The provisions made for the division of parishes in the General Court at New Castle on May 13, 1675, did not satisfy the Dutch members of the churches of New Castle and the Crane Hook, as on the first day of June they address to Governor Andros the following letter, in which they profess to be Lutherans.

"To the Noble, Right Honorable, Major Edmond Andros, Governor General of all his Royal Highness, James, Duke of York and Albany, etc., territories in America."

"Show with all reverence the subscribed petitioners, the community of the unchangeable Augsburg Confession, called the Lutheran, which has its residence on the Southriver, that after the petitioners had addressed an humble petition to the Right Honorable Governor on the 13th of May Anno 1675, together with a document, drawn up in Council at New Castle on the 10th of December 1672, and presented by petitioners' minister, whereby they divided the river into two parishes, so that all above Verdritige Hook is and shall remain under the pastorate of Mr. Lars (Laurentius Lokenius) and all below Verdritige Hook under the pastorate of Magister Jacobus Fabricius, and requested and asked with due humility, that your Noble Honor would please to confirm the action and the division for the sake of God's glory and good order, the petitioners expected hereupon a favorable answer and decision and had hoped to receive the same through Captain Ed. Cantwell, but as the speedy journey and many troubles have prevented your Noble Honor, the petitioners do not know, how to act and they come therefore again to your Noble Right Honorable Worship with the humble request, to confirm the act and the division, also their minister Magister Jacobus Fabricius and to grant a favorable reply to the petitioners, doing which they remain your Noble Right Honorable Worship's subjects and mediators with God."

"The Community of the Unchangeable Confession
of Augsburg on the Southriver belonging to the Churches
of Swanewyck and Crane Hook."

The Finns had denied the Rev. Fabricius the right to preach in the Crane Hook Church and in order to understand this situation it is necessary to us to look into the career of the Rev. Jacobus Fabricius. On December 6, 1664, the Finns in New York, whose Lutheran religion had been suppressed by the Dutch authorities, received a permission of the English governor, Richard Nicolls, to send for a minister of their religion. No other suitable and willing man however could readily be procured but a Dutch speaking German Lutheran, Magister Jacobus Fabricius, who then arrived to New York on February 20, 1669. In April, the Rev. Fabricius however went to Albany where he fell in trouble with the magistrates and was suspended of preaching there by Governor Lovelace. He however was allowed to preach in New York, where he returned, but was in trouble with his congregation in the summer of 1671. On the 6th day of July of that year the congregation petitions in the court "that they may have nothing further to do with him, nor that he may any more molest them, and that a person be appointed to settle accounts." Complaints had been made at this time to Governor Lovelace by the members of the Lutheran Church against the Rev. Fabricius, wherein they charge him with several matters unbefitting one of his profession. An alderman and two others were appointed to examine and settle the differences between the congregation and the pastor. Becoming tired of the situation, the Rev. Fabricius petitioned on August 21st "for liberty to give his congregation a valedictory sermon, and to install the new-come minister (Arsen-

ius), according to the custom used by those of their religion."
Thereafter he appears in New Castle on the Delaware and on the
10th of December 1672, the people there at their own consent
were divided into two parishes, between the Rev. Lokenius and
the Rev. Fabricius. To the latter minister belonged the Finns
and the converted Dutch in New Castle and dependencies, up to
the Verdritige Hook. And all above that point, being mostly
all Finns, belonged to the Rev. Lokenius.

When the Dutch rule again befell over the Delaware in 1673,
and Peter Alrichs, the commander at the River was instructed
"To see that sincere, true Christian religion in conformity with
the Synod of Dortrecht be taught and to maintain it by all
proper means, without tolerating, that people holding another
belief may make the least attempt against it." It was here that
the Rev. Fabricius fell in trouble and we find him again in
New York, where he in the court on March 1, 1674, appears
indicted of marrying a couple, "without having any legal authority to do so, and without any previous publication." The Englishman whom he married to a Dutch girl, previously had confessed
in the court of having presented a forged certificate for the
performance, but the fiscal demanded that the defendant "be
brought to the place where justice is usually executed and there
severely flogged, and further for ever banished of this province,
with costs." The Dutch governor, Anthony Colve and his Coun-
cii in passing sentence professed to be "unwilling out of respect
for his old age and the office he last filled, to proceed rigorously
against him, but condemn and declare the defendant incapable
for the space of one current year, of performing within this
province the duty of clergyman, and what depends thereon."
Immediately after the first sentence Mr. Fabricius was indicted
for beating a woman. To this the defendant answered that the
woman provoked him with harsh language. The case ended with
Fabricius being fined two beavers, with costs.

On the 18th of the following month, Fabricius petitions for
permission to baptize, but his request was denied. Nothing im-
moral ever appears against the minister, but he had a nasty

temper and at this time his troubles came mostly from the religious intolerance of the Dutch.

After the English again became the rulers of the New Netherland territory, the Rev. Fabricius appears in the ministerial office in New Castle, 1675. Some of the members of the congregation of the church at Crane Hook did not want the Rev. Fabricius to hold services in their church, as he had done before, alternately with the Rev. Lokenius. For reason they gave in their letter to Captain Cantwell on August 14th that they do not understand him, as he was preaching in Dutch. They further say that if the priest desires to teach, let him remain among his own people at Swanewyck (a place above New Castle) and preach before the Dutch.

During the past fifty years there had been made attempts to settle on the New Jersey side of the Delaware River. Both the Dutch and Swedes had had a fort there. Settlements were also attempted by the English from Connecticut, but for several reasons the entire territory remained unsettled by the white man until about 1661, when some Finnish settlers had established themselves there permanently, especially along the Delaware River between the Racoon Creek and the Salem Creek. This territory about this time and after is referred to as Finns' land and Finns' Point and in a map made by a Londoner in 1685, the present Lower Pennsneck is marked as Finns' Town and the little creek between the Upper and Lower Pennsneck is marked as Finnish River. Thus the Finns became the first permanent colonists and settlers in the western New Jersey as well as they were in the part of continental Maryland, east of the Chesapeake Bay and in the present states of Delaware and Pennsylvania.

At the north end of the town of New Castle was a large marshland, called Carr's Meadow, as Captain Carr had assigned it for himself during his stay in the colony. In the General Court, at New Castle, attended by Governor Andros, on May 14, 1675, the marsh was under discussion. It was represented "to be a general nuisance to the place and country as it then was, there being neither bridge nor fitting way to pass by, or through it, and that the Town is in great straight for want of it, as they might improve it. It was therefore ordered by the Court, that the said meadow ground shall be appraised by indifferent persons, and the Town to have the refusal, but whosoever shall enjoy it shall be obliged to maintain sufficient bridges and ways through the limits thereof, with a cartway; the appraisers to be two persons appointed by the magistrates of this place, and two more, by the Court of Upland and the appraisement to be returned in to the next Court held in New Castle."

The magistrates chosen to appraise the marshland were Peter Cock, Lars Andersson (Lasse the Finn), Peter Alrichs and Johannes de Haas, who after inspection judged the marsh to be of no value on account of the great cost by which it could be improved. Thereupon the magistrates of New Castle assembled and considered, that the order of the General Court, regarding the construction of a highway could not be carried out, unless an outside dike with sluices was first made along the Delaware River and they commanded therefore that all and every male inhabitant of the district of New Castle, shall go to work on the following Monday to build the dike and continue with his work until the dike is completed. Those who did not go to work themselves were to pay others who therefore were doing more than their share. The inhabitants of New Castle were to do as much work pro rata, as the country people work or pay for. The dike was to be ten feet wide at the bottom, five feet high and three feet wide on the top, to be well made and have strong flood-gates. After the dike is finished the country people would not be obliged to worry for its repairs, but the same would be done by the people of New Castle, under condition that they shall also derive the profits from the aforesaid marsh and have it as their own.

There was also another small marsh north of the town, belonging to the magistrate Hans Block, and was already protected against the tide in the river by a dike. The magistrates considered necessary to the public that this dike should be repaired and they ordered accordingly. The work was to be done by the public in the same manner as in the larger marsh and the owner will afterwards take care of the repairs.

The people of the New Castle Court jurisdiction, reaching as far up the river as the Christiana Creek, were called to assemble in the town on the 4th day of June 1675, when the above orders of the court would be read in the church. But the people outside of the town had knowledge of the court's decision in advance of the meeting and could see that somebody was trying to take undue advantage upon them. The order of the General Court provided that whosoever shall enjoy the marshland shall also be obliged to maintain sufficient bridges and ways through the limits thereof. While the order of the Court of New Castle was that the people of the town shall derive the profits from the marshland and have it as their own in return of making necessary repairs in the dike. Besides magistrate Hans Block's meadow being a private property and enjoyed by himself. When then the order was read in the meeting, in presence of the magistrates, one John Ogle answered in the name of others that "we will not make Hans Block's dike, nor the other dike either." Upon which Captain Cantwell replied "You John Ogle, are an Englishman, but it does not behoof to make such an ado among so many people," taking him by the arm and shoved him out of the church. Whereupon one Mathys Smith said "That man speaks the truth and we repeat what he says." This irritated Captain Cantwell, he called for constable to put the man into the stocks, but as the constable was not at hand and Smith supported his argument with new statements the captain struck him several times with his rattan. The Rev. Fabricius then said "That man has done no wrong, he speaks the truth. If he must go to prison, then I too will go." As the constable could not be found, Captain Cantwell and the magistrates seized Mathys Smith and the Rev. Fabricius, bringing them down to a yacht in the river, in order to send them as prisoners to New York. They however later found advisable to release the prisoners as there was rising a great tumult among the people, some having swords, some pistols and others sticks with them. The Finns are much blamed for the opposition in the letters written to Governor Andros by the New Castle magistrates. One statement says that they were most

drunk and another says if they had been drunk no good would
have come of it. And William Tom says the Swedes and Finns
are such a sort of people that must be kept under else they will
rebell. In this Mr. Tom was right, the Finns having the distinc-
tion of being the only people of mankind who do not know about
slavery. While the poor people among the English in Virginia
and Maryland, who were brought here, were satisfied to be sold
as slaves for their more fortunate brethren, the English never
did have in America a Finnish slave. The Swedish Governor
Rising intended to imitate the English system of slavery, but
he had the luck of being shipped back to the "old country" by
the Dutch, before he could realize the fruits of it, although he
had his troubles. As late as 1748, white slavery existed among
the English in Pennsylvania. Professor Kalm of Finland who
visited America in 1748-51, tells of it and says that the emigrants
coming in the English ship, on which he came over to Philadelphia, were not allowed to land before they were sold as slaves.
The buyer paying the captain for the passage.

After the meeting and the tumult, Captain Evert Hendriks-
son (Evert the Finn) in behalf of the Crane Hook militia company and Lieutenant Thomas Jacobsson and Ensign Jacob John-
son for the Christiana Creek militia company, addressed a letter
to Governor Andros, in which they explain their standing in
the matter of the building of the dikes. They say that John
Ogle and Domine Fabricius had been named by the inhabitants
of their locality to speak for them, and that their people were
willing to take part in the building of the dike, and a highway
over the marsh and also to do their part in maintaining the
same, on the condition that they also are allowed to enjoy their
share of profits derived from the drained land. But Hans Block's
meadow being a private property and enjoyed by him, therefore
the repairs in his dike should be made by himself. They also
say their nominated speakers had been sorely beaten without
cause, but only speaking for the rights and interests of their
people, who are even willing to buy the marsh and take care of
the improvement in it.

Another letter was addressed to the Court of New Castle on the next day after the meeting, signed by the same officers of the Finnish militia companies as the above letter and also by John Ogle and five Dutchmen. This letter reads: "Pursuant to the permission, which your Honors have given us, to make our complaints and requests in writing, we remonstrate with due reverence against being obliged to help making Mr. Hans Block's dike and are resolved not to do it, as we see no reason for it, unless the Honorable General expressly commands it; we therefore altogether respectfully request and ask to have a copy of the order, to act accordingly. As to the marshland, formerly belonging to Captain Carr, we are ready to help the inhabitants of New Castle in the construction of the dike, provided that we may have part of the marsh for us and our heirs, then we will keep our portion of the dike in repairs. We request your Honors to delay this work, until we have planted our corn and remain, hoping to receive a favorable decision."

On June 8th, the above petition was sent to Governor Andros in New York, with explanations of the whole affairs by William Tom the clerk. Under the document had been written the decision of the New Castle Court upon the petition. It says: "The petitioners are directed, to obey our former order and in case of refusal the High Sheriff shall execute the work at the double amount of their expenses, pursuant to the order of the Honorable General."

This shows that the New Castle magistrates further insist in giving a false interpretation to the governor's orders in the General Court held on the 13th and 14th of May 1675, in New Castle. The order about highways, bridges, etc., was to be put in execution by the magistrates of each district in their respective territories within three months, or else the sheriff shall have power to have the work done and the country to pay double the charge. But on the other hand, the decision about the Carr's meadow, desired by the town of New Castle to take possession of, was that "whosoever shall enjoy it shall be obliged to maintain sufficient bridges and ways through the limits thereof, with a cartway."

If the New Castle magistrates had been on the square and permitted the farmers to enjoy their share of the drained land in return of doing their share in the improvements, or had let the people of the town to make the improvements and hold the meadow, as opportunity had been offered to them, there had been no cause for a public commotion. The explanations of the New Castle magistrates about the affair to Governor Andros are most false. As an example Wm. Tom says in his letter that the town was to pay double of what the country people were to pay in the building of the dike. The truth had been that the town people were to pay a fraction of what the country people were to pay with their work, as most of the people of the jurisdiction lived in the country, south of Christiana Creek and at Swanewyck. The magistrates also ask for two files of soldiers for their protection and "to keep the people in awe."

At a council meeting in New York, on June 23rd, the disturbances in Delaware were taken up, and it was ordered that some person from New York and Connecticut be sent thither to investigate, accompanied with two files of soldiers. On the 24th of the following month the matter was again discussed in the council, the former order was respited and new order was issued to send a warrant for Magister Jacobus Fabricius and John Ogle to make their appearance in New York to answer before the governor for the misdemeanors objected against them concerning the late disturbance. The persons who subscribed the petition for the council of New Castle on June 5th, were "to be bound over to the next General Court there. In the meantime to be of the good behavior."

In a letter of August 15th, the New Castle magistrates notify Governor Andros that his order concerning the petitioners had been executed and that Magister Fabricius and Mr. Ogle are on their way to New York. Mr. Fabricius felt quite certain of his release as can be judged of his letter to the governor on his arrival to New York, in which he, in answer to charges in the warrant says in part that "therefore, it is your honor's petitioner's humble request, that an order may be given with a commission to examine the burghers and inhabitants of New Castle whether your honor's petitioner has been tumultious against the magistrates and likewise whether he has given base language to the powers, or came armed, or has any weapon, or made any resistance. On the contrary thereof your honor's petitioner, being desired by the people to speak for them, was affrontously dealt by the commander there: upon the return of the examination your honor's petitioner hope your honor to be better informed, and shall know the very truth, and to judge that your honor's petitioner is much wronged and damaged in coming here, in losing his time, and leaving his employment with daily expenses, which your honor be pleased to consider, and to give such order, that after your honor's petitioner is cleared of the accusations laid on him his costs, expenses, damages and loss of time may be allowed to him, not being reasonable to be so much trouble in a vexatious cause."

At a council meeting in New York on September 15th the case of Fabricius and the Delaware insurrection were handled and the following judgments passed. "Magister Jacobus Fabricius being ordered by special warrant to make his personal appearance before the Governor here to answer to a complaint made against him by the high sheriff and court at New Castle in Delaware for causing a disturbance and uproar against the Magistrate. It is ordered, that the said Magister Fabricius in regard of his being guilty of what is laid to his charge and his former irregular life and conversation, be suspended from exercising his function as a minister, or preaching any more within this government either in public or private. The orders of the Court at New Castle for making the dikes to be confirmed. The out-people there to have like or proportionable benefit of the commonage of the meadow adjoining to the dikes they have helpt to make with those of the town."

On the eastern side of the Delaware River, in New Jersey, the Finns had started permanent settlements about 1661, between the Raccoon Creek and the Salem Creek which they called Varken kill (from the Swedish Varg) or Wolf's Creek. This territory and further to the north was covered with pine forests, which had been long time utilized by the Finns for burning tar as well as for building purposes.

After the Finns had settled on the east side, some Dutchmen of New Castle also bought some land from the Indians within the Finnish Territory, however without settling on their lands immediately.

Soon after the New Netherland territory had been granted to the Duke of York, he conveyed a part of it, which he named New Jersey, to two of his countrymen, Lord Berkley and Sir George Carteret. In 1665, Philip Carteret, a relative of Sir George Carteret, arrived from England as Governor of New Jersey, and established himself at a point which he called Elizabethtown. The inhabitants of his territory were required to take an oath of allegiance for which purpose the people of the Finnish Territory commissioned Fopp Outhout and Peter Jegou, two New Castle Dutchmen who had claimed land in New Jersey. On November 3, 1668, they appeared in the New Jersey Assembly at Elizabethtown as the deputies of the Finnish Territory.

When the Dutch in 1673 recaptured their old New Netherland, the Finnish Territory became again united to the rest of the Delaware settlements in administration. The territory lying north of the Christiana Creek (on the opposite side) belonged to the jurisdiction of the Court of Upland and the territory south of the said creek, to the jurisdiction of the Court of New Amstel. After New Netherland again fell back to the English, the proprietorship in New Jersey became rather vexed by grants, purchases and assignments, which resulted in disagreements between the proprietors. In June, 1675, arrived from England Major John Fenwick, a Quaker, with his children, relatives and servants, and purported to be the proprietor of the land settled by the Finns and in which parcels were claimed by purchase from the Indians, by several magistrates, Captain Cantwell and other inhabitants of New Castle, several of whom had grants or deeds to their lands by Governor Carteret and other authorities. Major Fenwick with his party landed on the Varken's kill, at the present Salem, where were some Finnish settlers, and started to manage the territory as the proprietor. In this he was however disclaimed by Governor Andros of New York and also by Governor Carteret of New Jersey. When complaints soon were made against Fenwick for having disturbed the earlier settlers in the possession of their estates and with force of arms pulled down and destroyed their farm houses, Governor Andros ordered, on September 25, 1676, Captain Cantwell to go over the River to investigate in the affairs.

On account of the troubles with Fenwick and for Indian affairs Governor Andros commissioned John Collier to be commander in Delaware. According to his instructions Captain Collier summoned Major Fenwick to appear in New Castle but Mr. Fenwick having refused to comply, Captain Collier visited him and having been rebuffed by Mr. Fenwick, he called on December 8, 1676, a meeting of the justices of New Castle who with him signed the following warrant: "These are in his Majesty's name to empower and appoint you Lieutenant Johannes d'Haas, Mr. Michael Baron and Mr. George Moore undersheriff of this place to levy twelve soldiers out of any of the militia of this River, and with them to repair to the house of Major John Fenwick to bring by force before us to this town of New Castle upon Delaware, giving and hereby granting unto you and every one of you full power and authority to pull down, break, burn, or destroy the said house for the apprehending of him the said Fenwick. And further to act and use all or any forceable act or acts as the expediency of the time shall offer to your judgment withal giving and hereby granting to you and every one of you and every respective soldier under you, full power in case of resistance or presenting any gun or guns to your detriment to fire upon him the said Fenwick or any other so presenting or intending to shoot and if in the case he the said Fenwick or any other resisting shall happen to be killed, you and every one of you shall be hereby absolutely and freely discharged and held innocent, as being done in pursuant of the Duke's Lieutenant's order and of us by his honor's order recommended."

Subsequently Major Fenwick was taken to New York as a

prisoner and appeared in the court on January 12, 1677, where he was fined 40 pounds and costs and was released on bail of 500 pounds.

However Mr. Fenwick insisted on his proprietorship and on the 30th of April 1678, convened the people of the Finnish Terri-tory, demanded them to submit to him and to take an oath of allegiance. He defied the authority of the Court of New Castle in the territory claimed by him and prohibited the people with threats to pay taxes to said court. The magistrates of New Castle, having claims on parcels of land in the territory, were very eager to prosecute against Major Fenwick and in July he was again secured and sent to New York.

On October 26th, Governor Andros commissioned out of Major Fenwick's people six men to be commissioners in the Fen-wick settlement "at Elsenburg, commonly called Salem." They were to determine all matters not exceeding five pounds, above which they were to admit an appeal to the Court of Justices at New Castle. Mr. Fobb Outhout, magistrate of New Castle and now living in the Finnish Territory, was to preside in their court in disputes between their people and the old settlers. An order was sent by Governor Andros to the Justices of New Castle to take care that the inhabitants on the east side of the Delaware River, within the jurisdiction of the New Castle Court, be not disturbed in the possession of their land by Major Fenwick or anybody else.

In 1676 there was a war between Maryland and the Susque-hanna Indians, and in the beginning of August a message inform-ing of Indian scare arrived to New Castle from Augustine Heer-man, who had settled in the neighborhood of the Finnish settle-ment on the Elk River, that he once visited on his way from New Amsterdam as commissioner of Governor Stuyvesant to Mary-land. One stray settler was said to have been cut off of communi-cation with the rest of the inhabitants by the Susquehannas. Upon the news three great guns were fired to scare the savages and four men out of each militia company were called to arms, for precaution while negotiations were taken up with the Indians.

On September 23, 1676, Governor Andros commissioned Captain John Collier to go to Maryland about the Indian affairs and on his return he was to stay at New Castle as commander, sub-collector of customs and receiver of the quit-rents and revenues. His commission as commander reads: "By virtue of the authority derived unto me, under his Royal Highness, I do hereby constitute and appoint you, Captain John Collier, to be Commander in Delaware River and Bay. You are therefore to take care that the Militia in the several places be well armed, duly exercised, and kept in good order and discipline. And the officers and soldiers thereof are required to obey you as their commander, and yourself to observe such orders, and directions, as you shall from time to time receive from me, or other your superior officers, according to the rules and disciplines of war and the trust reposed in you."

The office of Captain Cantwell hereafter was as High Sheriff, whose duty was to represent matters to the courts, and to execute the laws or court orders, but not to preside or have any vote in the courts.

On September 25th, Captain Cantwell was fined 200 guilders for striking Captain Hans Jurriaen or Yrjanen of the Finnish militia company of Upland and many other things at this period appears against Cantwell, which were the causes for his reduction in office.

Captain Collier whose instructions were to take some fit person from the Delaware River to go with him to Maryland, brought with him from Governor Andros commissions for magistrates and for the high sheriff and also appointment of Ephraim Herman as clerk for the courts, instead of William Tom. The commission for the Finnish magistrates of Upland reads: "By virtue of authority derived unto me, I do hereby in his Majesty's name constitute, appoint and authorize you Mr. Peter Cock, Mr. Peter Rambo, Mr. Israel Helme, Mr. Lars Andriesson (Lasse the Finn), Mr. Wuolle Swain (Swenson) and Mr. Otto Ernest Cock, to be Justices of the Peace, in the Jurisdiction of Delaware River, and Dependences, and any three or more of you, to be a Court of Judicature. Giving you, and every of you, full power to act in the said Employment, according to law, and the trust reposed in you, of which all persons concerned, are to take notice, and give you the due respect and obedience, belonging to your places, in discharging of your duties. This commission to be of force for the space of one year, after the hereof, or till further order. Given under my hand and seal, in New York, the 23rd of September, in the 25th year of his Majesty's reign.

"Anno Domini 1676.

E. Andros."

By Delaware River in the commission is meaned the Finnish Settlements, while the other districts were called New Castle and Delaware Bay or the Hoornkill. The jurisdiction of the Finnish Court of Upland reached from Christiana Creek up to the head waters of the Delaware River in the Catskill Mountains. South of the Christiana Creek down to Bombay Hook belonged to the New Castle Court jurisdiction, a large part, if not the majority of the population of this district were also Finns, only in the town of New Castle the majority of the people were Dutch. The people in the New Jersey side of the Delaware River belonged to the jurisdiction of the court in the west side opposide which area they lived.

Captain Collier also brought with him an ordinance, drafted by Governor Andros, for the government of Delaware, in which it is said that the laws established by his Royal Highness shall be practiced in the Delaware River and precincts. A constable to be chosen in each place for the preservation of his Majesty's peace. That there be three courts held as formerly, viz., one in the town of New Castle and Upland and one in the Hoornkill. The said courts to consist of Justices of the Peace whereof three to make a coram, and to have the power of a Court of Sessions and decide all matters under twenty pounds without appeal, in which Court the oldest Justice is to preside, unless otherwise agreed amongst themselves. Above twenty pounds and for crime extend ing to life, limb or banishment, to admit appeal to the Court of Assizes (in New York). That all small matters under the value of five pounds may be determined by the Court without a jury, unless desired by the parties, as also matters of equity. That all necessary by-laws or orders (not repugnant to the laws of the government) made by the said courts, be of force and binding, for the space of one whole year, in the several places where made. That there be fitting books provided for the records in which all judicial proceedings to be duly and fairly entered as also all public orders from the governor, and the names of the magistrates and officers authorized, with the time of their admission. The said records to be kept in English, to which all persons concerned may have free recourse at due or seasonable time. That a fit person for secretary, when vacant, be recommended by each court to the governor for his approbation in whose hands the said records to be kept. All writs, warrants and proceedings at law, to be issued in his Majesty's name. No rates to be imposed or levies of money made, without the approbation of the governor, except in extraordinary occasion of which the governor be presently informed. A full record to be kept of all public incomes and expenses, which is to be yearly given to the General Court in the River to be passed and then sent to the governor. Persons desiring land were to make application to the court in whose bounds the land was situated and the courts were to grant no more than 50 acres per head, except in extraordinary occasion and were to issue warrants for the surveyor to survey the same. These warrants with the surveyor's certificates were to be sent to New York for the governor's approbation. The courts were to sit for the land affairs once a month or oftener.

The first court under the new commissions and ordinances sat at Upland on the 14th of November, 1676, where Captain John Collier and Captain Edmond Cantwell administered the oath (according to their warrant from Governor Andros of September 27th) to the justices of the court. All of the six Finnish justices were present. A new record of the court was opened by the new clerk Ephraim Herman, it begins with the names of the justices after which the different commissions and instructions from the governor are recorded. Then follows a court order that William Tom, the former clerk should deliver to the present clerk Ephraim

Herman, the records and other public books and writings belonging
to the Upland Court. After that a case was called in, at which
Thomas Spry appears as plaintiff and the estate of Hendrik Johnsson as defendant. The plaintiff not appearing, the Court ordered
a non suit to be entered against the plaintiff with costs. The old
clerk William Tom then petitioned that execution be entered upon
the record, against all those who shall deny to pay him old fees
earned by him during the time that he was secretary of the court.
The court ordered that execution should be granted against those
who should prove unwilling to pay the said Mr. Tom's just fees.
Justice Israel Helme petitioned for some recompense of having
been the official interpreter at the River between the Indians and
the English officers. The court answered to this that they will
order the clerk to write to his honor the Governor about the same.
Guardians were nominated for the children of Hendrik Johnsson,
deceased, who were to make inventory of the estate and bring into
the office of the court to be recorded.

The Court then thought fit to write to his Honor the Governor
the following letter:
"Right Honorable Governor.
Sir:

"Since it had Graciously pleased your honor to commissionate
us Justices of the Court and Jurisdiction at Upland in Delaware
River, we find it our duty humbly to present to his honor the
hereafter mentioned particulars for which we Intreat your honor's
favorable grant and approbation, viz.:

"1. That your honor will be pleased to Confirm the orders
made at the Last General Court here about the wolves' heads.

"2. That his Honor will prescribe a way and order how the
charges of this Court when they sit may be found, considering
that we all live at a very great distance from our court place, and
the amercements (by reason of the small number of actions)
amounting to little; and that your honor will be pleased to empower us, so that the old debts of the Court together with the
debts of your honor's government may also be satisfied by the
same way which your honor shall prescribe.

"Lastly Mr. Israel Helme has been often employed by Captain Cantwell, as interpreter with the Indians, who now makes application to this Court for some recompense for his trouble and loss of time of which we are all sensible. We therefore desire his honor either to prescribe a way how we may recompense him, or order the same other ways, so as your honor in his wisdom shall think fit; so praying God for his honor's health and prosperity we remain,

"Your Honor's humble and faithful subjects the magistrates of the Court at Upland.

"By order of the same,

November 14, 1676.   Eph. Herman, clerk."

The Court made then accounts with Neels Laersen for the charges of keeping the court in his house and for the diet of the justices. They found that the same rose to 452 guilders, whereof 200 guilders had been paid during last year, the balance being 252 guilders.

After that the Court adjourned until the 2d Tuesday in March next, and no sooner by reason of the season, and so is to be continued and be kept quarterly.

At this period there was over the world the idea prevailing that cities were the foundations and sources of wealth and progress. Laws were therefore enacted, privileges granted and people arbitrarily prevailed upon to move into certain cities to practice their trades. The system was believed in and followed by the patrons of the early Dutch and English colonies in America, with the result that the early settlers of these nations died for hunger by the hundreds.

The town of New Castle on the Delaware which had been founded by its patrons to exploit the river, had constantly tried to lay upon the Finns, who had been so far the only producers of wealth in that territory. But the ship captains persistently found their way to trade directly with the Finns. This made the merchants of New Castle to sit in their stores waiting for customers who did not come, while the ships were supplying the people and the merchants up the river. The magistrates of New Castle, being the merchants of the town, therefore on November 8, 1676, appealed to Governor Andros upon this injustice towards them, telling that two ships at the very movement were trading up the river. They say if the ships are allowed to trade up the river, the whole river will be ruined and become "as bad as Maryland." And they continue "wherefore we in all humility entreat your honor (considering the necessity for it) to prohibit the going of all sloops and vessels, up and down the River and Bay on the said accompt, as it was in the time of your Honor's predecessors and likewise that this town as being the only medium and best place of loading and unloading, and keeping stores for all merchants." For this and other favors they say "tradesmen and merchants will resort hither and the place will not only be populated but also the whole River will thrive by it."

At a council held in New York on November 20, 1676, it was resolved "that former orders, prohibiting sloops and vessels going up the River above New Castle to trade, be duly observed as heretofore."

On the same day an order made about killing of wolves at the Delaware was confirmed by the governor. The wolves had become so over frequent and had been doing daily damage to sheep, cattle and hogs, that it was decided in the General Court held on May 9-11, 1676, in New Castle, to pay forty guilders of each wolf's scalp brought to any of the magistrates on the River. To defray this and other public charges, all fines since the second coming of the English rule, up to the last day of 1676, were granted by the governor to be applied for public uses, also that a levy be made of one penny in the pound upon every man's estate, to be taxed by indifferent persons thereunto appointed by the respective courts and by the said courts to be disposed of accordingly whereof an account be given to the governor.

On March 13, 1677, there was a court again held in Upland. Of the Finnish Justices present were Peter Cock, Peter Rambo, Israel Helme, Lasse Andries (Lasse the Finn) and Otto Ernest (Cock).

The first case handled in this court was an attachment of

goods for debt. Sheriff Cantwell being the plaintiff and John Ashman the defendant. The case was continued until the next court. The High Sheriff then appeared as plaintiff against an Englishman Richard Duckert and a negro woman, a servant of Lasse Cock. This case also was continued until the next court. Justice Israel Helme then appeared as plaintiff against Oele Oolsen (Kukko). The defendant is accused of an attack upon Justice Helme. A witness Lace Coleman testifies that he had seen it and that Israel Helme's shirt was torn all in pieces. The defendant remaining absent, the court ordered him to appear at the next court to defend himself, or in case of further default judgment will be passed against him according to law and merit. Thereafter Morten Mortensen appears as plaintiff against Mouns Staeck. The defendant is accused of killing the plaintiff's ox. The witnesses not appearing, the case was continued until the next court when the witnesses were ordered to appear upon fine. The same plaintiff again appear against the same defendant in a case of assault and battery. The witnesses being heard the case was continued until further order and the parties were recommended to settle their differences in the meantime. In the next case Anthony Nealson was the plaintiff and Lace Dalboo the defendant. The plaintiff not appearing by himself or by attorney a non suit was ordered against the plaintiff with costs. A petition was presented by Johannes d'Haes in which he says of having obtained a patent from the late Governor Lovelace upon a piece of land at the bend of the river, between the land of Oole Fransen and Company and the creek called Naaman's Creek; which said land was not yet surveyed, so that the petitioner is uncertain of the quantity of his land and therefore desired that the court would be pleased to give order and issue a warrant for the laying out of this land. The court did grant the request and that warrant will be issued for the survey of the land.

The charges for keeping the court in the house of Neales Laersen and the diet of the justices and their guest Captain Collier amounted this day 100 guilders, which sum was allowed by the court.

The court adjourned until the 2d Tuesday of June next. After which there is a land deal, Jan Hendrickse acknowledging a deed for a parcel of land transferred by him to William Orian. The latter again conveys half of the land to Michill Izard.

After the court session there was a council held about the Indian affairs by the commander and the justices. A news had reached the River about the coming of the Simeco (Seneca) Indians to fetch the Susquehannos that were keeping themselves amongst the Delaware River Indians. It was concluded upon the motion of Rinowehan the Indian Sachamore for the most quiet Indians at the River, that Captain Collier and Justice Israel Helme go up to Sachamexin (Shackamaxon) where a great number of Simeco and other Indians had gathered and that they endeavor to persuade the Simecos, the Susquehannos and the Delaware River Indians to send each a Sachamore or Deputy to his honor the Governor at New York, and that justice Israel Helme goes with them to hear and receive the governor's resolutions and answer to the demands of the Indians.

A complaint had been made about the order of prohibiting ships to go up the River in Delaware to trade among the Finnish farmers, therefore Governor Andros wrote on April 6, 1677, to Commander Collier, granting liberty to vessels to go up the River as formerly "for this year's effects or former debts."

In compliance of the order of the General Court in 1675, the Finnish magistrates had caused a church be built in Wiccaco, for the people leaving above or about the Schuylkill River. This was done by converting to this purpose a block house, that the Finns had built few years earlier for retreat in case of an Indian attack. But the Rev. Lokenius had then three churches to attain which he in his old age could not very well do. The Finns therefore were obliged to obtain Jacobus Fabricius to officiate in the Wiccaco church, he being now allowed to resume his office as minister. The Rev. Fabricius preached his first sermon in the Wiccaco church on the Trinity Sunday, 1677. He officiated in the Dutch language with which the Finns had become acquainted during the Dutch rule of the Delaware and by contact with the Dutch colonists during the later years.

On the 13th of June, 1677, the Upland Court again convened, all the Finnish justices being present. Among the cases handled in this court was that an Englishman John Test brought his slave named William Still, a tailor by trade, whom he acknowledged of having sold to Captain Edmond Cantwell for the space and term of four years, beginning from the first of April last. The said William Still declared in the court to be willing to serve the captain the above said term of four years.

The two cases between Morten Mortense and Mouns Staeck, which were continued from the last court, had been settled and the parties had agreed to pay half of the costs each. Mortense and Staeck were neighbors, living at Calceon Hook. The former had come from the province of Pohjanmaa, Finland, and the latter from the city of Turku (Abo), Finland. Mr. Staeck was a new arrival to the Delaware Colony, having earlier lived in New Amsterdam, where he in 1660 was a house owner. He married Magdalenja van Tellickleus and moved to the new village of Harlem where he with another Finn, Johan Gogu, was running a brick factory, being also one of the magistrates of the town. In 1665 Staeck was heavily fined for beating the cattle herder of the village and moved thereafter to Elizabeth, N. J., as farmer. Later he moved to the Finnish colony at the Delaware, but his three sons, Peter, Mathew and Israel, settled in their home town of New York, where their descendants use the name Stuck.

The Upland Court sat two days at this session. On the second day, June 14th, Lasse Cock brought in an account of expenses incurred during the conference with the Indians at the Finnish village of Shackamaxon, in the spring. It appears that Captain Collier and Israel Helme and some other Finnish magistrates had lived in his house in Shackamaxon during four days, from March 14 to 18. Also that he had spent for gifts given to the Indians at this conference. His expenses being 250 guilders, which the court ordered to be paid of the levy that was to be laid.

A new Englishman in the colony, John Ashman, who had ventured into considerable business deals, appears in financial difficulties and several judgments in this and following courts are entered against him.

On July 8, 1677, Captain Collier was censured by Governor Andros in a letter, for going to sit as judge in the courts. The captain was told to act according to his known authority. On August 13th a commission was given by the governor to Captain Christopher Billop to be commander and sub-collector of customs at the Delaware. In a letter the new commander brought with him to the magistrates of New Castle, Governor Andros says: "I find no need of a General or High Court in the river, every court having power to make fitting rates for the highways, poor, or other necessaries, as is practiced in England, and unless otherwise ordered by said courts the clerk proper to be receiver and pay all by order of court, for which you need no further authority or directions from the governor, than former orders and rules for keeping due accompts to be yearly examined and past in court and copies remitted here."

The western New Jersey had fallen into the management of William Penn and others, who sold lands for the settlement of the country. Two companies of Quakers, altogether 230 souls, arrived with a ship on the 16th of August, 1677, to the Delaware and soon after landed in the Finnish settlement at Racoon Creek. Not enough dwellings could be found in the settlement to accommodate so many persons, so that the cow-stalls and barns had to be converted for the shelter of the people. Three purchases of land were made, by the new settlers, from the Indians by the aid of Israel Helms, Peter Rambo and Lars (Lasse) Cock, who recommended the newcomers favorably to the Indians. Those of the new emigrants coming from London selected their land in the vicinity where formerly stood Fort Nassau, present Gloucester City, and those coming from Yorkshire occupied the land from Rancocas Creek to the Falls of Delaware. Both parties settled however together to live at the Burlington Island, where they built a town. In October another ship arrived bringing 114 new emigrants to the Yorkshire Colony and in November one more ship arrived from London, bringing 60 or 70 passengers, some of whom settled at Salem and some at Burlington.

A court was again held at Upland on September 11, 1677, all

the Finnish magistrates being present. In the last court and in this a larger number of cases appear than ever before and many grants for lands were made in this session, more than three thousand acres being granted, mostly within the area of the present city of Philadelphia.

The clerk of the court was ordered to send a copy of the public debts to the governor, which was done on September 27, 1677. The debts were:

"To Neels Laersen for the Court expenses to this day, except 200 guilders already paid to him by Captain Cantwell..................................... 639 guilders

"To Lace Cock for expenses by the Commander and Simico Indians last spring, the account having been allowed by the Court.......................... 250 "

"The wolves heads in this Court not all brought in yet but computed by the Court to................... 420 "

"To the clerk allotted by the Court for his several extraordinary services (besides salary).............. 200 "

"To Justice Israel Helme for his several services to the country as interpreter with the Indians.. 400 "

"To Captain Cantwell for having paid to Neels Laersen for the accommodations of the Court.. 200 "

"To Justice Otto Ernest (Cock) for sundry expenses on the public account............................. 300 "

"To Lasse Cock for expenses when his honor the governor was here.................................... 112 "

"To Peter Rambo for his expenses when his honor the governor was here .... 800 "

"To Captain Cantwell, the Court having proffered to pay him 400 guilders (as a gift) which he refused, so that this is left to his honor (the governor) to judge of..............................

"Total in Guilders.. 3321 "

In October, 1677, Governor Andros was preparing to go to England and to return in the spring. He addressed therefore a letter to Commander Billop, warning him to do anything else than he is authorized and ordered. A letter was also sent to the magistrates of Upland, New Castle and Hoornkill, informing about the governor's departure. The letter to the magistrates of Upland reads:

"Gentlemen:

"I have written to the commander and this is to acquaint you also that having his Royal Highness' leave for my own occasion this winter so as to return in the spring, all things being all well throughout the Government. I intend, God willing, going home in a ship bound here for London, leaving all things to remain in all parts of the government as now settled, and therefore recommend your being very vigilant and careful (which I will not doubt) for the due administration of justice in your several stations and particularly that inferior officers do their duty for the good and quiet of their respective places according to law. Any appeals to be to the Court of Assizes, which on extraordinaries may be sent to the secretary Captain Nicholls here, and if occasion to be communicated to the Council. I am,

"Your affectionate friend to serve you,

E. Andros."

A Court was held at Upland on Tuesday the 13th of November, 1677, all the Finnish justices being present. On account of the new English emigrants there was a large number of cases to be handled in this session, the law suits being mostly debts for business transactions, as money was not used the goods promised in place of money were often delayed. A large number of new grants for lands were issued again, totaling 2,550 acres, mostly in the neighborhood of the Schuylkill River. A petition was also addressed "to the Worshipful Court of Upland" by twenty-four persons, mostly Finns, who desired to build a farming colony near the Delaware falls. In their petition they say "that they the petitioners being all inhabitants and for the most part born and brought up in this River and parts have a great inclination (as well for the strength of the River, as for the convenience of travel and other ways) to settle together in a town at the west side of

191

this River just below the falls, do therefore humbly request this worshipful Court to move the case to his honor the governor that they the petitioners may have each of them in lots laid out one hundred acres of land with a fit proportion of marsh, as also that a fit place for a town may be laid out, in the most convenient place there about with such privileges and liberties for their encouragement as shall be thought fit and that the same may be confirmed unto them by his honor the governor and the petitioners will forthwith settle accordingly."

The Court promised to send the petition to his honor the governor, with recommendations and request in behalf of the petitioners.

The former clerk of the court William Tom, who was present, was ordered to deliver the records of the court to the new clerk Ephraim Herman. This was the second time he was requested to do so and he promised to do it, but he never did and the records are lost to the history.

The taxation to pay the public debts was taken up for final discussion and they found that twenty-six guilders had to be collected from each of the 136 taxable persons within the Upland jurisdiction. It was ordered to be paid in either of the following species: Wheat at five guilders per scipple (bushel) and rye and barley at four. Indian corn at three guilders per scipple, tobacco at eight stivers per pound. Pork at eight and bacon at sixteen stivers per pound. Or else in wampum or skins at current prices. The court further ordered and empowered the high sheriff Captain Cantwell to receive and collect the tax, allowing him five shillings per pound for his work.

The court allowed to Neels Laersen, in whose house the court was held and where the justices and officers had their meals, two hundred guilder for the sitting of this court.

The court adjourned till the second Tuesday of March next.

In the record then follows a letter from the governor to the Upland magistrates, which reads:

"New York, August 14, 1677.
"Gentlemen:
"These are to desire and authorize you to treat with the

Indian Proprietors for the purchasing of a small tract of land which I am informed is not yet purchased and is about half Dutch or two English miles long, along the River side between your land and the late purchase up to the falls, which done I shall forthwith take care for settling those parts. I do not think of making any change in your Court this year, not doubting your continued care, for the king's and country's service, and remain,

"Your affectionate friend,

"E. Andros."

Then follows a declaration by the governor, which says that:

"By virtue of my authority under his Royal Highness I do hereby desire and request all persons that have or claim any land in Delaware River and Bay that they do without delay or as soon as conveniently may be, make a due return to the clerk of the Court in whose jurisdiction said land lies, of the quantity and situation of their land, according to the surveyors' plats or cards thereof, and the said Courts to make a return of the whole unto me, and whether seated and improved, that such wanting grants or patents may have them dispatched and sent. This order to be published in the several courts which to take care therein, and surveyors also to give notice and see it be observed where he shall know or find the defect acturn. In New York, this 13th day of August, 1677.

"E. Andros."

The following resolution of the governor and council was read for the second time in the court.

"Fort James, 19th of May, 1677.

"Governor and whole Council.

"Resolved and ordered that pleading attorneys be no longer allowed to practice in the government, but for the depending causes."

The house of Neels Laersen becoming too small for the court, it was ordered that Hans Yrjanen, captain of the Finnish militia of Upland, with the men belonging to his company fit up and finish the house of defence at Upland fit for the Court to sit in, for the next session. This house of defence was the block house built by the Finns during the time of Governor Lovelace, for a retreat in case of Indian attack.

On March 12, 1678, the Upland Court sat in the House of Defence, all the Finnish magistrates being present. On account of the long interval in the court sessions and for the new English emigrants there were now a great number of cases to be handled. Two cases of slavery appears in this session. Robert Hutchinsson as attorney for his brother Ralph, sold to Israel Helme an Englishman William Bromfield for the term of four years. The price being 1,200 guilders. The above named slave William Bromfield promised in the court to serve the Justice Israel Helme faithfully and truly for the said term of four years. Another Englishman, William Goaf, was brought to the court by Anthony Nealson who had bought him from Moens Petersen for the term of three years servitude. The slave promised to serve his new master honestly and truly the above said term of three years.

New land grants were made in this court to the amount of 2,100 acres, mostly on the Schuylkill River, and land conveyances between parties in the town of Upland was recorded.

"It being represented to the Court that by reason of the peoples daily taking up land near the mill of Carkoen Creek, the said mill would be left destitute of any land to get timber for the use of the said mill, the Court therefore ordered that on the west side of the said mill branch should be laid out 100 acres of land for the said mill's use." This was the mill erected by the Finns in 1643, for the public use and was the first water mill in the Delaware country.

The expenses of the court were now smaller, on account of the new court house, Neels Laersen being allowed seventy guilders only, for the diet of the justices and officers.

The high sheriff was ordered to bring in his account of the receipt of the taxes, on the 25th day of March, instant, for which the court appointed a meeting to be held by them on the first day of April at Upland.

The court then adjourned until the second Tuesday of June next.

The meeting for the settlement of accounts with the high sheriff was held at the house of the president of the Upland Court, Peter Cock, in Passayunk, on April 3, 1678. The justices Peter Cock, Peter Rambo, Israel Helme and Oele Swensen were present at the meeting.

On the 18th and 19th day of June the Upland Court sat in the House of Defence, but four pages of the original record being missing, all the transactions are not known. A great number of debts in business transactions were handled in this session, and several persons in Moyamensing and Justice Oele Swenson were granted to take up twenty-five acres of marsh each.

Another case of slavery appears in this court, an Englishman, Benjamin Goodman, a slave of Justice Oele Swenson, appeared and desired to be free as he said he had served his time. The case was continued for the next session for witness.

An insane asylum was ordered to be established. Jan Cornelissen of Amesland complaining in the court that his son Erik had become insane, and he being a poor man could not take care of his unhappy son. The court therefore ordered that three or four men be hired to build a little Blockhouse at Amesland where the madman can be placed and in the next court a levy will be laid for the building of the house and maintaining of the madman, according to laws of the government.

Land conveyances are recorded for Englishmen in the Finnish town of Marcus Hook. The whole tract of the town had been confirmed by patent from Governor Andros on March 28, 1676, to six Finns, among which was Hans Hofman who formerly lived in New York and came to collect money at the Delaware when the Finnish church in New York was built in 1672.

The court resolved to impose a levy of five guilders per head for every taxable person to pay the expenses of the court. The tax was to be paid before the sixth day of October next, at Tinicum Island to Justice Otto Ernest Cock, who now owned the island and the Printz Hall of the former Swedish governor Printz.

The court adjourned till the second Tuesday of September next.

During the absence of Governor Andros, Commander Billop and Walter Wharton the surveyor had behaved quite self-righteously and had overstepped their commissions. On the 8th of March, 1678, complains were made against Billop by the magistrates of New Castle, that the commander uses the fort as a stable, and keeps the court room filled with hay and fodder, that he keeps hogs in the fort and debars the court from sitting in their usual place in the fort, besides that he makes use of the militia about his own private affairs. After the dispute with the court the commander promises to remove his horses. In the latter part of July, the governor was expected to return from London, therefore on the 17th of that month a long list of complaints was drafted by the New Castle magistrates against Commander Billop and Surveyor Wharton. Wharton is accused of neglecting his office to a great obstruction and hindrance of the people, that he had performed, while being a reader in the New Castle church, his own marriage, that he gives lands to people who have not obtained any grant for the same in the courts, and in one instance had confiscated a man's land for himself only for the surveyor's fees. Against Commander Billop they say that since his coming to the River he had all along publicly blamed and defamed the governor, and during the controversies with Major Fenwick about the lands and authority in the east side of the Delaware River, the commander had contrary to his duty stood up for and held with the major, so that the inhabitants of the eastern shore have not known whom to obey. That the commander in several occasions had declared that he has the power to command the courts. That the commander had confiscated the goods, horses and swine of several persons without valid cause or any lawful proceedings and had converted the same to his own use. Also that the commander had issued marriage licenses, whereby the common usages of the Delaware River Colony were laid aside.

On September 3, 1678, Captain Billop was ordered by Governor Andros to appear in New York, leaving the charge of the military and civil matters to Justice Peter Alrichs. Thomas Woolaston was appointed sub-collector of customs and on December 15, Philip Pocock was appointed surveyor.

The Upland Court sat again on November 12, 1678, all the Finnish justices, except Israel Helme being present. An order from Governor Andros about lands that had been taken up but not settled, was proclaimed in the open court.

A case in which 167 guilders was involved, in business deals between William Orian and John D'Haes, that had been in the court before, was debated before the jury of twelve men and the case was continued to the next court when the parties were ordered to bring in their account books.

A large number of Englishmen appeared in the court in connection of business debts, and 1,200 acres of land was granted for new farms.

The slave of Justice Oele Swenson, Benjamin Goodman, who had been bought from Maryland, was freed, Lasse Cock his witness being of the opinion that he had been sold for three years' servitude.

It was considered very necessary that a new water mill be built at the Schuylkill River and there being no fitter place than the fall called Captain Hans Moens' falls, the court therefore is of the opinion that Captain Hans Moens ought to build a mill there (as he says that he will) or else suffer another to build it for the common good of the part of the country.

Captain Lawrence (Lasse) Cock appeared in the court acknowledging the sale of his plantation in the Finnish town of Shackamaxon to Elizabet Kinsey, the daughter and heir of John Kinsey, late of Herefordshire, England.

The town of Shackamaxon originally contained 1,800 acres of land besides marshland and was owned by six Finnish families, each having equal part of the land and marsh.

The Upland Court this day ordered that every person should within two months, as far as his land reaches, make good and passable ways, from neighbor to neighbor with bridges where it needs, to the end that neighbors on occasion may come together. Those neglecting the order will forfeit twenty-five guilders.

The boundary between the Upland and New Castle Counties had been the Christiana Creek, but it seems that the New Castle people desired to get part of the population of the Upland County whose population was constantly increasing. The limits and divisions were today agreed upon and settled in the Upland Court between John Moll the president of New Castle Court and the Upland magistrates. The County of Upland was to begin from the north side of Oele Fransen's Creek (Stone Creek), lying in the bend of the Delaware River, above Verdrietige Hook, and from the said creek over to the Single Tree Point (Oldman's Point) on the eastside of the Delaware.

Town lots were now sold in Upland, as complaints had been made to the court by the church wardens that Neels Laersen had taken in, with the lots that he had bought from the Rev. Lokenius in Upland, some of the land preserved for the church purposes. It was therefore ordered that Neels Laersen shall have what belongs to the two lots that he had bought, but what he had taken in more he must leave out annexed to the church lots.

A number of surveyors returns were brought in, which were recorded and ordered to be sent to New York.

The court adjourned till the second Tuesday of March, 1679.

On the 12th and the 13th of March, 1679, the Upland Court was in session, the justices Peter Cock, Israel Helme, Otto Ernest Cock and Lasse Andries being present.

The vexatious case between William Orian and Johannes D'Haes was the first one handled. Both parties produced their account books and the accounts of William Orian were found to be defective, he was then sentenced to pay the costs and 150 guilders for damages to the defendant.

There were a large number of cases in this session, many of which were withdrawn and some were dismissed. The former Commander Christopher Billop is sued for a horse that he had taken to his plantation in Staten Island against the wishes of its owner Peter Bacon. The estate of former Surveyor Walter Wharton in Upland was sued for house rent and other debts, he himself being dead. A school master Edmund Draufton sued Dunck Williams for 200 guilders for having taught the defendant's children to read the Bible, according to agreement. The Rev. Lokenius is sued for two small debts, and the Rev. Fabricius is granted to take up 300 acres of land.

The land transactions are getting very numerous at this time, the land speculation having started in the towns of Marcus Hook and Upland. More than a thousand acres of new lands were granted and several conveyances of land were recorded in this session of the court.

Justice Peter Rambo claimed by a late grant of the Upland Court, a certain tract of land at Wiccaco and Justice Oele Swensen and his brothers Swen and Andries (sons of Swen Gunnarson), pleaded that the same land was within the bounds of their patent, which difference together with the allegations of both parties were heard and the court ordered that since the Swensen brothers have the same land in their patent, which is of old standing and that Peter Rambo's grant was but of late, therefore the Swensens or Swensons do keep the land and in case more land be found within the bound of the said patent, than is set down, the Swensons to have the preference to take it up before others.

Neeles Laersen was ordered to leave open the street between the Upland Creek and the House of Defence or the Country House, where the courts were held, between this and the next court and in default thereof to be fined according to the discretion of the court.

The court adjourned till the second Tuesday in June next.

In the summer of 1679, there was an epidemic ravaging in the country, therefore the court session had to be adjourned from June to September and from September again to November. On November 25th the court finally convened and was in session two days. The justices present in this sitting of the court were the presiding judge or president Peter Cock and the justices Israel Helme, Otto Ernest Cock and Lasse Andries. While Peter Rambo and Oele Swenson were missing.

The case of the former commander Captain Christopher Billop and Peter Bacon was taken up again and Bacon was allowed 1,080 guilders for damages sustained when Captain Billop was keeping his horse. The captain, who had his plantation in Staten Island, had a servant in the custody of Lasse Cock, which was attached for the benefit of Bacon.

The Dutch trader Peter Jegou declared in the court that in the year 1668 he obtained a permit and grant of Governor Philip Carteret, to take up the land called Leasy Point, lying opposite Mattinagcong Island (Burlington Island), to settle himself there and to build and keep a house of entertainment for the accommodation of travelers. All which the plaintiff accordingly had done and moreover had purchased of Cornelis Jorissen, Jurian Macelis and Jan Claessen their houses and lands at Leasy Point, which lands had been given them by the Dutch governor (?) in the year 1666. For the lands Governor Carteret had promised patent to Jegou and he had been in lawful possession of the property until the year 1670, at which time he was plundered by the Indians and became utterly ruined "as is well known to all the world," so that he then for a time was forced to leave his land and possession aforesaid and to seek his livelihood and to repair his losses in other places. He was therefore forced to leave his land with the intention to return when occasion should present, but now "with the arrival of these new comers called Quakers out of England, these defendants Thomas Wright and Godfrey Hancock have violently entered upon your plaintiff's said land and there have by force planted corn, cut timber for houses, mowed hay and made fences notwithstanding that they were forewarned by your plaintiff's friend Henry Jacobs, in your plaintiff's behalf, in the presence of Captain Edmund Cantwell, and afterwards by the plaintiff summoned before the magistrates of Burlington, who making no end of it, the case was with the said magistrates' and defendants' consent removed here before your worships, wherefore plaintiff humbly craves your worships to order the defendants and all others not to molest the plaintiff in the quiet possession of his land."

The defendants in the court declared to be very willing to stand to the verdict and judgment of the Upland Court, whereupon the court, after having heard the debates of both parties and examined all the papers concerning the land, expressed the opinion that since Peter Jegou had Governor Carteret's grant and had been in quiet possession of the land, before the land was sold by John Berkeley to Edward Bylling and that he the said Jegou had also bought the land and paid the Indians for the same, that therefore Peter Jegou ought to enjoy the land and appurtenances peaceably and quietly, according to grant and purchase.

Only three hundred acres of new land was granted in this session of the court, which indicates that all the choice land along the Delaware River and the Schuylkill had been occupied. There was a great speculation going on about the lands near the River, as can be seen of the following: John Test, merchant of Upland, acknowledged in the court of having sold his plantation in Upland to Richard Friends of Weymouth, England. The land had been first granted by patent from Governor Francis Lovelace, on June 7, 1672, to Neeles Mattson and since by the said Mattson sold to John Test, by John Test to Richard Guy, by Richard Guy to John Hayles, by John Hayles again to John Test and now by John Test to Richard Friends. James Sanderlin as attorney of Richard Friends, acknowledged in the court the assignment and conveyance of the above said plantation to Stephen Chambers of Weymouth, England, Stephen Chambers having received deed upon the land, made in New York on August 8, 1679. At present William Oxle (Ogle?) was a tenant upon the farm and James Sanderlin (Sandyland) declared that he as attorney for Stephen Chambers will take possession of the plantation with the cattle and appurtenances.

Jonas Nielsen appeared in the court asking to be paid 106 guilders as expenses for the burial of Peter Veltscheerder and Christian Samuels, who were murdered by the Indians at Tinnagcong Islan (Burlington Island) in the service of Peter Alrichs, in 1672. The court was of the opinion that either Mr. Alrichs whose servants they were must pay the expenses or else the said Jonas should be paid out of the estate of the deceased, if there was any.

It being represented to the court by the church wardens of Tinicum and Wiccaco churches, that the fences about the church yards and other church buildings are much out of repairs and that some of the people, members of the said churches are neglecting to make the same up. The court having taken the premises into consideration, found it necessary to order, authorize and empower the church wardens of the respective two churches to order and summon the respective members of the two churches from time to time and at all times when it shall be found necessary to build, make good and keep in repair the said churchyard fences, as also the churches and all other appurtenances thereof. And if any of the said members upon warning do prove neglective in the doing of their proportion to the same, they and each of them shall forfeit fifty guilders for each such neglect, to be levied out of their goods and chattels, lands and teniments.

The court, after having handled a large number of cases, adjourned till the second Tuesday of March 1680.

On March 10, 1680, a court again was held in Upland, all the Finnish magistrates being present.

Among the debt cases handled in this court was a sum of forty-six guilders, Francis Steevens being the plaintiff and Claes Jansen the defendant. The court ordered the debt paid, twenty guilders in wheat and twenty-six in pumpkins at sixteen guilders per hundred.

The surveyor of Upland County, Richard Noble, delivered his commission from Governor Andros, dated December 15, 1679.

Only 700 acres of new lands were granted at this session, besides 100 acres granted to Peter Nealson for a watermill.

Justice Israel Helme acknowledged the sale of his house and plantation at Upland to James Sanderlins. The deed had been made on March 9, 1680.

The Duke of York's law allowed to the court for every judgment two shillings and six pence. This had not been required so far but now the court found itself compelled to collect it, to defray the expenses of the diet of the judges during the court sessions. The Under-Sheriff William Warner was, therefore empowered to collect the said sum for each judgment since June 13, 1677. The whole sum of the court fees amounted to five pounds or two hundred guilders and was to be collected before the next court day.

The court adjourned till the second Tuesday of June next.

Although the colonists in the Duke of York territories in America had made great progress during the rule of Governor Andros, the duke apparently was not satisfied to his income from the exploitation of the colonies, therefore on May 24, 1680, a commission was given by the duke to one John Levin, to proceed to America and "by all good and reasonable ways and means, to apply himself to inquire and find out all the estate, rents and revenues, profits and perquisites, which in any sort do of right belong and appertain to me (the duke), and arise in any of those places."

On the same day a letter was written by the duke to Governor Andros, in which he says that having had lately some propositions tendered to him about "farming out" (leasing) his revenues in New York and therefore sends Mr. Levin to make thorough inquiry relating thereunto. The duke requests Governor Andros to come to England by the first opportunity, the better to inform the duke in all particulars, and in the meantime leave Lieutenant Anthony Brockholls in charge of the government.

Meanwhile all things were going on as usual on the Delaware. New Commissions for magistrates or justices were issued by Governor Andros on May 28, 1680. A new county became also established on the Delaware, that of St. Jones, whose jurisdiction reached from the south side of Duck Creek to north side of Cedar Creek, at the Delaware Bay, in present State of Delaware.

The Upland Court convened on June 8, 1680, and the new commission for magistrates was publicly read. Here is the copy of the commission.

"Sir Edmund Andros, Knight, Lieutenant and Governor-General and vice-admiral under his Royal Highness James Duke of York and Albany etc. in America. By virtue of the authority derived unto me I do hereby in his majesty's name constitute, appoint and authorize you Mr. Otto Ernest Cock, Mr. Israel Helme, Mr. Henry Jones, Mr. Lasse Cock and Mr. Geo. Brown to be Justices of the Peace in the Jurisdiction of Upland Court or County in Delaware River and dependencies and any three or more of you to be a Court of Judicature giving you and every one of you full power to act in the said employment according to law and the trust reposed in you, of which all persons are to take notice, and give you the due respect and obedience belonging to your places in discharging of your duties.

"This commission to be of force for the space of one year from the date hereof or till further order. Given under my hand and seal of the Province in New York this 28th day of May Anno Domini 1680.

E. Andros."

"Past the office,

 Mathias Nicolls, Secretary."

Among the justices we now miss the venerable names of Peter Cock, Peter Rambo, Lasse Andreas and Oele Swenson. Otto Ernest Cock hereafter appears as the presiding judge or president of the Upland Court, in his father's place. Captain Lasse Cock was also a son of Peter Cock.

The new justices were sworn to their office, except George Brown who was not present.

Only a small number of cases appear in this court. One thousand acres of land was granted, of which two hundred acres was for Peter Cock. The surveyor, Richard Noble brought a number of certificates in of his surveys, which were approved and ordered to be sent to New York.

In order to defray the expenses of the court a tax of one scipple of wheat or five guilders was levied to be paid yearly by each taxable person. It was also ordered that all the arrears of the former taxations be delivered and paid to Justice Otto Ernest Cock at the estate of Tinicum Island and "such who prove neglective to be fetched by the constable by way of restraint." Andries Homman (Andries Andriesson the Finn) appears as the constable of the Upland County.

The Upland Court now found the town of Upland to be situated in the lower end of their county. Therefore for the greater convenience of the people it was decided that the court hereafter will sit in the Finnish town of Kingsesse (Kingsessing) on the Schuylkill River.

The court adjourned till October 13, 1680.

On October 13, the court convened at Kingsesse, all the justices being present and George Brown, who was absent in the last session of the court, was sworn into the office of a justice.

Among the cases handled in this court was Moens Staeck being fined one thousand guilders for slandering Justice Otto Ernest Cock. The defendant asked for forgiveness and at the request of Justice Cock the fine was remitted.

Former Justice Peter Rambo appeared in the court as defendant in a dispute about a marsh, upon which Rambo had a patent. The jury brought in a verdict for Rambo's favor and it was allowed to pass by the court.

Seven hundred acres of new lands were granted in this court.

The court found it necessary for the due preservation of peace that one more constable be appointed and authorized to officiate between the Schuylkill and Neshaminy Kill. It was therefore ordered and resolved and Mr. Erik Cock (son of Peter Cock) was nominated, appointed and sworn as constable for one year till another be appointed in his place.

The court likewise found it necessary that some fit persons be appointed as overseers of the highways and roads and as overseers and viewers of all fences throughout the Upland County. It was therefore resolved and Mr. John Cock (son of Peter Cock) and Lasse Dalbo were appointed and sworn overseers and viewers of the highways, roads and fences within the county for one year or till others be appointed in their said places.

Richard Noble, the surveyor of Upland County brought in his certificate of a survey made by him upon the governor's special order, dated June 1, 1680, for the benefit of Ephraim Herman and Lasse Cock, on a tract of land called Hataorackan containing 602 acres. The survey had been made on August 4, 1680 and the tract was later included in the Pennsbury Manor.

The court adjourned till the second Tuesday of March 1681.

On March 8, 1681 the court convened in the Town of Kingsessing, the justices present were Otto Ernest Cock, Henry Jones and Lasse Cock.

In this court 1,890 acres of new lands were **granted**, several of these grants were up the river, in the neighborhood of the Delaware Falls.

Not many cases appear in this court. The **next court** day was to be the second Tuesday of June 1681.

CHAPTER XVII.

The Third Period of the Finnish Settlements under the English Rule.

A CHANGE in the government of the Delaware River was taking place at this period. William Penn, who had inherited from his father Vice-Admiral Sir William Penn a considerable wealth, had become interested in the proprietorship of New Jersey in America and thus having obtained information about the land in that section of the country, proposed to King Charles II., to receive land in America in lieu of 15,000 pounds that the government owed to his father. To this the king was very willing and after the boundaries had been defined, the charter, constituting William Penn proprietary of Pennsylvania, was signed by the king on March 4, 1681. The boundaries of Pennsylvania were to be, on the east, the Delaware River, starting from a point twelve miles distance northward of New Castle town, up the river as far as forty-third degree of northern latitude, if the said river extends so far northwards, otherwise as far as the river extends, and from that point along the meridian line to the said forty-third degree. The land was to extend westward five degrees of longitude from the eastern bounds. On the north the forty-third degree of northern latitude was to be the boundary and on the south a circle drawn at twelve miles distance from New Castle, northward and westward, for the fortieth degree of northern latitude, along which degree it was to continue to the above mentioned limits of longitude.

For this area, named by the king Pennsylvania, William Penn and his heirs were to pay to the king and his successors two beaver skins yearly, on the first of January at the castle of Windsor.

Nearly a month after the charter had been signed, the following declaration was addressed by the king's command to the inhabitants of Pennsylvania:

"Charles R.—Whereas his majesty, in consideration of the great merit and faithful services of Sir William Penn, deceased, and for divers other good causes him thereunto moving, hath been graciously pleased, by letters-patent bearing date the 4th day of March last past, to give and grant unto William Penn, Esq., son and heir of the said Sir William Penn, all that tract, etc. (as described above).

"His majesty does, therefore, hereby publish and declare his royal will and pleasure, that all persons settled or inhabiting within the limits of the said province, do yield all due obedience to the said William Penn, his heirs and assigns, as absolute proprietaries and governors thereof, as also to the deputies, agents, or lieutenants, lawfully commissioned by him or them, according to the powers and authorities granted by the said letters-patent, wherewith his majesty expects and requires as ready compliance for all persons whom it may concern, as they tender his majesty's displeasure.

"Given at the court, etc., 2d April, 1681, thirty-third year of reign. By his majesty's command,

Conway."

William Penn, who commissioned his cousin William Markham, to be deputy-governor for him in the province of Pennsylvania, prepared with his own hand, the following letter for the inhabitants of the province, to be read by Deputy-Governor Markham at his arrival to the colony.

"My friends.—I wish you all happiness, here and hereafter. These are to let you know that it hath pleased God, in his providence, to cast you within my lot and care. It is a business that, though I never undertook before, yet God has given me an understanding of my duty, and an honest mind to do it uprightly. I hope you will not be troubled at your change, and the king's choice, for you are now fixed at the mercy of no governor that comes to make his fortune great; you shall be governed by laws of your own making, and live a free, and, if you will, a sober and industrious people. I shall not usurp the right of any, or oppress his person. God has furnished me with a better resolution, and has given me his grace to keep it. In short, whatever sober and free men can reasonably desire for the security and improvement of their own happiness, I shall heartily comply with and in five months resolve, if it pleases God, to see you. In the mean time, pray submit to the commands of my deputy so far as they are consistent with the law, and pay him those dues, (that formerly you paid to the order of the governor of New York), for my use and benefit, and so I beseech God to direct you in the way of righteousness, and therein prosper you and your children after you. I am your true friend,

"William Penn.

"London, 8th of the month called April, 1681."

William Penn's commission to his deputy governor reads as follows:

"The commission given by William Penn, governor and proprietor of the province of Pennsylvania, to his cousin, William Markham, to be deputy governor for him, of the aforesaid province.

"At Westminster, this 10th of (2d mo.) April 1681.

"Whereas the king has graciously pleased, upon divers good considerations, to settle upon me and my heirs for ever, by his letters-patent, under the great seal of England, dated the 4th of March last, a tract of land in America, by the name of Pennsylvania, lying and bounded as in the said letters-patent is particularly expressed, with ample powers and authorities requisite for the well-governing of the same, to be exercised by me or my deputy. Out of the special regard that I have to the care and fidelity of my cousin, William Markham, I do hereby appoint him my deputy, and fully authorize him in my stead and for my behoof, and for the benefit of the said province, to act and perform what may be fully needful to the peace and safety thereof, till I myself shall arrive, or he shall receive further orders; that is to say, he has hereby power.

"First. To call a council, and that to consist of nine, he presiding.

"Second. That he does there read my letter to the inhabitants, and the king's declaration of subjection; then (or there) take the inhabitants' acknowledgements of my authority and propriety.

"Third. To settle bounds between me and my neighbours; to survey, set out, rent, or sell land, according to (my) instructions bearing date the 8th of the month called April, 1681.

"Fourth. To erect courts, make sheriffs, justices of the peace, and other requisite inferior officers, that right may be done, the peace kept, and all vice punished, without partiality, according to the good laws of England.

"Fifth. To call to his aid, and command the assistance of any of the inhabitants of those provinces, for the legal suppression of tumults or riots, and conviction of the offenders, according to law, and to make or ordain any ordinances, and to do any thing or things that to the peace and safety of the said province he may lawfully do, by the power granted to me in the letters-patent, calling assemblies to make laws only excepted. Given under my hand and seal, this 10th day of the month called April, 1681.

William Penn.

"Witnesses—Henry West, John West."

Penn now desired emigrants to his colony, and therefore issued a lengthy proposal, in which he explains the profits of colonization to the country by which colonies are planted. Then he proceeds to enumerate the benefits derived by the colonists themselves in the enterprise, and among other things says: "Such as could not only marry here, but hardly live and allow themselves clothes, do marry there, and bestow thrice more in all necessaries and conveniences, (and not a little in ornamental things too), for themselves, their wives and children, both as to apparel and household stuff."

After describing the colony as to its convenience for navigation, capability in production of commodities, the making of its laws, and the conditions of the distribution of land, he speaks of the persons that are most fitted for plantations. He desires farmers and farm laborers, tradesmen, and also poor "ingenious spirits" may have time and opportunity, for the easy subsistence in the colony, to gratify their inclinations and thereby improve science. And another sort of people, he says, that are not only fit but necessary in plantations, are "men of universal spirits," who have not gained recognition under settled customs, referring in this connection to parallels in the ancient Greece and Rome.

Next he advises about the journey, what goods are fit to take with for the use or for selling with profit, also about the charges for the voyage and how to start living on arrival to the colony. And lastly concludes by urging people not to make rash or hasty decisions but maturely consider all inconveniences as well as future ease and plenty.

In the whole the document unravels William Penn, as a practical dreamer, as a man of learning, and considering to the soft life in which he had been brought up, a wonderful observer of all conditions in human society, besides being a man of perfect knowledge of the things that appeal to the different types of human mind.

While these events of historical consequences were taking place in London, Mr. John Levin appeared at the Delaware River, on April 8th, to inquire into the sources of revenue for the Duke of York.

The Upland County Court was sitting at the town of Kingsessing, on June 14, 1681. The justices present were Otto Ernest Cock, Israel Helme and Lasse Cock.

The justices Henry Jones and George Brown who had failed to attend the court, were fined ten pounds each, according to the law. Justice George Brown later appeared and became seated in the court, having been hindered to come sooner for want of passage over the creek.

As the cattle, hogs and horses were running wild in the forests, the ordinances of the Delaware River required all domestic animals marked. Claes Janson on this day brought in the earmark of his cattle and hogs, desiring it recorded, which the court granted. The earmark being: the foremost side of the ears half cut away.

Land was getting so valuable along the river that in every

court at this time there were disputes about tracts that formerly were not cared about. In this court Lasse Dalbo claimed a piece of land on the Schuylkill, which was occupied by Sven Loom. The defendant replied that he has had the first grant and survey and has paid the quit-rent for the land. The plaintiff desired the case settled by a jury which was granted and the jury bringing in their verdict in favor of the defendant the court passed judgment accordingly.

The president of the court, Otto Ernest Cock, acquainted the court, that he had bought and paid, of the Indian proprietors a certain swampy or marshy island, called by the Indians Quist-conck, (the present Hog Island), lying at the upper end of Tinicum Island in the river, opposite Andreas Boone's Creek; and desired the court's approbation. The court having well informed themselves about the premises, did approve the same.

A petition was presented to the court by the Rev. Jacobus Fabricius, upon which the court ordered that the church wardens of the petitioner's church do take care that everyone of those who have signed and promised towards the minister's maintenance, do pay him the sums promised, upon pain of execution against the defaulters.

Upon complaint made by the overseers of the highways, the court condemned John Champion to pay a fine of twenty-five guilders, for not working upon the highway when due warning had been given to him.

William Warner and William Orian presented a request to the court, upon which it was ordered that the several people who hold lands, of the tract which the petitioners had bought from the Indians on the Schuylkill River, everyone to repay to the petitioners proportionable to the quantity of land they hold there. The whole purchasing price being 335 guilders and the following persons were holding parts of the land: Andreas Inckoren 200 acres. Andreas Homman 200 acres, Pelle Larsson 100 acres, Peter Erickson 200 acres, William Warner 100 acres, William Orian 100 acres, John Boyles and John Schoeten 400 acres and Swen Loom 300 acres.

Upon petition the court granted lands to the following persons: Reinier Petersen 200 acres, Andries Boon 200 acres, William Warner Senior 400 acres, Richard Tucker 100 acres, Otto Ernest Cock 400 acres, Lionel Brittain and Jan Classen 200 acres.

William Boyles, the Upland County constable at the Delaware Falls, complained to the court that Gilbert Wheeler, at the said falls, is selling liquors by retail to the Indians, contrary to the law and forewarning of the said constable. The said information was ratified by Justice George Brown, upon which the court condemned the said Gilbert Wheeler to pay four pounds and costs as fine for his trespass, according to law of the government.

The court appointed and authorized William Boyles to be surveyor and overseer of the highways from the falls to Poetquessing creek. He was to take care that the highways be made good and passable, with bridges over all marshy places. The work upon the highways was to be performed between this and the next court and all the inhabitants living within the above said area were ordered to be ready to work and to complete a certain highway upon due notice by the overseer. The unwilling to be fined according to former order and practice.

The court adjourned till the second Tuesday of September next, but it never met any more. Here ends the local government of the Finns in the country today known as the State of Pennsylvania. The government had been managed by the Finnish magistrates with such fairness and orderliness that there is no equal in example among the early American colonies.

About ten days after the above court day, in June 1681, Deputy-Governor Markham arrived to take charge of the Province of Pennsylvania and Lieutenant Anthony Brockholls of New York issued the following proclamation, releasing the justices and other officers who fell within the new province, from their allegiance to the Duke of York.

"Whereas his majesty hath been graciously pleased, by his letters-patent bearing date 4th March last, to give and grant to William Penn, Esquire, all the tract of land in America, now called by the name of Pennsylvania, formerly under the protection and government of his royal highness, (then follows the description of the boundaries), with all powers, pre-eminences, and jurisdictions necessary for the government of a province, as by letters-patent doth at large appear, which, with his majesty's gracious letter, directed to the inhabitants and planters within the said limits, and a commission from the said William Penn to the bearer hereof, William Markham, Esquire, to be his deputy governor of the said province, have been produced and shown to us, and are entered upon record in the office of records for this province, and by us highly approved of, as his majesty's royal will and pleasure, therefore thought fit to intimate the same to you, to prevent any doubt or trouble that might arise, and to give you our thanks for your good service done in your several offices and stations, during the time you remained under his royal highness' government, expecting no further account than that you readily submit and yield all due obedience to the said letters-patent, according to the true intent and meaning thereof, in the performance and enjoyments of which we wish you all happiness.

"New York, June 21, 1681."

The above document is copied in the Upland Court Record, by which the record becomes to a close.

Soon after his arrival to the Delaware, Deputy-Governor Markham, according to his instructions, nominated a council of nine men. Seven of these were Englishmen and two were Finns, namely Otto Ernest Cock and Lasse Cock.

The following "Obligation of Councilmen" was signed by the newly appointed. "Whereas we whose hands and seals are hereunto set are chosen by Wm. Markham (agent of Wm. Penn, Esq., Proprietor of the Province of Pennsylvania) to be of the Council for the said province, do hereby bind ourselves by our hands and seals, that we will neither act nor advise, nor consent unto anything that shall not be according to our own consciences the best for the true and well Government of the said Province, and likewise to keep secret all the votes and acts of us, the said Council, unless such as by the general consent of us are to be published. Dated at Upland the third day of August, 1681."

The Finns at this time were handicapped for the lack of knowledge in the English language. In their affairs with the Dutch they had used the Swedish language rather than the Dutch. Swedish in those days being very similar to the Dutch language, it could be therefore easily mastered by the Dutch colonists. Swedish had become the language of communication on the Delaware River between the different nationalities, although there was scarcely a Swede in the colony since the downfall of the Swedish rule. Many of the Finns on their arrival to the colony did not speak Swedish, as Papegoja who was appointed commander of the colonists that arrived on the ship Mercurius in 1656, was compelled to employ an interpreter as he could not speak Finnish and the passenger did not understand Swedish. Also Trotzig writes in his letter in the spring of 1664, that of the one hundred and forty Finnish colonists, then in Amsterdam on their way to the Delaware Colony, but some of the men could speak Swedish. The greatest part of the Delaware Finns came from the Finnish settlements in the south-central Sweden where some of the Finns still retain their language, despite arbitrary measures during more than two centuries to compel them to learn Swedish.

In the colony most of the Finns seem to have acquired the Swedish rather than the Dutch language, although a report of a Finnish commission investigating a land dispute in Kingsessing on June 4, 1673, was left to the Upland Court in the Dutch language.

Despite the Delaware Colony had been under the English rule about seventeen years, before it came under William Penn, the Englishmen were few and only newly arrived among the Finns. Therefore there had not been need of the English language, nor opportunity to practice it, except to some of the magistrates who came in contact with the English commanders at the river and with the correspondence, orders and commissions of the governors of New York. An English colonist, Thomas Paschall, in a letter to his friend in England refers to the Finns as ingenious, who speak English, Swedish, Finnish, Dutch and the Indian languages. But Mr. Paschall must have been rather optimistic as far as the Finns' knowledge of English concern. This was unfortunate, as the Finns had the experience of twenty-six years in self-government in the colony, having been more or less by themselves since the downfall of the Swedish rule on the Delaware. They would have been valuable as stabilizers in the new government and undoubtedly would have saved much disappointment and sorrow from William Penn.

Deputy-Governor Markham established himself first in Upland, where a newly organized court met the first time on September 13, 1681, according to the resolution of the former court. Among the nine justices present four were of the old Finnish colony, namely, Otto Ernest Cock, Lasse Cock, Sven Svenson and Andreas Bankson. In the jury drawn in this court, two of the twelve members were Finns, namely, Lasse Dalbo and Peter Rambo, Jr.

On the 30th of September, 1681, Proprietor Penn appointed three commissioners, who were to proceed to Pennsylvania, with instruction having the following points: They were to take special care that the people embarking with them shall be well accommodated on their arrival to the colony. They were to warn the old inhabitants, if found taking advantages of the new immigrants by raising the prices of food supplies, etc. They were to let the rivers and creeks sounded, especially at Upland, in order to settle a great town. In founding a navigable, high, dry and healthy place, suitable for the town they were to lay out ten thousand acres of land for that purpose. No more land to be surveyed till the town be fixed and the people settled upon it. The sixth article of the instructions reads: "If it should happen that the most convenient place for the great town should be already taken up, in greater quantity of land than is consistent with the town-plot, and that land not already improved, use utmost skill to persuade them to part with so much as will be necessary, that so necessary and good a design be not spoiled; that is, where they have ten acres by the water side, to abate five, and to take five more backward, and so proportionably, because that, by the settlement of this town, the remaining five, in two or three years' time, will be worth twice as much as those before, yea, what they take backward for their water side land, will, in a little more time, be really more valuable than all their ten forward was before; urging my regard to them if they will not break this great and good contrivance, and in my name promise them what gratuity or privilege you think fit, as having a new grant at their old rent; nay, half their quit rent abated, yea, make them as free as purchasers, rather than disappoint my mind in this township; though herein be as sparing as ever you can, and urge the weak bottom of their grant, the Duke of York having never had a grant from the king, etc. Be impartially just and courteous to all, that is both pleasing to the Lord and wise in itself."

The commissaries further are instructed in the plan of the town. And the Indians were to be summoned in conference and Penn's conditions with the purchasers of land to be read to them in their own tongue, that they will see they are fairly treated. Their chieftains were to be given presents sent by Penn, and the commissioners were to make a league of friendship with them. Penn further warns the commissaries to appear grave in the conference, as the Indians do not love to be smiled on.

The commissaries were to buy land from the Indians from time to time, but to see that they do not sell one another's land as the ownership between themselves is not always settled. But the commissaries were by no means allowed to sell any land before Penn himself arrives to the colony, nor to allow old patents, that have been forfeited by not planting in time according to the old law of the place. The forfeiters were to be paid their expenses of patent and surveying.

In the middle of the town the commissaries were to leave space for a storehouse, market and state houses. And on the river bank, in the middle of the town plan, they were to lay aside three hundred acres for the situation of Penn's own house.

A quarter of a mile or at least two hundred feet along the shore were to be left for harbor purposes.

The fifteenth article of the instruction reads: "Let every house be placed, if the person pleases, in the middle of its plat, as to the breadth way of it, that so there may be ground on each side for gardens or orchards, or fields, that it may be a green country town, which will never be burnt, and always be wholesome."

Lastly Penn leaves the town plan to the commissaries as they will find the situation.

The following letter was sent by Penn with the commissaries to the Indians:

"London, 18th of October, 1681.

"My friends—There is one great God and power that hath made the world and all things therein, to whom you and I, and all people owe their being and well-being, and to whom you and I must one day give an account for all that we do in the world; this great God hath written his law in our hearts, by which we are taught and commanded to love and help, and do good to one another, and not to do harm and mischief one to another. Now this great God hath been pleased to make me concerned in your parts of the world, and the king of the country where I live hath given unto me a great province, but I desire to enjoy it with your love and consent, that we may always live together as neighbors and friends, else what would the great God say to us, who hath made us not to devour and destroy one another, but live soberly and kindly together in the world? Now I would have you well observe, that I am very sensible of the unkindness and injustice that hath been too much exercised towards you by the people of these parts of the world, who sought themselves, and make great advantages by you, rather than be examples of justice and goodness unto you, which I hear hath been matter of trouble to you, and caused great grudgings and animosities, sometimes to the shedding of blood, which hath made the great God angry; but I am not such a man, as is well known in my own country; I have great love and regards towards you, and I desire to win and gain your love and friendship, by a kind, just, and peaceable life, and the people I send are of the same mind, and shall in all things behave themselves accordingly; and if in anything any shall offend you or your people, you shall have a full and speedy satisfaction for the same, by an equal number of just men on both sides, that by no means you may have just occasion of being offended against them I shall shortly come to you myself, at what time we may more largely and freely confer and discourse of these matters. In the meantime, I have sent my commissioners to treat with you about land, and a firm league of peace. Let me desire you to be kind to them and the people, and receive these presents and tokens which I have sent to you, as a testimony of my good will to you, and my resolution to live justly, peaceably, and friendly with you.

"I am your loving friend,

"William Penn."

The commissioners were given to bring over a letter of recommendation to the Finns from Liembergh, the Swedish ambassador in London, written in the "Norse" language, as Penn says, and to be delivered by Deputy-Governor Markham to the Rev. Fabricius, for publication among the people.

In the meantime the Indians presented in Upland the following petition to the Governor and Council of Pennsylvania:

"Whereas, the selling of strong liquors was prohibited in Pennsylvania and not at New Castle, we find it a greater ill-convenience than before, our Indians going down to New Castle, and there buying rum, and making themselves more debauched than before.

"Therefore we, whose names are hereunder written, do desire that the prohibition may be taken off, and rum and strong liquors may be sold as formerly, until it be prohibited in New Castle, and in that government in Delaware.

"Pesienk (Passayunk) in Pennsylvania, 8th October, 1681."

On November 30th, the second court of the Province of Pennsylvania was held at Upland. Present were Governor William Markham and twelve justices of which seven were Englishmen and five of the old inhabitants, viz., Otto Ernest Cock, Lasse Cock, Swen Swenson, Andreas Bankson and Hendrick Bankson. Among the jurors were John Cock, Erik Cock, Mons Peterson and Peter Joakum.

The third court of the new province was held on March 4, 1682, in which nine overseers of highways were appointed, having their specified districts from Marcus Creek to the neighborhood of the Delaware Falls and along the Schuylkill. They were selected mostly from the older inhabitants, among which was Andreas Rambo, son of Peter Rambo, Senior.

During the winter and spring of 1682, Penn was busy in England, selling lands in the colony and negotiating about the organization of a commercial company, the "Free Society of Traders," which was incorporated and granted special privileges in the colony. He had also worked a constitution, to his province, having a lengthy preface and twenty-four articles. The constitution is headed as follows:

"The frame of the government of the province of Pennsylvania, in America, together with certain laws agreed upon in England, by the governor and divers freemen of the aforesaid province, (those in England who had bought land from Penn in the province), to be further explained and continued there by the first provincial council that shall be held, if they see meet."

In the preamble for the articles of the constitution he says among other things that: "Now know ye, that for the well-being and government of the said province and for the encouragement of all the freemen and planters that may be therein concerned, in pursuance of the powers aforementioned, I, the said William Penn, have declared, granted, and confirmed, and by these presents, for me, my heirs and assignees, do declare, grant, and confirm, unto all the freemen, planters, and adventurers, of, in, and to the said province, these liberties, franchises, and properties, to be held, enjoyed, and kept by the freemen, planters, and inhabitants of the said province of Pennsylvania, for ever."

The first and second articles read as follows:

"I. That the government of this province shall, according to the powers of the patent, consist of the governor and freemen of the said province, in form of a provincial council and general assembly, by whom all laws shall be made, officers chosen, and public affairs transacted, as is hereafter respectively declared. That is to say:

"II. That the freemen of the said provinces shall, on the 20th day of the twelfth month, which shall be in this present year one thousand six hundred eighty and two, meet and assemble in some fit place, of which timely notice shall be beforehand given by the governor or his deputy, and then and there shall choose out of themselves seventy-two persons, of most note for their wisdom, virtue, and ability, who shall meet on the 10th of the first month, next ensuing, and always be called and act as the provincial council of the said province."

In the third and fourth articles Penn gives the rules of re-election, in the fifth he establishes the quorum, in the sixth he retains the presidency of the provincial council for himself or his deputy. In the seventh article he defines the preparation of bills for the general assembly, in the eighth the execution of laws, in the ninth the inviolability of the "Frame of Government." The tenth, eleventh and the twelfth articles deal with the settlement of towns, with the management of the treasury and about schools and learning. The thirteenth article deals with committees of the provincial council and the duties of each committee in the government of the province.

The fourteenth article reads as follows: "And to the end that all laws prepared by the governor and provincial council aforesaid, may yet have the more full concurrence of the freemen of the province, it is declared, granted, and confirmed, that at the time and place or places for the choice of a provincial council as afore-said, the said freemen shall yearly choose members to serve in a general assembly as their representatives, not exceeding two hundred persons, who shall yearly meet, from the 20th day of the second month, which shall be in the year one thousand six hundred eighty and three following, in the capital town or city of the said province, where during eight days the several members may freely confer with one another, and if any of them see meet, with a committee of the provincial council, (consisting of three out of each of the committees aforesaid, being twelve in all,) which shall be at the time purposely appointed to receive from any of them proposals for the alterations or amendments of any of the said proposed and promulgated bills; and on the ninth day from their so meeting, the said general assembly, after reading over the proposed bills by the clerk of the provincial council, and the occasion and motives for them being opened by the governor or his deputy, shall give their affirmative or negative, which to them seemeth best, in such manner as hereinafter is expressed. But not less than two-thirds, shall make a quorum in the passing of laws, and choice of such officers as are by them to be chosen."

The articles from fifteenth to the twenty-first, inclusive, deal with the enrollment of the laws, about increase of the members in the assembly, (Penn proposing that in the first year all the freemen in the province shall or may take part in the assembly), how the courts are established and the officers chosen, (Penn appointing the first officers), the duties of the assembly, election to be by ballot, and lastly provisions are made in case of infancy of the governor or proprietor.

The twenty-second article makes provisions in case any day mentioned in the articles falls on Sunday. Article twenty-three provides that any change in this constitution requires the consent of the governor, his heirs or assigns, and six parts of seven of the freemen in the provincial council and general assembly.

The twenty-fourth and last article reads:

"And lastly, that I, the said William Penn, for myself, my heirs and assigns, have solemnly declared, granted, and confirmed, and do hereby solemnly declare, grant, and confirm, that neither I, my heirs nor assigns, shall procure or do any thing or things whereby the liberties in this charter contained and expressed shall be infringed or broken; and if any thing be procured by any person or persons, contrary to these premises, it shall be held of no force or effect."

The charter or frame of government was signed by William Penn, on the 25th of April, 1682.

Shortly after the issuance of the "Frame of Government," Penn with some freemen that were coming to the colony from England, agreed upon forty laws, which were to be presented to the assembly in the colony for ratification. The laws were titled as "Laws agreed upon in England." They further amplified and confirmed the Penn's "Frame of Government." The first act reads: "That the Charter of liberties, (the Fame of Government), declared, and confirmed the five and twentieth days of the second month, called April, (Quaker calculation of time), 1682, before divers witnesses, by William Penn, governor and chief proprietor of Pennsylvania, to all the freemen and planters of the said province, is declared and appointed, and shall be forever held as fundamental in the government thereof, according to the limitations mentioned in the said charter."

The sixteenth act provides: "That seven years' quiet possession (of land) shall give an unquestionable right."

The thirty-ninth act reads as follows: "That there shall be no time any alterations of any of these laws, without the consent of the governor, his heirs or assigns, and six parts of seven of the freemen, met in provincial council and general assembly."

The last act of the laws says, "That all other matters and things not herein provided for, which shall and may concern the public justice, peace, or safety of the said province, and the raising and imposing taxes, customs, duties, or other charges whatsoever, shall be, and are hereby referred to the order, prudence, and determination of the governor and freemen in provincial council and general assembly to be held from time to time in the said province."

The above referred laws were ratified and signed by William Penn and the party of freemen in England, on May 5, 1682.

Deputy-Governor Markham, with the commissioners appointed by Penn on September 30, 1681, had been diligently looking for a suitable place, where to lay off ten thousand acres of land for the site of a great town, according to the orders of the proprietary. In this they were seriously hampered for the reason that the Finns had occupied and settled the western side of the Delaware River, within the Province of Pennsylvania, as far up the river as above the Neshaminy creek. The land about Upland, which Penn had especially in his mind for the town, had been all occupied far to the inland, besides the boundary question between Pennsylvania and Maryland had become threatening on account of Lord Baltimore's claims. The deputy-governor and the commissaries therefore had selected the land between the Finnish settlements of Wiccaco and Shackamaxon, called by the Indians Coquannock or Coaquannock. This land, being kind of a ridge along the Delaware River, had only lately been occupied by the Finns, on account of it being less adapted for agriculture and being covered with heavy pine forest. Two hundred and fifty acres of this shore was granted on Tuesday the 13th of November, 1677, to Justice Peter Rambo, by the Upland Court and at the same court on March 13th, 1679, Rambo claimed the land upon the grant, but Justice Oele Swensson and his brothers Swen and Andreas pleaded that the same land was within the bounds of their patent of the Wicaco tract, which was granted to them and their father Swen Gunnarrson by Governor Stuyvesant on May 5, 1664, and confirmed to them by Governor Lovelace on May 3, 1669. The court decided in favor of the Swensons.

However was the statute of this land, Richard Noble, Surveyor of the Upland County, upon warrant of the Upland Court, surveyed the shore land between Wicaco and Cooconocon Creek (Pegg's Run), on June 21, 1681, to the Swensons or Swansons, as they are hereafter referred to. This tract contained 345 acres and was an addition to their former land, called Wicaco, which contained 800 acres.

It was the custom on the Delaware that with each grant of land a proportionate amount of pasture land was assigned besides the land described in the patent. In some patents the area of the pasture land was given in acres, but was free from the quit-rent. This explains why the Swanson brothers claimed the Coaquannock although it was not mentioned in their patent. In order to make their ownership certain they got the land surveyed for them, but were too late to receive a patent upon the tract from the Duke of York, as the Province of Pennsylvania was transferred by Lieutenant Brockholls to William Penn on the same day as Richard Noble made the survey. This undoubtedly had much to do with the decision of Markham and the commissaries to locate the town of Philadelphia on that site.

When the location of Philadelphia was decided is not recorded, but it was known in London in July, 1682, as James Claypoole, treasurer of the Free Society of Traders, writes to his brother on the 14th of that month that "I have 100 acres where our capital city is to be, upon the river near Schuylkill and Peter Cock; there I intend to plant and build my first house."

The first purchase of land in Pennsylvania made in the name of William Penn from the Indians was that of the territory on the west side of Delaware River between the Neshaminy and Towsissink creeks. The deed was signed on July 15, 1682, Lasse Cock acting as interpreter. The site of Philadelphia was not purchased from the Indians, it had long belonged to the Finns as commonage, and the Swanson brothers were later given for their Coaquannock tract nearly twice as much land further inland by William Penn. Some amendments, or rather explanations and amplifications were made in the first land purchase of William Penn from the Indians on the following first day of August. The document says that it was made "at the house of Captain Lasse Cock," who was the only white witness in the deal, and the interpreter in all of the early transactions between Deputy-Governor Markham and William Penn with the Indians.

On August 24, 1682, the Duke of York transferred the rest of his territory on the west side of the Delaware River, from twelve miles above New Castle to Cape Henlopen, for William Penn. All the Finns and other old settlers, on the west side of the river now fell under the same government.

Having arranged his affairs in England, William Penn with about one hundred Quaker colonists left for Pennsylvania about the first day of September, 1682. Numerous English immigrants had already arrived to the province and all the houses of the early colonists were filled by the new arrivals. In the autumn of 1682, lots were drawn for the immigrants in Philadelphia and the building of houses had already started, but none was ready on the arrival of Penn. The first residences for the Englishmen in Philadelphia were caves dug into the river bank, some of which had been left there by the Indians.

William Penn, with his diminished party of immigrants, nearly one-third of which had died on the way for smallpox, arrived before the town of New Castle on the 27th day of October, 1682, and produced deeds of feoffment from James, Duke of York, upon which he received possession of the town in the following day and the two counties below New Castle, few days later. On the 29th, Penn appeared in Upland, which he selected as his temporary capital and residence, and changed its name to Chester.

Immediately after his arrival, Penn was a busy man. Twenty-three ships, with more than thousand immigrants, arrived in the Delaware during 1682, these needed much of his care. The boundary question between Penn's province and that of Lord Baltimore had become acute and disturbing, requiring Penn's immediate attention. Besides he felt it to be his duty to the Duke of York to visit his colony of New York.

But Penn could not escape of meeting the Indian chieftains, as he had promised in his letter, sent to them by his commissaries. The Indians had been accustomed to receive presents from every new deputy-governor, director or commander at their arrival. And when the presents were not forthcoming, the Indians were not shy to make a remark about it. Penn had already sent preliminary presents to them and the Indians had been made to regard the proprietary as a great dignitary, for which the greater were their anticipations.

An ancient tradition, very popular in connection of the early American colonial history, relates that "a treaty of amity and friendship" was made by Penn with the Indians, at Shackamaxon, under the branches of a great elm tree. The elm, to which the tradition was attached grew on the bank of the Delaware River, at the house built and formerly owned by Captain Lasse Cock, Penn's official interpreter in the Indian affairs. The house and plantation was sold by Captain Cock in 1678, to Elizabeth Kinsey, and by marriage became the property of Thomas Fairman. A monthly meeting of the Quakers was held in the house on the 8th of November, 1682, the record of the Society of Friends telling of Penn arriving to Philadelphia at that time, therefore it is most probable that the celebrated Penn-Indian treaty was then made.

The elm tree, known as "The Treaty Tree," became an object of veneration and was carefully protected, even the British officers posted guards around it during the Revolutionary War. The Great Elm Tree was blown down in 1810, being two hundred and eighty-three years of age, as proved by its rings. A monument now marks the site of the tree, under which branches William Penn spoke his message of trust in humanity, in which he was never disappointed as far as concern the Indian nations represented at the noble occasion.

On the fourth of December, 1682, agreeably to earlier summons, the first General-Assembly met at Upland, now known as Chester. The members of the assembly were few and Quaker in color. The Finns and other old settlers were found to be foreigners, by the Quaker advisers of Penn, and therefore not eligible as members of the assembly. This constituted a violation of Penn's charter from the king, as in the document the planters and inhabitants in the province are always referred to as the king's subjects before there was any suggestion of new colonists. By the governor's of New York these Delaware colonists were always referred to as his Majesty's subjects and oath of allegiance had been required in behalf of the inhabitants when the river fell under English rule.

The old Finnish county of Upland having been divided into three separate counties, these three counties and the three old counties down the river, called the lower counties, each elected twelve members to the assembly, of which three from each county were to be members of the provincial council. Penn's noble Frame of Government was thus broken from the very start.

On the third day of the session a petition was presented by the freemen of the three lower counties, New Castle, Jones and New Deal, "humbly desiring that they may be favored with an act of union, by the governor and assembly, for their incorporation in and with the province of Pennsylvania, in order to the enjoyment of all the rights and privileges of the aforesaid province, and that they might ever after be esteemed and accounted as freemen of the before-mentioned province."

On the same day the Finns and other old inhabitants of Delaware presented that the governor would be pleased to make them as free as the English members of the province, and that their lands may be entailed on them and their heirs for ever. This had been granted to them when England took possession of the Delaware River in 1664. While the patents granted in name of the

Duke of York, were issued to guarantee the lands for the colonists and their heirs for ever. William Penn likewise in the preamble of his "Frame of Government" solemnly says that, "Now know ye, that for the well-being and government of the said province, and for the encouragement of all the freemen and planters that may be therein concerned, in pursuance of the powers aforementioned, I, the said William Penn, have declared, granted, and confirmed, and by these presents, for me, my heirs and assigns, do declare, grant, and confirm, unto all the freemen, planters, and adventurers of, in, and to the said province, these liberties, franchises, and properties, to be held, enjoyed, and kept by the freemen, planters, and inhabitants of the said province of Pennsylvania, for ever."

The two above mentioned petitions caused an act of union and naturalization to be made, by which, firstly, the three lower counties became annexed to the province of Pennsylvania, to enjoy the privileges granted in the "Frame of Government." Secondly, it is said in the act: "And forasmuch as it is apparent that the just encouragement of the inhabitants of this province and territories thereunto belonging, is likely to be an effectual way for the improvement thereof, and since some of the people that live therein, and are like to come thereinto, are foreigners, and so not freemen, according to the acceptation of the law of England, the consequences of which might prove very detrimental to them in their estates and traffic, and so injurious to the prosperity of this province and territories thereof, be it enacted by the governor and proprietary of the province and counties aforesaid, by and with the consent of the deputies of the freemen thereof, in assembly met, that all persons who are strangers and foreigners, that do now inhabit this province and counties aforesaid, that hold land in fee in the same, according to the law of a freeman, and who shall solemnly promise, within three months after the publication hereof, in their respective county courts where they live, upon record, faith and allegiance unto the King of England, and his lawful heirs and successors, and fidelity and lawful obedience to William Penn, proprietary and governor of these provinces, etc., and his heirs and assigns, according to the king's letters-patent, shall be held and reputed freemen of the province and counties aforesaid, in as ample and full manner as any person residing therein; and it is hereby further enacted by the authority aforesaid, that when at any time person that is a foreigner shall make his request to the proprietary of this province, for the aforesaid freedom, the said person shall be admitted on the condition herein expressed, paying, at admission, twenty shillings sterling, and no more, any thing in this law, or any other law, act, or thing in this province, to the contrary in anywise notwithstanding.

"Given at Chester, alias Upland, the 7th of December, 1672, under the hand and broad seal of William Penn, proprietary and governor of this province and the territories thereunto belonging, being the second year of his government, by the king's authority.

William Penn."

It is regrettable that Penn, in keeping and conveying his "Friends," had so exhausted his means, despite having sold lands in the colony for tens of thousands of pounds, that he had to resort to so heinous proceedings as to extract head money for privileges that by right were possessed alone by the people who had to pay it, who had pioneered and settled the land, bought it from the Indians and to most of them the land was now their native country.

But the Finns had learned to expect injustice of any foreign domination and did not seem to mind of it as Penn is quoted of having said that the act of naturalization "much pleased the people." "The Swedes (as Penn calls the Finns), for themselves, deputed Lasse Cock to acquaint him, on one occasion, that they would love, serve, and obey him with all they had, declaring it was the best day they ever saw."

In order to secure the Quaker interests on the Delaware River, it was found that not such a large general assembly and provincial council could be formed as provided in the "Frame of Government," therefore it was necessary to re-frame an "Act of Settlement," to cut the number of members in the provincial council from seventy-two to eighteen, and the assembly which was "the first year to consist of the whole body of the freeholders, and ever after of an elected number, not exceeding two hundred persons, without the consent of the provincial council and general assembly," was cut to thirty-six members.

Finally the liberal conditions and laws proposed and agreed upon by Penn with the colonists in England, were presented to the assembly and received their final shape. Sixty-nine laws were passed on a day, the collection being titled: "The Great Law, or, the body of Laws of the province of Pennsylvania and territories thereunto belonging, passed at an assembly at Chester, alias Upland, the 7th day of the 10th month, December, 1682."

The set of laws begins with a lofty preamble, and the first law purports to establish the liberty of conscience. However in the law number two it is said: "And be it further enacted, by the authority aforesaid, that all officers and persons commissioned and employed in the service of the government of this province, and all members and deputies elected to serve in assembly thereof, and all that have right to elect such deputies, shall be such as profess and declare they believe in Jesus Christ to be the son of God, and Saviour of the world."

The fortieth act of the Great Law says: "And be it further enacted by the authority aforesaid, that the days of the week, and the months of the year, shall be called as in Scripture, and not by heathen names (as are vulgarly used) as, the first, second and third days of the week; and first, second, and third months of the year, etc., beginning with the day called Sunday, and the month called March."

The session of the first assembly lasted four days.

Undoubtedly William Penn, in the beginning of his colonial enterprise earnestly meaned good, but having been raised in soft life, he had missed the opportunity to develop his character in the respect of firmness of carrying his good and noble resolutions into effect when he became in contact with and was prevailed upon by evil influences. This defect in his character caused him much disappointment, sorrow and even calamity in the near future.

Soon after the meeting of the assembly, Penn set out to meet at West River, in Maryland, Lord Baltimore about the threatening boundary question. This matter had been a nightmare to every one who claimed the right to rule at the west side of the Delaware River. On June 20, 1632, Charles I., king of England, confirmed to Cecilius Calvert, Baron of Baltimore, a charter, upon a territory in America, which in the charter was named Maryland. The eastern and northern boundary of the territory is defined in the charter to be a line drawn from the ocean "unto that part of the Bay of Delaware on the north, which lyeth under the fortieth degree of north latitude from the equinoctial, where New England is terminated; and all the tract of land within the metes underwritten (that is to say), passing from the said bay, called Delaware bay, in a right line, by the degree aforesaid unto the true meridian of the fountain of the river of Pottowmack" (Potomac). This definition of the boundary had been made of early defective maps. The Delaware Bay, in modern maps does not extend to the fortieth degree of north latitude at all, but the said degree crosses the Delaware River few miles above present city of Philadelphia. Lord Baltimore's map of 1635, shows the northern boundary of Maryland to be at about Appoquiniminck Creek on the Delaware Bay, but when the true position of the fortieth degree of north latitude became known, Lord Baltimore's heirs claimed the right to the added territory. Then the Delaware colonies became under the rule of the Duke of York, and Lord Baltimore's heirs could not vigorously force their claim against the king's brother.

When Charles II., king of England, granted to William Penn the territory in America, named Pennsylvania in the charter, a new mistake was made. The fortieth degree of north latitude was supposed to cross the Delaware River at about the present city of Wilmington. The southern boundary of Pennsylvania was therefore defined in the charter to be from the Delaware River the circumference of a circle drawn with twelve miles' radius from the town of New Castle, as its center, as far as it meets the fortieth degree of northern latitude, and along that degree westward to a certain limit of longitude. Lord Baltimore's surveyors had however taken accurate bearings and as the Delaware territory now had fallen into the hands of a private party, Lord Baltimore saw opportunity to push immediately his claims, he visited Deputy-Governor Markham in Upland and in the interview it was discovered by actual observations, that Upland itself was at least twelve miles south of the fortieth degree of north latitude, which discovery ended the conference.

In the conference between William Penn and Lord Baltimore at West River in Maryland, on December 12, 1682, no settlement about the boundary could be made. The dispute continued, with temporary agreements until it was finally settled that the boundary lines between Pennsylvania and Maryland were to be about the same as meaned and intended in the charter and the deeds of feoffment to William Penn. This was ratified by King George III., in 1769.

The winter of 1682-1683 witnessed a great building activity in Philadelphia and in the spring there was already accommodations for the Provincial Council and the Assembly to meet. On the 10th of March, 1683, the Council came together in the new town and the Assembly two days later. The council having eighteen members, all Englishmen, except Lasse Cock. The assembly at this meeting still had fifty-four members, all Englishmen, except Andreas Bengtsson, Swen Swensson, Gasparus Herman, Peter Alrichs and Cornelis Verhoof.

Some opposition had been expressed in the colony against the breaking of the original charter, or the "Frame of Government" and Dr. Nicholas Moore, president of the Society of Free Traders, was commanded before the council on the 13th of March to duly apologize for his utterance against the General Assembly "that they have this day broken the Charter, and therefore all that you do will come to nothing, and that hundreds in England will curse you for what you have done, and their children after them, and that you may be hereafter be impeached for treason for what you do."

A new Frame of Government was signed, sealed and delivered through the council and the assembly to the inhabitants of the province on the second day of April, fourteen members of the council and forty-four of the assembly being present. The council and assembly were to be called the General Assembly, and the assembly was to consist hereafter thirty-six members.

During the year of 1683, the old settlers and native inhabitants
of Pennsylvania became far outnumbered by the new English immigrants, and being scattered all along the river, they could not pool
their votes for their own representatives in the General Assembly,
they fell in oblivion politically, but economically they were in the
advantage. They had occupied the entire river shore that was
the first one to advance in value, and having their plantations
brought up to productive stage, they at once became the most prosperous part of the population. On the other hand the newcomers
profited for the accommodations that already existed in the colony,
for the knowledge that the old settlers had gained in the cultivation of the soil in the new conditions and for the mutual trust and
good relations that existed between the Indians and the old colonists. While the history of all other colonies in North America are
full of horrible massacres, the Finnish settlers on the Delaware
scarcely lost a night's sleep on account of the Indians. The Finns
and the Delaware Indians each relied upon the other as a protector
against the attacks of strange Indian tribes living further inland.
At the time of the arrival of William Penn, the names of the
Indian chiefs were very much Finnish, mostly animal names, as
was the habit of the Indians to adopt. Thus the great king of the
Lenni-Lenape nations had adopted the name "Tammanen," (also
spelled Tammany and adopted by a political association in New
York City), which is a Finnish name for mare horse. There were
also Indian names like "Secane," or "Sikane," which in Finnish
mean hog. The Indian moccasins likewise are the ancient Finnish
low shoes and undoubtedly were acquired by the Indians from the
Delaware Finns. The Finnish name for these shoes is "Lapatos-
sut," but in their simplest form were called "muokasin," or make-
shift shoes, from which the Indian name of the same may have
been derived.

All the letters, sent by William Penn, or by the members of his
colony to England, after their arrival to the Delaware River, speak
with great satisfaction of the accommodations and wealth that
already had been created in the colony. William Penn in his letter
to the Committee of the Free Society of Traders, in 1683, says:

"We have no want of horses, and some are very good and shapely enough; two ships have been freighted to Barbadoes with horses and pipe-staves, since my coming in. Here is also plenty of cow-cattle, and some sheep; the people plow mostly with oxen." The newcomers were cheerfully received, mutual respect prevailed and none needed to go hungry, for the lack of provisions. In the above mentioned letters Penn says about the Finns (whom he most of the time refers as Swedes), "they kindly received me, as well as the English, who were few before the concerned with me came among them; I must needs commend their Respect to Authority, and kind behaviour to the English. As they are people proper and strong in body, so they have fine children, and almost every house full; rare to find one of them without three or four boys and as many girls; some six, seven and eight sons; and I must do them that right, I see few young men more sober and laborious." And Penn further continues in his letter: "We are daily in hopes of shipping to add to our number; for blessed be God, here is both room and accommodation for them; the stories of our necessity being either the fear of our friends, or the scare-crows of our enemies."

In a letter to his steward, William Penn says: "Pray send us some two or three smoked haunches of venision and pork, get them of the Swedes (Finns), also some smoked shadds and beelf—the old priest at Philadelphia had rare shadds." By the "old priest" Penn refers to the Rev. Fabricius, the minister of the Finns of Wicaco parish. This shows that at this period the rare shad, that is caught on the other side of the river at Gloucester, N. J., was then already made use of.

A new English colonist, Thomas Paschall, who lived among the Finns on the west side of the Schuylkill, says in his letter to his friend, in 1683, among other things that: "The River is taken up all along by the Swedes and Finns, and some Dutch, before the English came, near eight score of miles, and the Englishmen some of them, buy their Plantations, and get room by the great River-side, and the rest get into creeks, and small rivers that run into it, and some go into woods seven or eight miles. . . . I have hired a house for my family for the winter, and I have gotten a little house in my land for my servants, and have cleared land about six acres; and this I can say, I never wish myself at Bristol again since my departure. I live in the Schuylkill Creek, near Philadelphia, about 100 miles up the River. Here have been 24 ships with passengers within this year, so that provisions are somewhat hard to come by in some places, though at no dear rate, there is yet enough in the River, but it is for to fetch, and suddainly there will be an order taken for continual supply. Now I shall give you an impartial account of the country as I find it, as followeth. When we came into Delaware Bay we saw an infinite number of small fish in sholes, also large fish leaping in the water. The River is a brave pleasant River as can be desired, affording divers sorts of fish in great plenty, it's planted all along the shore, and some creeks, especially in Pennsylvania side, mostly of Swedes, Finns and Dutch, and now at least, English throng among them, and have filled all about 160 miles up the great River; some English that are about the Rivers and creeks a great way in the woods, and have settled the falls, have sowed this year 30 or 40 bushels of wheat, and have great stocks of cattle. Most of the Swedes and Finns are ingenious people, they speak English, Swedish, Finnish, Dutch and the Indian. They plant but little Indian corn, nor tobacco; their women make most of the linnen cloath they wear, they spinn and weave it and make fine linen, and are many of them curious housewives. The people generally eat rye bread, being approved of best by them, not but that here is good wheat, for I have eaten as good bread and drank as good drink as ever I did in England, as also very good butter and cheese, as most in England. Here is three sorts of wheat, as Winter, Summer and Buck Wheat; the Winter Wheat they sow at the fall, the Summer Wheat in March, these two sorts are ripe in June; then having taken in this, they plow the same land, and sow Buck Wheat, which is ripe in September. I have not given above 2 s. 6 d. per skipple (which is 3 English pecks) for the best wheat and that in goods which cost little more than half so much in England, here is very good Rye at 2 s. per skipple, also barley of 2 sorts, as Winter and Summer, at 4 guilders per skipple; also oats, and 3 sorts of Indian Corn, (two of which sorts they can malt and make good beer of as of barley), at four guilders per skipple, a guilder is four pence halfpenny. I have bought good beef, pork and mutton at two pence per pound and some cheaper. also turkeys and wild geese at the value of two or three pounds of shot apiece, and ducks at one pound of shot, or like value, and in great plenty: here is great store of poultry, but for curlews, pigeons and pheasants, they will hardly bestow a shot upon them. I have venision of the Indians very cheap, although they formerly sold it as cheap again to the Swedes; I have four dear for two yards of trading cloath, which cost five shillings, and most times I purchased it cheaper. We had bearsflesh this fall for little or nothing, it is good food, tasting much like beef. There have been many horses sold of late to Barbadoes, and here is plenty of rum, sugar, ginger and molasses. I was lately at Bridlington-fair, where were a great resort of people, with cattle and all sorts of goods, sold at very reasonable rates.

"Here are gardens with all sorts of herbs and some more than in England, also gooseberries and rose-trees, but what other flowers I know not yet. Turnips, parsnips, and cabbages, beyond compare. Here are peaches in abundance of three sorts I have seen rot on the ground, and the hogs eat them, they make good spirits from them, also from corn and cherries, and a sort of wild plums, and grapes, and most people have stills of copper for that use. Here are apples, and pears, of several sorts, cherries both black and red, and plums and quinces; in some places peach stones grow up to bear in three years."

In the letter of William Penn, from which we already have quoted, it is said that the early settlers had not paid great attention for the propagation of fruit trees, but the above letter of Thomas Paschall shows that a good deal had been accomplished, especially when we take into consideration that fruit trees, like peach, apple and pear were introduced in the colony by the settlers.

On the 12th of December, 1685, Penn writes in his "Further account of the Province of Pennsylvania," that a considerable quantity of flax and hemp is dressed yearly in the province, and that peaches are cultivated in great quantities, the people drying them in the sunshine and lay them up in lofts to be stewed in the winter with meat. He further says that: "It has been often said we were starved for want of food; some were apt to suggest their fears, others to insinuate their prejudices, and when this was contradicted, and they assured we had plenty, both of bread, fish and flesh, then it was objected that we were forced to fetch it from other places at great charges: but neither is all this true, tho all the world will think we must either carry provisions with us, or get it of the neighbourhood till we had gotten houses over our heads and a little land in tillage, we fetcht none, nor were we wholly helpt by neighbours. The old inhabitants supplied us with most of the corn we wanted and a good share of pork and beef. It is true New York, New England, and Rhode Island did with their provisions fetch our goods and money, but at such rates, that some sold for almost what they gave, and others carried their provisions back, expecting a better market nearer, which showed no scarcity, and that we were totally destitute on our own River."

This was rather well done by the old settlers, as Penn says that since the beginning of 1682, 7,200 new people had arrived to the province. Besides there was immigration going on to the east side of Delaware River, in the western New Jersey.

On the 13th of September, 1686, Dr. Nicholas Moore, president of the company of the Free Traders, wrote to William Penn, who was then in England, that some corn already had been exported from the Province of Pennsylvania and that some thousand of bushels of wheat were exported at the season at hand.

On October 2, 1686, David Lloyd, attorney-general of Pennsylvania, writes to William Penn that: "I shall only add, that five ships are come in since our arrival (July 15, 1686), one from Bristol, with 100 passengers; one from Hull with 160 passengers; one from New England for corn, and two from Barbadoes; all of them, and ours (of above 300 Tun) had their loading here, ours for New England, and the rest for Barbadoes; and for all this wheat (as good, I think, as any in England) is sold for three shillings six pence per bushel, this country money, and for three shillings ready money (which makes two shilling five pence English)."

Most of this production was done by the Finns, as the English were engaged with the building of the city and those who engaged in farming could not realise much in the first years, not enough for themselves. The City of Philadelphia grew in three years more than New York and Boston had done in fifty years, but we must take into consideration that there was forty years of productive labor of the old inhabitants behind it. It was this that made such a rapid development possible. Penn's colony was laid on a firm foundation of labor of the early settlers, otherwise the colony, for the manner it was started, had resulted in the greatest disaster in the early colonial history of America.

The year 1683, was spent with a great activity in the Province of Pennsylvania. At the end of that year 80 houses had been finished in Philadelplhia, besides hundreds of newcomers were living in the caves that they built for temporary shelter, while preparing for houses. The council met during the year fifty-seven times and several land purchases were made during the summer from the Indians. From King Tammanen and others, Penn bought the land between the Pennypack and Neshaminy Creeks; from Chief Wingebone the land on the west side of the Schuylkill River, above the falls; from Chief Secane and Icquoquehan the inland between the Schuylkill River and the Chester Creek; from Chief Neneshickon and others the inland between the Schuylkill River and Pennypack Creek; from Chief Kekerappan and Chief Machaloha the vast back forest as far south and west as Chesapeake Bay and the Susquehanna River. In these deals Captain Lasse Cock acted as interpreter and among the witnesses appear Peter Cock, Peter Rambo and Swan Swensson.

Before the council, held at Philadelphia on February 7, 1684, there was heard a case of witchcraft, the accused parties appearing to be Finns. Two women, Margaret Mattson and Gerdrud Hendrickson, were suspected of being witches and having bewitched cows. The case of Margaret Mattson was tried before the jury on February 27th, when several witnesses were heard. The jury found the prisoner "guilty of having the common fame of a witch, but not guilty in manner and form." Nils Mattson, her husband,

and Anthony Nilsson, her son, entered into recognizance of fifty pounds each for the good behavior of Margaret Mattson for six months. Similarly Jacob Hendrickson, husband of Gerdrud Hendrickson, entered into the recognizance of fifty pounds for the good behavior of his wife for six months. The superstitious parties that appeared as hearsay witnesses were Englishmen and William Penn acted as the judge. Among the Finns present were Lasse Cock, member of the court, who acted as interpreter for Margaret Mattson. Gunnar Rambo was in the grand jury and Johan Cock was a witness, but did not know anything about the matter. Annakey Coolin denied of having even uttered anything she was alleged.

The controversy between William Penn and Lord Baltimore, concerning the boundaries, and other matters, required Penn's presence in England, where he sailed on June 12, 1684, after having left the care of government in the hands of the Provincial Council, of which Thomas Lloyd was made president. The town of Philadelphia now had two thousand five hundred inhabitants and had three hundred houses, while hundreds of the people lived in caves along the river bank. Soon after the arrival of Penn to England, Charles II. died and was succeeded by James, Duke of York, in whose favor Penn had stood, for his father having fought under the flag of James. This helped Penn in obtaining from the king's council a favorable decree in his dispute with Lord Baltimore. But the period of Penn's absence from the Province is marked by unhappy differences between the assembly and the council, and between the members of the three lower counties and those of Pennsylvania proper. In the assemblies of 1685 and 1686, disagreements prevailed and undignified scenes took place. In 1686, Penn changed the form of executive government to a board of five commissioners, but the next session of the assembly continued with the usual lack of harmony. Penn made another change, by appointing, in 1688, Captain John Blackwell as governor of the province. But Captain Blackwell, who was not a Quaker, fell into dissention with some of the members of the council and returned to England in February, 1690, after which the government of the province again devolved on the council, with Thomas Lloyd as president.

At this period grave events took place in England. A revolution in 1688, drove James from the throne, and the new rulers, William and Mary, decided to make war on the French king. A letter, announcing of immediate hostilities, was laid before the council at Philadelphia, on October 1, 1689, and during the following year atrocities were made at the borders of Pennsylvania, by the French and Indians from the French territory of the Middle West of North America. The Delaware territory was threatened by a hostile invasion by land and sea, but the Quakers whose doctrines forbade them to carry arms did not want to concern themselves with the war, which brought much controversy when the English king was seeking for funds to carry on the long war against France.

The Finns were willing and ready to bear arms to defend the colony, as they show in the petition of the officers of their old militia to the council on April 24, 1690. The petition was also signed by William Markham, the secretary of the province, and by John Holme. It reads as follows:

"To the Honorable Provincial Council, now Deputy Governor of the Province of Pennsylvania.

"The humble petition of some of the inhabitants willing and ready to bear arms for the service and difence of this government, shewith:

"That whereas, there is war between the crowns of England and France and that our enemies, the French, have barbarously murdered many his Majesty's subjects, very near the confines of this Province, which have struck no small terror in us and our families, and may happen to attack us when we least think of it, we humbly pray that you, our Governor, will be pleased forthwith to settle the country in such a posture that we may to be able by force of arms, to defend it against any assault of our enemies; and as in duty bound, shall pray."

This is signed by

> Wm. Markham,
> Lassi Cock,
> Swan Swansson,
> John Holme,
> Andreas Benksson.

This is the only occasion that the Quakers gave any attention to the dangers of invasion by the enemy. The step taken by the Council was the following decision:

"The board being informed that Lassi Cock intends up the Schuylkill among our Indians, the beginning of the next week, do request that the president, with the present members, give instruction to the said Lassi Cock to make particular enquiry concerning the store and quantity of ammunition in the custody of the few French families seated up the said River, and in case he shall find greater store than shall be judged expedient to be left there, to have the same secured, in order to be brought to Barnabas Willcox's store, assuring the owner's reasonable satisfaction for the same; and further, that such of the said French who may be justly suspected of unfaithfulness to this province, may be by the most suitable means, persuaded down here; and that the chief sachem of our Indians may be assured of our good intention toward them and their people, and that we desire a meeting with their chief men as soon as they can conveniently, giving us notice of the time nine or ten days before, and if he sees occasion to employ four or six likely and trusty persons of them to range along the most likely parts for the discovering of any designs of the French, or their Indians, against the peace, who shall have competent satisfaction at their return to us. And our desire is that Captain Markham, Rob. Turner, with such credible persons as may be persuaded upon this service, go along with the said Lasse Cock, and that he upon all occasions, take the advice and concurrence of the said persons; and in the meantime, care be taken for suitable presents for them at their meeting with us."

On the 22d of May, 1690, delegates of the Delaware Indians appeared in Philadelphia to confer about the hostilities, for which the council ordered that Captain Lassi Cock be sent for, to be in town by eight of the following morning, to interpret between the council and the Indians.

When James, former Duke of York, was driven from the throne, Penn lost all influence at the English court. Penn's intimacy with the deposed monarch covered him with suspicion of conspiring the restoration of James. He was thrice examined before the privy council, was held in bail and tried in the court, however no evidence appearing against him. Penn was preparing to return to Pennsylvania with five hundred emigrants, when an infamous person accused him, on oath, with being engaged in a conspiracy of the papists in Lancashire to raise a rebellion, and restore James to the crown. Penn narrowly escaped arrest on his return from the funeral of George Fox, the founder of the Quaker "Society of Friends." At this time Penn deemed it prudent to retire in concealment.

After the departure of Deputy Governor Blackwell from Pennsylvania in 1690, the Council, according to the constitution, assumed executive power, and elected Thomas Lloyd as its president. But the struggle between the Quaker and the non Quaker interests continued in the Province and in 1691, six councilors from the Lower Counties, formed themselves into a separate council, assuming upon themselves the executive power in the Lower Counties.

When all the efforts of Penn, to bring about a union between the two sections of the Province failed, he conferred the government of the Upper Counties to Thomas Lloyd and that of the Lower Counties to William Markham.

The dissensions in the Province furnished the new rulers of England, William and Mary, an opportunity to punish Penn for his attachment to the deposed king. William Penn was deprived of his province and Benjamin Fletcher, Governor-General of New York, was commissioned by their majesties, on October 21, 1692, to assume the governorship of Pennsylvania and the territories as "Captain-General." The commission to Fletcher reads in part as: "And whereas, by reason of great neglect in America, and the absence of the proprietor, the same is fallen (Pennsylvania) into disorder and confusion, by means whereof not only the public peace and administration of Justice (whereby the properties of our subjects should be preserved in those parts) is broken and violated, but there is also great want of provision for the guard and defence of our said province against our enemies, whereby our said province, and the adjacent colonies, are much exposed, and in danger of being lost from the crown of England. For the prevention whereof, as much as in us lies, and for the better defence and security of our subjects inhabiting those parts during this time of war, we find it absolutely necessary to take the government of our province of Pennsylvania into our own hands, and under our immediate care and protection."

Governor Fletcher came to Philadelphia on April 26, 1693, and had his commission read in the market place. Later he demanded the oath, or its substitute, (according to the act of the English Parliament), from the members of the Council, which Thomas Lloyd refused to take, but the other members, among which were William Markham and Lasse Cock, all subscribed. Fletcher appointed Markham his Lieutenant-Governor, to preside over the Council, in the Captain-General's absence in New York. The Upper and Lower Counties were again united under one government, but the differences now swinged to the united opposition of the General Assembly against the efforts of Fletcher to extract money and men for the defence of the colony against French invasion. This worked to the interest of William Penn, who had many friends among the nobles that surrounded the king. These friends made the true character of Penn known among the royals, and a new hearing was granted to Penn before the privy council, where he was honorably acquitted, and was restored to his proprietary rights by patent, dated August, 1694, in which the disorders in the province were ascribed solely to his absence. Penn's wife, Gulielma Maria, was ill at this time and died in February, 1694.

William Markham was once more appointed by Penn, on September 24, 1694, to be Deputy Governor of Pennsylvania and territories. After some difficulties between Markham and the General Assembly, a new Frame of Government or Constitution was drawn and adopted on November 7, 1696. The Council was to consist of two representatives, chosen biennially from each county, the Assembly of four representatives from each county and the election for the Assembly was to take place on the 10th of March each year. The constitution further provided, "that the representatives of the freemen when met in Assembly, shall have power to prepare and propose to the Governor and Council all such bills as they or the major part of them shall at any time see needful to be passed into law within the said province and territories." Another important victory for the popular cause was the provision in the constitution declaring the General Assembly indissoluble for the time for which its members were elected and giving it power to sit upon its own adjournments and committees, and to continue its sessions in order to propose and prepare bills, redress grievances, and impeach criminals. This constitution was never formally sanctioned by Penn, but to keep the people quiet, it was continued until 1701, when a new one was substituted in its place, under which the people finally began to settle down.

On the first day of December, 1699, William Penn, accompanied by his second wife and children, arrived in the Delaware, where he was cordially welcomed. In the autumn of 1701, Penn was again obliged to return to England, to fight a bill, then before the Lords, to change the proprietary governments in America into regal ones. Before sailing away, Penn convened the Assembly on September 16, 1701. A new constitution that had been pending since Penn's arrival to the colony, was agreed and signed by Penn and by the Assembly and Council, on October 28, 1701. The Constitution or "The Charter of Privileges" provided to the Lower Counties the right to separate from the Upper Counties by forming an Assembly of their own within three years if they wanted.

The new "Charter of Privileges" annulled the right of the people to choose the members of the Council. Penn appointed himself ten of his friends, chiefly Quakers, to be "Council of State," who were empowered by their commission of October 28, 1701, to consult and assist, with the best of their advice and counsel, the Proprietary himself or his deputies, in all public affairs and matters relating to the government. And in his absence, or on the death or incapacity of his deputy, they, or any five of them, were authorized to execute all the Proprietary powers in the administration of the government.

The new constitution plainly shows of a more autocratic spirit in Penn, after his own unpleasant experiences and the strifes in the

Province. From the other hand it shows the more conciliatory spirit of the people of the Province, when there was a question of them becoming directly under the royal government, that they did not however want.

After having appointed Andrew Hamilton, formerly Governor of East and West New Jersey, to be his Deputy Governor in Pennsylvania, William Penn sailed for England, arriving at Portsmouth about the middle of December, 1701. The bill, for reducing the proprietary provinces into regal ones, pending in Parliament, was entirely dropped. King William died on the 18th of March, 1702, and was succeeded by the Princess Anne of Denmark, with whom William Penn was in great favor.

The administration of Deputy Governor Hamilton was not very long, for he died in April, 1703. Thereafter the government of the Province again devolved upon the Council and the Lower Counties, taking advantage of the clause in the constitution, providing them the right to separate from the Upper Counties within three years if they chose, composed their own Assembly in 1703.

As successor to Deputy Governor Hamilton, Penn had selected John Evans, an officer of the Queen's household and a man of twenty-six years. He was to be however rather as a figure-head governor, under Secretary James Logan, who was a steadfast supporter of the Proprietary and the Quaker interests. Evans arrived in the Province in February, 1704, settled in a stately house of the old Lasse Cock's plantation, in the Finnish village of Shackamaxon, and soon fell in odds with the Assembly in trying to raise an armed force, according to the order of the Queen, who was then at war with France and Spain. Besides there soon ensued a misunderstanding between the Deputy Governor and Secretary Logan, which all tended to the removal of Evans from his office in the beginning of 1709, and Captain Charles Gookin was dispatched by the Proprietary to assume the office of the Deputy Governor of Pennsylvania.

At this time William Penn, for his generosity towards the cause of the Quaker sect, had fallen in financial embarrassment. Already, in 1707, Penn was involved in a lawsuit with the executors of the estate of his former steward, who preferred large claims against him, and was obliged to spend some time in debtors' prison, from which he got out at the end of December, 1708, by mortgaging the Province of Pennsylvania for the sum of 6,600 pounds. The strifes in the province were going on, the Assembly had demanded the impeachment of Secretary James Logan, and his retention brought much grievances. Finally in 1714, Penn entered into an agreement with Queen Anne to cede to her the Province of Pennsylvania and the Lower Counties, for the sum of 12,000 pounds sterling. But before the legal forms were completed, an apoleptic stroke reduced him to the feebleness of infancy. On the 30th day of July, 1718, William Penn died at Rushcombe, in Buckinghamshire, England, aged seventy-four. His heirs continued as Proprietaries of Pennsylvania until 1776, when the Revolution, resulting to the independence of the United States of America, made an end to the proprietary rights.

The political turmoils and petty strifes between the Quaker and non-Quaker interests in Pennsylvania and in the Lower Counties (the present State of Delaware), had not much effect upon the Finnish element of these territories. But there was another issue, the land troubles, that vitally hurt the descendants of the early Finnish colonists. The Finnish pioneers of these territories had during more than forty years before the arrival of Penn and his Quakers, selected and settled at their leisure, the most suitable lands along the Delaware River and its western tributaries. This much displeased the Quakers, who, as Proprietary Penn's proteges, felt privileged and justified to own these lands and pleasant grounds for themselves. During those times when the Finns were the only ones on the River who cared to take up and cultivate land, the surveyors were not very accurate in their surveys, for the abundance of land and fewness of the cultivators, they rather saw that the pioneers had enough land within the boundaries and acreages described in their certificate of survey. Besides there were allotted "meadow land" or "marshy land" outside of the boundaries and acreages of the farm plots. These extra lands were free of quitrents and were sometimes defined in the patents by their acreage or as "besides marshy land proportionately," but often were not mentioned in the patents at all, the settlers having established commonages of forests or of lowlands that were covered with water during the flood-tide, but were useful during the ebb, for the pasturage of cattle. In these commonages each surrounding farmer had his equal right for cutting of timber or for hay making and pasturage and the rights had been respected by the courts and the governors of the Duke of York. Besides these, there were farmers, who did not have patents upon their lands, as they had bought their lands from the Indians, whom they considered the rightful owners of the lands, and therefore had not hurried for the patents from authorities that were established by conquest and without any moral rights upon the lands. Others had taken up their lands only some time before the country was transferred under William Penn's government and were therefore too late to receive their patents from the Duke of York. These colonists held only the grants of the local courts, or also the surveyors' certificates. On June 14, 1683, William Penn issued an order to the old inhabitants of the Province, to bring in their surveyors' certificates in order to receive patents, and those who had patents were ordered to bring them in likewise, in order to receive new ones. Many of the Finnish farmers, for being orderly and abiding to regulations, handed in confidence their patents and certificates to Penn's Surveyor-General Thomas Holme. Soon afterwards an order was issued for the resurvey of these old homesteads, and when the farmers applied for their promised new patents, their lands were resurveyed and the commonages, pasture lands and good measures in the original surveys were taken off. Others did not hurry with such a resurvey and their old patents, that they had given up to the Surveyor-General, disappeared and their lands were put under higher taxes than had been originally granted to them, while their occupuancy fell to the class not considered to rest upon "a good and equitable right." Some of the Finns for the many and constant changes in the government of the Delaware River territory, were not as quick to hand in their patents, thinking that those they had obtained from the Duke of York were always safe, and they had reasoned it right, as they never were molested and troubled in the occupation of their lands, but held all that rightly belonged to them.

Among the forty laws, agreed upon by Penn and some freemen in England, who were preparing to come to the colony, the sixteenth act provided "that seven years' quiet possession (of land) shall give an unquestionable right." These laws were ratified and signed by William Penn and party of freemen, on May 5, 1682. The first General Assembly passed these acts, but the act of seven years' quiet possession of land was found to be not in conformity with the Quaker interests and did not become a law. The charter by which the Province of Pennsylvania was granted to William Penn, provided that all laws which shall be made in the province must be within five years transmitted and delivered to the Privy Council of the king of England, where within six months of their delivery they will be repealed or otherwise become a law. During the years that William Penn had influence in the English royal court, his opinions were respected in passing or repealing the laws.

When William Penn returned to the colony in 1699, there immediately started a movement to make room for the Quakers in their coveted places, the validity of the old settlers' occupancy of land was vigorously questioned, and in order to induce Finns who stubbornly held on upon their ancient lands, to vacate, a parcel of ten thousand acres was assigned for them in the back woods, sixty miles up the Schuylkill at Manatawny. Some Finnish families moved to settle there.

The "overplus lands," as the parcels cut off from the old homesteads were called, became the subjects of much discussion at this time, both in the Council and the Assembly. Many Englishmen had bought farms from the Finns, others had become owners of the old plantations by marriage, besides there were some Dutch, who were possessing old farms, all these became united in the maintenance of their rights to the lands. On November 8, 1700, the Assembly, by two delegates, delivered a message to William Penn and his Council, at New Castle, desiring the law of seven years' quiet possession to be held in force. Upon which Penn desired the delegates to acquaint the Assembly, that he desired a conference with them about that matter. On November 27, 1700, the Assembly passed "An Act of Privileges to a Freeman," providing that no freeman in the province and territories could be disseized of his freehold, except by the decision of a committee composed of twelve freemen or by the law of the province. It appears that this act was delivered by Penn's agents to the privy council in London near the expiration of the five years' time limit and was repealed by the queen in council, on February 7, 1705, Penn being then in England.

On the same day as the Assembly passed the above mentioned act, it also passed "An Act for the effectual establishment and confirmation of the Freeholders of this province and territories, their heirs and assigns, in their lands and tenements." In its first section this act provided, "that all grants and parcels of land taken up within this province and territories, and duly seated by virtue of letters patent or warrants obtained from governors or lawful commissioners under the Crown of England, before the King's grant to the proprietary and governor for this province (except the same was held by fraud or deceit) shall be quietly enjoyed by the actual possessors, their heirs and assigns. . . . "And although no patent hath been granted, yet if peaceable entry and possession hath been obtained by warrants or otherwise as aforesaid, and thereupon quiet possession hath been held during the space of seven years or more, such possession or such entry as aforesaid shall give an unquestionable title to all such lands according to the quantity they were taken up for, and shall be deemed and held good and be confirmed by the proprietary to the settlers or possessors thereof their heirs and assigns forever. . . . "And whereas our proprietary and governor did formerly in a clause of our charter of privileges give and grant to all and every one of the inhabitants of this province and territories full and quiet enjoyment of their respective lands to which they had any lawful or equitable claim, saving only such rents and services for the same as were or customarily ought to be reserved to the proprietary, his heirs and assigns, which clause upon delivering up our said charter was reserved and our said proprietary and governor was pleased to reserve to us. We therefore desire it may be enacted, and be it enacted by the authority aforesaid, that the said clause shall be in as full force, power and virtue as if the surrender of the charter as aforesaid had never been made."

The above act was passed by the Assembly, on November 27, 1700, and was repealed by the queen in council, on February 7, 1705. The Assembly once more tried its luck by passing again on January 12, 1706, an act providing, "that seven years' quiet possession of lands within this province, which were first entered on upon an equitable right, shall forever give an unquestionable title to the same against all, during the estate whereof they are or shall be possessed." This act having been considered by the queen in council, on October 24, 1709, was allowed to become a law.

The clause in the above act, "which were first entered on upon an equitable right," was insisted upon and inserted to the bill by the Quaker council in Philadelphia, on December 27, 1705, when the bill was considered by them, and it worked against the Finns, whose patents, grants and certificates had been taken away and been destroyed or become lost. Other provisions were left out of the bill by the same council.

On January 8, 1706, the council considered another bill, submitted by the assembly, namely, "The bill for confirming grants and patents from the proprietor," and it was ordered, "that the clause, obliging the proprietor to appoint commissaries upon reasonable demands to confirm all lands, etc., to be left out as being unfit for the governor to pass without the Proprietary's immediate assent."

The more the Finns by their hard farm labor advanced in prosperity, the more they became the envy of the Quakers who as Penn's protégés felt that they were wronged and deprived of something that should be theirs. The Quakers had missed the opportunity to see how the early Finns had opened their farms in the wilds of Delaware. There was more than fifty million acres of uncultivated land in Pennsylvania and better adapted to agriculture than the Delaware shores, but farms cannot be created by impulse, they required hard labor and self denial of the best time of man's life, this the Quakers did not want to do.

Finally on June 1, 1709, the Finns presented to the Assembly a petition, (in which they call themselves Swedes as Finland was then united with Sweden and the Finns were commonly called in Pennsylvania as Swedes, also the parents of these Finns had mostly come from the Finnish colonies in Sweden, where most of them were born), complaining that, "Whereas we the Swedes, ancient settlers and first inhabitants of this Province, with great difficulty, hazard and loss of several of our lives, having at last obtained peace and quietness with the Indians—and after the changes that have happened by reason of the divers sorts of governments, we have lived peaceably and quietly, enjoying our lands and estates, which we first settled, under our own government. And since we are informed that upon the surrendering of this province to the crown of England, in lieu of Surinam to the Dutch, it was agreed on both sides, that the inhabitants were in no wise to be disturbed either in their lives, liberties, or estates; we after that being summoned to appear before the government which then resided at New York, were obliged to take patents or grants for what land we held before, or desired after. But since this Province has been granted to William Penn, he and his officers called for our patents and grants under pretence of renewing them, which having obtained would not return them again, but instead thereof resurveyed great parts of our lands, and took it from some of us: others were required to pay greater quit-rents than before; and because some of us refused the payment of such quit-rents, being on some tracts of land three or four times more than we ought or used to pay, when under the government of New York, we being, as we suppose, the Queen's tenants, and not liable to pay any at all to the proprietor—the collector, James Logan, threatened to make distress upon our goods for the said rents, using at the same time many harsh and opprobrious epithets:

"We, therefore, presuming that the same justice which, under similar cases, is dispensed by the Parliament of England, may be obtained here, solicit from you our representative, some help in our distress, that we may have our patents restored to us, together with all the overplus of the quit-rents which have been unjustly exacted from us these twenty years past: For which we shall always pray."

The above petition was signed by twenty-four members of the Finnish community, among which was Otto Ernest Cock, who originally owned the Tinicum Island and Hog Island and few hundred acres other land besides. Three other descendants of Peter Cock signed the petition. Several of the signers had purely English names at this period already.

The Assembly delivered a copy of the above petition to Governor Charles Gookin and his Council, signed by David Lloyd, the speaker, and several members of the Assembly. For this the governor and the council, after discussing the petition on June 11, 1709, inserted, by James Logan, the secretary, to its record that: "James Logan being present, in answer to those allegations, affirmed it was utterly false that he ever had any of those ancient grants in his keeping, and informed the board that as far as he could understand that matter, the Swedes had delivered up those old grants, in order to obtain more firm titles for their lands from the proprietor, which most of them had accordingly obtained; he said that he never demanded more from any of them than one bushel of wheat for every hundred acres of the land they held, and so proportionately, which was the quit-rent first agreed to be paid under the English government; that when he first arrived these people, with all the old settlers, were in the practice of paying the said rent and that he had never attempted to alter or augment it. That this petition he was certainly informed was carried on purely by the instigation of two or three persons concerned in lands in Chester County, most eminently disaffected to the proprietor and the government."

In the morning of August 17, 1709, three commissaries from amongst the Finns appeared before the Assembly in Philadelphia, in order to receive a reply for the above quoted petition, upon which the assembly by verbal message requested it from the governor. The messenger having told to the governor that the "Swedes" were urgent with the House to have an answer, and if they could not obtain relief here, designed to apply to the Swedish ambassador in England. This threat much displeased the governor and council and it was ordered that the House for preventing mistakes, should be required to send their said message in writing, as also to send a perfect copy of the said petition, with the names of all the subscribers to the same, in which the copy delivered to the governor was deficient. Samuel Preston, member of the Council, was ordered to go to the House and deliver the request.

Samuel Preston returning from the House, reported that they answered that they would send the solicitors of the said petition, who were waiting on the House, to the governor, that he might be satisfied with themselves, in what he desired of them.

Upon this, the secretary, James Logan, was immediately ordered to the House and require of them a perfect copy of the petition, with all names added, also to require an account of the persons who had threatened to apply to the Swedish ambassador. The speaker of the Assembly answered to the secretary's demand that the House would take the first part of the message into consideration, but that if the members of Assembly who brought the said message to the governor in the morning, had mentioned anything of the Swedes applying to the ambassador of that nation in England, it was a mistake, for that the House had no such thing in charge, to prove which they read to Secretary Logan the minute made upon it, in which no such expression was contained.

During Secretary Logan's absence in the House, the message of the Assembly, that had been delivered verbally to the governor in the morning, arrived to the Council, now drawn up in writing in these words: "Ordered that Joshua Hoopes, Abraham Bickley and Henry Lewis, do wait upon the governor, and acquaint him that some of the Swedes have been with the Assembly, requesting an answer to their petition, a copy whereof the House had lately sent to the governor, therefore do desire to know the governor's result and conclusion upon the said petition."

The solicitors of the petition, by direction from the House, appeared before the governor, and being asked whether they came to speak to the aforesaid petition, they answered yes. The petition then was read to them and they were asked if they owned it as theirs, to which they answered in the affirmative. The matter of the said petition was then largely spoken to by most of the members present and the grievances belittled and minimized. The solicitors were informed that they had taken wrong steps to obtain relief, if they were really injured, for that this could be had only by application to the proprietor himself, or his commissioners, or else by law, the only method of redress amongst the English, when other means fail; that if it was intended that they thought themselves injured by being obliged to pay a bushel of wheat for every hundred acres they held, this was no injury, but pursuant to the first agreement with the English government for their lands, and with which the English and those of all other nations here, as well as "Swedes" complied; that if any of them had been injured in losing a part of their lands, upon the first settlement of the proprietary's great colony amongst them, (the secretary affirming he knew but one instance of the kind and never heard of more than two), the persons suffering ought to complain in a proper way and not those of the nation conspire together, to make themselves a faction; that several at the board were sensible what they had done was not of themselves, but at the instigation of some very ill disposed persons, highly disaffected against the proprietor and his government; that they were extremely ungrateful to the proprietor, to suffer themselves to be thus made use of by his late enemies, for that it was most certain no people in the province had been more kindly treated, or more highly indulged by the proprietor, ever since his first settlement of this colony, than the "Swedes" had constantly been; and therefore, that if they behaved themselves so unworthily of those favors, they might find their error when they could not so well remedy themselves: for that if they caballed with the enemies of the government, they could not be considered otherwise than as such, but as they had always behaved themselves peaceably and as good subjects hitherto, so they ought for their own sake, to continue such, and if any particular of them had any cause of complaint, if they would apply themselves properly, as the English and all other subjects must do, they would certainly be as much regarded as any other.

Secretary Logan in his "Record of the Council" further declares the solicitors as ignorant of the laws and no masters of the English language, and the slick secretary finally clears himself, in his narrative, of the charges against him in the said petition and made it appear that he had not given any occasion for the accusation against him. And the secretary further declares that upon the whole it being most manifest, that the petitioners had been seduced by such ill disposed persons as have been mentioned and used only to serve a malicious end, they were advised to take more care of themselves for the future, and not to render themselves obnoxious to their best friends, by facetious caballing, only to gratify the ill-nature of those who never intended nor were capable of serving them.

The petition of the Finns was communicated to William Penn, in England, who in return communicated the matter to Count Charles Gyllenberg, the Swedish ambassador in London, and the affair was brought to the notice of the king and royal council of Sweden, by which an admonition was dispatched to the descendants of the old Swedish subjects, on the Delaware. But the Finns were not satisfied to be branded as disorderly, if they were standing for their manifest rights of property. A new petition was presented to the Assembly, in 1713, by the Finns, requesting the Assembly's good testimony that during all the time the Delaware Colony had been under English rule, they had conducted themselves as quiet and loyal subjects. The testimony was to be delivered by their messenger to the English and Swedish courts, followed by a letter to the Swedish ambassador in London, which in part says: "The Right Honorable Count Gyllenberg, the Swedish Envoy in London.

"May it please your Excellency.

"We are much concerned that Mr. Penn should complain of us in such general terms as renders it difficult to make any particular defence, as he seems to do in our case. We can with all sincerity assure your Excellency, that we and our predecessors, have been ready upon all occasions, to serve Mr. Penn, and never as far as we know, gave him the least cause of complaint. But, the manifest wrongs we received, gave us frequent and just occasion to complain. That this may appear, we respectfully ask your impartial consideration of our case and grievances, which in part, may appear to your Excellency in these following particulars, viz:

"When this country was surrendered to the English, all the inhabitants were confirmed in their lands, but required by the Governor of New York (to whom they were then annexed) to take patents out there for the same, and to become tenants to the kings of England, under the rent of a bushel of wheat per annum, for every hundred acres. But may it please your excellency, when this province was granted to the present governor by the late King Charles II., we find, that lands held by the Indians, and not the lands confirmed before to our predecessors, much less the rents reserved to the crown of England, were granted to Mr. Penn; who, nevertheless, by an order under his hand and provincial seal, dated the 14th of June, 1683, did require all that had not patents, or were willing to have their patents renewed, to send their certificates of survey, and old patents to the surveyor-general's office; whereupon many of the said patents and certificates were taken in, and have been detained ever since from the owners; and instead of having patents upon the said certificates of survey, or the old patents renewed, the governor and his commissioners caused the lands therein mentioned, without any warrant of law, or consent of the possessors, to be actually surveyed, and the greatest and best part thereof patented to new purchasers under Mr. Penn; and the rent of what was left, advanced to some three, and others fourfold more, than was reserved by the old patent."

The above letter shows that the Finns were somewhat misinformed concerning the grant of the territory to William Penn. According to the charter, the inhabitants of the Delaware Colony were to be William Penn's tenants and consequently were to pay their quit-rents to him, although remaining as the king's subjects. This wrong idea may be the result of the naturalization and exaction of 20 shillings per head from the old settlers at the first arrival of Penn, although they were the king's subjects.

To settle the land question for once and all, a bill was passed in 1712, called "An Act Confirming Patents and Grants." This new act at large reads as follows:

"Be it enacted by Charles Gookin, Esquire, by the Queen's royal approbation Lieutenant-Governor under William Penn, Esquire, absolute Proprietary and Governor-in-Chief of the Province of Pennsylvania, by and with the advise and consent of the freemen of the said Province in General Assembly met, and by the authority of the same, that all lands and hereditaments which any person or persons do hold and enjoy, or ought to have, hold and enjoy within this province, as well by or under any gift, grant or estate made or granted by the said Proprietary and Governor, William Penn, or his commissioners of property and agents, pursuant to the said person's right of purchase, demise or grant from him the said propietary, as also by or under any old grant, patent or warrant obtained or had from governors or lawful commissioners, under the crown of England, before the date of the late King Charles the Second, his letters patent to the said proprietary, or by any other legal or equitable grant, right, title, entry, possession or estate whatsoever, shall, by virtue of this act, be held and enjoyed by such person or persons according to the purport and intent (of the) respective right, grant, patent, purchase or demise, and for and in the estate or estates thereby granted or intended to be thereby granted or settled.

Provided always, that nothing herein contained shall be construed or adjudged to confirm any lands taken up by virtue of the said old grants and not duly seated or improved by the grantees or their assigns before the year one thousand six hundred and eighty-two, nor to create or confirm any right or interest to any person or persons whatsoever for or to any more or greater quantity of lands, marsh, meadow or cripple than shall appear, by gift, grant, demise or purchase from the said proprietary or his commissioners or agents, or from his predecessors, the former governors or commissioners aforesaid to be the said person or persons' just due (over and above the six acres by the said proprietary allowed to be added to every hundred acres of land for roads and barrens, and the four acres over or under, to be accounted for difference of surveys), nor shall create a right to the possessor or claimer of any lands that were not taken up or surveyed by virtue of a warrant or order from persons empowered to grant the same, and by a surveyor appointed for that purpose; anything herein or in any patent, grant or survey to the contrary in anywise notwithstanding.

"And be it further enacted, that the governor and council shall and will from time to time, and at all times hereafter, upon all reasonable demands, make and execute, or cause so to be, all and every such patents, grants or assurances, as may be necessary according to the laws and constitutions of this province, to grant, assure and confirm all and singular the lands, tenements and herediteaments in the said province by him, the said proprietary, or his commissioners or agents heretofore sold, granted or disposed, or which by him, his heirs or assigns, or by his or their commissioners or agents shall hereafter be sold, granted or disposed to any person or persons, bodies politic or corporate to hold the said lands, herediteaments and premises, with their appurtenances, to the grantee or persons interested therein, for such estate or estates, term or terms of life, lives or years, and for such uses and under such rents or acknowledgements as the same lands and premises were, are or shall be sold, granted or disposed of as aforesaid. Saving to all persons, their rights, titles, estates and interests in lands (granted, derived or claimed by, from or under the said old patents or grants made before the date of the said letters patent) seated and improved as aforesaid.

"And whereas several persons before the date of the said late King's royal charter obtained grants or patents for more lands than they had any right unto by their original warrants or orders for the surveying or laying out the same, in which case it has been the method of the said proprietary and his commissioners, by their warrants to order resurveys of those lands, and allot to the possessors thereof or to the heirs or assigns of the old patentees or grantees so many acres of land and meadow or marsh, as really belonged unto them by virtue of the said respective original warrants or orders, or by the right of occupancy or improvement, and confirm the same by new patents, and dispose the residue as other vacant lands which had never been surveyed. Nevertheless, no effectual care has been hitherto taken for excavating and annulling the record of those old exhorbitant grants, patents, surveys or locations; and for securing the new patentees against the demands of the old patentees and possessors, or such as claim by, from or under them:

"Therefore be it enacted by the authority aforesaid, that nothing herein contained shall extend to revive, make good or confirm any of the said old grants or patents, nor give to the grantees or patentees of the same, nor their heirs, executors or assigns, any right, title, interest, or estates of, in, to or for any more or greater quantity of lands, marsh, meadow or cripple, than were expressly granted or really intended to be granted in and by the said original first warrants or orders for survey to which the old patents respectively relate. But that all and every said old grants or patents, as to the residue or overplus of the said lands and hereditaments contained therein, shall be and are hereby declared to be null and void and of none effect; and that all and every the grants, patents, conveyances and assurances made or to be made and granted for the said residue or overplus lands, to any person or persons whatsoever, and all the estate and estates, rights, interests and possessions of any person or persons of, in or to the said overplus lands, shall, notwithstanding any of the said old grants or patents, be and continue and are hereby declared to be good and available in law against the said old patents and against all others claiming or to claim the said overplus land or any part thereof by, from or under them or any of them, as if the same lands had never been surveyed or located before the date of the said King's letters patent: saving always to all and every person and persons (other than those who will set up or insist on any of the said old grants or patents to maintain or make good their demands or claims to any more of the said overplus land than what they or those under whom they claim have occupied, built upon or improved) all and every such right, title, interest, use, possession, estate, rents, reversions, commons, profits and advantages whatsoever, as he, they or any of them, should or might have had before the making of this act, anything herein contained to the contrary notwithstanding.

"And whereas, by a late law of this province, passed in the year one thousand seven hundred, and confirmed in the year one thousand seven hundred and one, it was (amongst other things) enacted that any person's lands in this province should be resurveyed; and if upon such resurvey (after allowance of four acres in the hundred, over or under, for difference of surveys, and six per cent for roads) an overplus should be found, the possessor thereof should have the refusal of it from the proprietary at reasonable rates; and in case of disagreements about such rates, the proprietary was to choose two men, and the possessor two more, who should either fix a price on the said overplus land or appoint where it should be taken off for the proprietary in one entire piece at an outside (saving to the purchaser or renter his improvements and best conveniences), any three of whom agreeing should be conclusive; and the charges of resurveying should be borne by the purchaser or renter of the main tract, if he bought the overplus or if not then by the proprietary; and that deficiencies should be made good by the proprietary, according as he received for overplus land as aforesaid.

"In pursuance of which act, resurveys have been made of divers lands, wherein overmeasure was found. But the act expiring before the same could be cut off, or the rates thereof settled as the said law directed, the proprietary is not satisfied for the overmeasure, and the owners of the land want confirmation of what is their just due.

"Be it, therefore, enacted, that where any overplus land has been found upon the said resurveys (after allowances are made for roads and difference of surveys as aforesaid) the proprietary, his heirs and assigns, and his or their commissioners or agents, shall give the possessor or owner of such land the refusal thereof at reasonable rates; and in case of disagreement with the said possessor about such rates, then the proprietary, his heirs and assigns, and his or their commissioners or agents, shall give the possessor or owner of such land the refusal thereof at reasonable rates; and in case of disagreement with the said possessor about such rates, then the proprietary, his heirs or assigns, or his or their commissioners or agents, shall forthwith choose two men, and the said possessor or owner shall at the same time choose two more, which persons so chosen, or any three of them, shall within thirty days after such choice either fix a price on the said overplus land to be paid by the said possessor or owner, or within the same time appoint where it shall be taken off for the proprietary, his heirs or assigns, in one entire and convenient piece at an end or outside; saving to the said possessor or owner his improvements and best conveniences."

The above act was passed on June 7, 1712, but was repealed by the Queen in Council on February 20, 1713, and therefore did not become a law. In the meantime the Penn's commissioners Richard Hill, Isaac Norris and James Logan continued to clip off pieces from the old lands of the Finns, through resurvey, although all previous acts for resurvey were likewise repealed by the queen and royal council of England. The descendants of the early Delaware colonists were through this ruling in England allowed to possess all the lands that their forefathers had occupied. Furthermore "the law about seven years' quiet possession," which was passed by the Provincial Assembly of Pennsylvania on January 12, 1706, was allowed to become a law by laspe of time in accordance with the proprietary charter, having been considered by the Queen in Council, on October 24, 1709. This law provided, that seven years' quiet possession of lands within the Province, which were first entered on upon an equitable right, shall forever give an unquestionable title to the same against all, during the estate whereof they are or shall be possessed.

The persistency of the Quaker government to get something for nothing resulted to another petition to the Assembly in 1722, by the Finns and their English relatives. The chief complaint of this petition was that the proprietor by his commissioners, especially within the last five years, had interfered with the lands that were occupied by the first Finnish colonists and those Englishmen who were here before the country was granted to William Penn, although they had their rights to the land not only from the English authorities before Penn's time, but were likewise confirmed by the law about seven years' quiet possession.

The Assembly communicated the petition to Governor Sir William Keith, who left it for consideration to the proprietary agents Richard Hill, Isaac Norris and James Logan. This petition, alike with the previous petition of the Finns, is not in the record of the Council. The secretary, James Logan, did not write there anything that might be prejudicial to the Quaker government, although their own replies to these petitions are at large in the record. The author of this work regrets of having not been able to secure the full text of the petition, and therefore cannot give it here for the reader. The answer of the proprietary agents, submitted to the governor on February 28, 1722, follows here.

"Having seriously considered the petition from certain persons amongst us called Swedes, addressed to the House of Representatives, which the Governor, by his letter of the 20th of last month was pleased to refer to us for our opinion, we with all due submission humbly offer our sentiments upon as follows:

"As we cannot find that any one of those persons whose names are put to that petition has had their title to land held by virtue of grants from the Governor of New York, called in question by the late Proprietor or any under him, within the compass of our knowledge. We have therefore just cause to apprehend that this petition arises from much different foundation. For of all men in this Province, those called the Swedes have certainly the least reason to complain of hard usage. The Proprietor at his first arrival, finding their ancestors possessed of the then most valuable tracts of land on the front of the River, without inquiring into the validity of their titles, but considering them as strangers in an English government, through his known benevolence to mankind, was pleased so far to distinguish them by his favors as to confirm to all such as applied to him all their just claims to the great disappointment of those English adventurers who embarked with him, and hazarded their lives and fortunes on the commendable design of peopling this colony. Or where it was found necessary to apply any of those claims to other purposes, he was pleased to make very ample compensation for them, a pregnant instance of which is his grant of six hundred acres of land to the Swansons in lieu of a very slender claim they had to about half that quantity in the

place where it was judged most convenient this city should be
built   The same measures also his commissioners, by his order,
from time to time pursued in relation to these people and himself
again on his second arrival, finding them much crowded in their old
possessions, through the same goodness in a most peculiar manner,
extended his favors by granting them in one tract, for their greater
conveniency, no less than ten thousand acres of land on Schuylkill
without any other consideration on their parts than the easy quit-
rent of one bushel of wheat for each one hundred acres yearly, of
which divers of them have, by sale of their rights without any
improvement, made considerable advantage. Yet, notwithstanding
these special marks of favor, which those people, when left to
themselves will duly acknowledge. In our former unhappy times,
when men who delighted in embarrassing the public, exerted their
endeavor to promote that end.   One of the measures then taken
was to spirit up those people to petition the Assembly, and to complain of grievances. So that this is not the first time that they
have been prevailed on by truly designing persons (to use the
words of the petition) to draw upon themselves the imputation of
ingratitude. In which nevertheless they may the more easily be
pardoned, since they were only made use of by others, and that it
might be truly said of them, as some of themselves have owned,
that they knew not what they did.

"But seeing the petition mentions the suit between Shae and
Justis, and as a groundless clamor has been raised and spread from
that and another affair, both grounded originally on the claims of
the Swansons, we shall beg leave, briefly and truly to represent both
cases, that the state of these matters may be the more clearly
understood.

"The Proprietor, after his first arrival, as we have already
observed, granted by his warrant to these brothers of the Swansons six hundred acres of land very near the city, and within the
bounds of its liberties, which was to be held under the yearly quit-
rent of only three bushels of wheat for the warrant. This the said
brothers, or their relicts or heirs, disposed of to two Englishmen
and another Swede, who married in the family, but having no other

title than a warrant and survey, they obliged themselves (as we have been credibly informed) by articles and bonds to procure a patent, and until that was done to pay the quit-rent. At the proprietor's return into the province all these three brothers being then dead, their widows, after a law had been passed for a general resurvey, applied to the proprietor requesting, according to the practice at that time, a resurvey and title to the said land, that they might be eased from the further payment of quit-rents and discharge their or their late husbands' bonds. Desiring that the overplus in measure might be cut off, for as no more than 600 acres were sold, they were obliged to make a title only to that quantity. A warrant was accordingly granted at their request, the land was resurveyed, and tho' it lay within the City Liberties, in which lands were wanted to answer the demands of the first original purchasers, who had not obtained the rights due to them by the proprietor's first concessions to purchasers in England. Yet to the manifest injury of those purchasers the allowance of ten acres in the hundred was also made to that land, six hundred and sixty acres, that there might be no room for complaint, instead of 600, were regularly laid out, most of the overmeasure above that quantity was cut off, on the side remotest from the Town adjoining to the City Liberty Land, and a patent was prepared confirming the whole 660 acres to those three widows according to their desire. But whether it was to make a firmer title to the vendees and their assigns, or for whatever other end, the widows applied to the proprietor again, and at the instance of those men requested that the tract might be divided into three equal parts of 200 acres each, with the mentioned allowance, and be severally confirmed to those vendees, etc., respectively, in which they were also gratified. The division lines and bounds were actually run, and returned into the office, and according to those returns three several patents to the vendees were drawn by the secretary and signed by the Proprietor in October, 1701, now above twenty years ago, and most of the overmeasure being thrown off, as has been observed, to the other City Liberty Lands, was about fourteen years after granted indifferently with others of the same, to Thomas Shute, who, having

at high rates bought divers rights to Liberty Land belonging to
original purchases, made of the Proprietor in England in the year
1681 and 1682, to the quantity of —— acres, as he fully made
appear to us, obtained warrants for the same, and the surveyor,
in laying it out taking in some part of (as he had good reason)
the overplus of the Swansons', which had so long before been cut
off from the tract, returned it accordingly into the office, and a
patent was thereupon granted to T. Shute in the usual manner
for all those Rights together. Now, though the Swansons had
never any pretence to the land there but from the Proprietor's
warrant of survey, nor their assignees any real title but from the
proprietor's patents. Though they have the utmost they can
claim either in Law or equity. Though the overplus in the first
erroneous survey was regularly cut off; and though T. Shute holds
his land by virtue of firm original deeds of lease and release, executed by the Proprietor in England before any one adventurer
came over into Pennsylvania; and had it as regularly surveyed
and confirmed by patent as any other lands have been in the
province, (all which can be largely proved). Yet some men not
only have the assurance to disturb him in his possession, but have
been so unjust as to raise a clamour and impose on many to believe,
that the rights of the good Swedes have in this case been invaded,
when in truth the question only lies in this whether or not the
assignees of the Swansons' shall hold much more than their due
and what they have no manner of right to, and thereby deprive
the assigns of the first English purchasers of their undoubted
rights that have been largely paid for. That is, whether a warrant
to the Swedes, with an erroneous survey upon it, shall give a better
right to what was never granted, nor intended to be granted, than
English deeds of lease and release, with a regular process through
the offices for a confirmation, will give for what was truly purchased
so many years before.

"The other case is this: The same three widows whom we
have mentioned, applied to the Proprietor in the same year, 1701,
for the grant of some unsurveyed marsh or cripple, which lay
contiguous to their or their children's lands in Wiccaco. The

Proprietor, with his usual indulgence to these people, the same day granted them a warrant for 50 acres; except that they yearly made use of the grass of it, but from this grant only. Some few years ago the unhappy heirs to two-thirds of those lands were induced to sell their rights in Wiccaco, both highland and marsh, to some English purchasers, for from such sales only those clamours here rose. Hereupon immediately the new purchasers were pleased to give out, that they had a right, not only to their respective shares of the fifty acres granted by the proprietor to the widows, but of all the marsh that lay there. (Upon the petition of Justice Oele Swanson, the Upland Court granted on June 19, 1678, twenty-five acres of the marsh to the Wiccaco plantation.—Author's remark.) This being wholly new to us, who were then about encouraging the improvement of the vacant marshes and cripples to the southward of this town, we appointed a day for all those to meet us, whom we understood to have any claim to those lands of Wiccaco. and having then accordingly being met, we desired them to acquaint us with the claim we understood they had made to the remainder of that marsh above the 50 acres, assuring them, that if they had any equitable right, of which we had never found the least footstep or probability, we were so far from desiring to deprive them of it that we should be ready to confirm it to them, but their lawyer, then with them, (for what reason he best knew,) advised them (as some of them have freely owned) against it, alleging at the same time something out of the Royal Charter to the Proprietor which was never there. On this head also, though more could not have been done on our parts, and nothwithstanding we have no foundation to believe they have any such right as they have pretended, the same kind of noise and clamour has been raised, fomented not much by the Swedes themselves, as by others more nearly related to Great Britain, who may justly be accounted the truly designing men to whom our divisions, whenever they arise will be owing.

"These (may it please the Governor) are the only cases we know, in which the Swedes in the late cry have been rendered as suffering persons; and perhaps it may exceed the belief of any rational man who is a stranger to the place, that such indirect uses could be made of them. Upon the whole, we shall briefly say, that all men who have fair and just rights might have had them confirmed, and those who neglect it, may undoubtedly have them hereafter upon a candid application; honest men want no other provisions, and it is presumed no Assembly of this Province now will espouse the cause of the other part of mankind. The greater part of those old claims are already confirmed by the Proprietor of or his commissioners; and if any yet want a confirmation, it has been owing, we conceive to a notion industriously instilled into those people, that a title from New York was preferable to any the Proprietor could give from the King's Letters Patent, and therefore it is unreasonable they should apply for an act derived from the Proprietor's authority to have them. Their titles from New York have never yet been called in question, for all that was said at the trial of their cause was intended to show the Proprietor's great favor and tenderness to that old settlement, who have not always made the best returns, of which this petition is an instance. But such an act as seems to be desired to confirm all men in all their claims to which they could plead quiet possession, would, under any administration, be highly unjust, seeing some persons (and such are seldom the best of men) have long possessed themselves of lands and lots without any right at all, of which divers instances could be given. Acts of such a nature, we say, could at no time be justly passed without the consent of the Proprietor or those intrusted by him in those cases. And we beg leave further to add, that the Governor himself is fully sensible, that at this time, while the affairs of the late Proprietor's family remain unsettled, none such can by any means be passed that may affect their estate and interest here; and we hope those men, who on a late occasion, were so tenderly concerned where there was no danger, that his heirs should not be wronged, will now abhor the thoughts of so manifest and flagrant an injustice.

"These men, called Swedes amongst us, we are sure have

never been injured by the proprietor or any under him; though they are very ill used by those who from time to time court their hands and names to carry designs that require such palliating. These people, as they are descended from a nation famed of their loyalty and obedience to government, may of themselves, and when not misled by others, be quiet honest men. But how far it is consistent with the peace, honor, or security of an English government, that they who by their birth are really English, and have had the utmost protection, should upon occasion be thus nationally distinguished, (as the Governor has most justly observed to us,) is humbly referred with what here offered to his further consideration."

CHAPTER XVIII.

The Last Stages of the Finnish Settlement on the Delaware.

IN 1688, the Rev. Laurentius Caroli Lokenius passed away, after having ministered the Finns on the Delaware for forty years. The other minister of the Finns, the Rev. Jacobus Fabricius, had become totally blind in 1683, however continuing his preaching until nearly his death in 1696. The Finnish descendants were now in dire need of a minister of their own faith, but as they originated mostly from the Finnish colonies in Sweden, they did not have connections in Finland, nor did they believe of getting any hearing in Sweden in the matter.

William Penn at his first return to England in 1684, communicated the desire of his Finnish subjects for a minister and books, to the Swedish Ambassador in London, and offered to forward the same to Pennsylvania, but nothing was done in Sweden upon that request.

A stray Swede had come to the colony, this was Charles Springer, a student who had gone to study the English language in London, and in one evening had been captured and carried to a merchant ship in the river Thames, loading for Virginia, where he was taken and sold as a slave. After five years of slavery, he obtained his freedom and journeyed to the Delaware River in search of his countrymen. For his education, he was employed as a schoolmaster by the Finns and it fell upon him to obtain a Lutheran minister from Europe. Two letters, written by him, in the matter, to the authorities in Sweden, bringing no reply, he was advised to write to the Lutheran Consistory in Amsterdam, Holland, who had sent the German student Magister Jacobus Fabricius to the Finns in New York, in 1669. In 1691, Springer wrote to the Consistory in Amsterdam, requesting them to send a Swedish student of theology to be minister for the Lutherans on the Delaware, as in those days students from Sweden and Finland frequented in the German and Dutch universities. And in case they would not know one, then to get the congregations to correspondence with some one in Sweden. But no reply came.

At this period arrived to Philadelphia an English ship having on board a Swedish sailor, Andrew Printz, nephew of John Printz the former Swedish governor of the Delaware Colony. As he again returned to Stockholm, he fell in conversation with John Thelin, postmaster of Gothenburg, to whom he told about the colonists' desire for a minister and religious books. The postmaster brought the matter to the knowledge of the king, Charles XI, who was interested to hear from the people of the long forgotten colony, and in a letter of January 11, 1692, requested Johan Gezelius, bishop of Turku, Finland, to select a suitable Finnish speaking minister and to buy thirty Finnish Bibles and two hundred psalm books on account of the Finnish families on the Delaware River. The Bishop recommended for the mission Magister Henning Fulda.

The sailor Andrew Printz was looked about for further information but had already disappeared, wherefore Postmaster Thelin wrote a letter on November 16, 1692, to the colonists for further information. The letter was answered by Charles Springer, on May 31, 1693, asking for two ministers "who are well learned and well exercised in the holy scriptures, and who may well defend both themselves as us against all the false teachers and strange sects by whom we are surrounded." He also assures that everything will be paid for, as for the books and ministers' salaries.

About the general conditions of the people he writes that they live well and "according to the laudable old Swedish customs," also that all the people now understand Swedish, that no Finnish minister is necessary. That the Rev. Lokenius had preached in Swedish and the Rev. Fabricius in the Dutch language. In the letter is enclosed a list of all the Finns in the Delaware

Colony, comprising of 188 families and altogether 942 souls. This however did not include all the Finns that had intermarried with the Dutch and English. The list included thirty-eight Finns who were born in Sweden or Finland, besides the writer, Charles Springer, who at least was a Swede. Among the old inhabitants was Peter Rambo from Vasa, Finland, who had been in the colony fifty-four years. In the Postmaster Thelin's letter, he is inquired for by his sister, an old woman in Gothenburg, where many Finns became stranded for lifetime during the expeditions to the colony, for not founding room on board the ships. The Rambo family on the Delaware now embraced twenty-nine members. Israel Helme was still living with a family of five people, besides some married daughters. Peter Cock, who died in 1688, had his family branched to forty-seven people, bearing his name.

In the meantime the affair had been forgotten in Sweden, as the king began to think of placing much confidence in the report of the said Andrew Printz, and the people being now under the rule of another country. Therefore, when the report of the colonists was presented to the king in December 1693, it did not bring any action from the side of the king.

At this time a Quaker reaction took place in Pennsylvania. A Quaker preacher, George Keith, who had been employed some time as head of the first grammar school in Philadelphia, started to agitate against some of the religious principles of the Friends, whereof he was dismissed from his position and from the Quaker clan, calling themselves the Society of Friends. Keith formed a Society of his own, known as the Christian or Baptist Quakers, but soon returned to England, leaving his disciples in Pennsylvania like sheep without a shepherd, until the fight was taken up by a German Heinrich Koester, who arrived to the colony in 1694.

This rupture in the ranks of the Quakers introduced some religious antagonism on the old River Delaware. Even the Finns suffered for it, although minding only their own business and quietly worshipped with the aid of their blind minister Fabricius in the Wacaco church and two lay readers, Charles Springer in

Crane Hook Church and Andreas Benkson in the Tinicum church. The Finns residing on the west side of the Schuylkill had been interfered in crossing the river on way to their church in Wicaco. Therefore they on May 11, 1693, presented to Governor Fletcher and his Council a petition, wherein they set forth that their meeting house is on the other side of the river, that they live three miles distant from the ferry, and that they are restricted from passing the river the nearest way to their worship on Sundays and Holidays by Philip England, keeper of the ferry at Schuylkill, opposite the High Street (present Market Street).

The governor offered his inclination to remove any obstruction that might be given to the worship, and in his regard to the interest of William Penn in the ferry, he desired the Council's advice.

The members of the Council were of the opinion that the petitioners may have liberty granted to them to transport themselves over the river to and from their worship, provided they do not abuse this liberty to other ends, to the prejudice of the ferry, the ferry monopoly having been retained by William Penn.

In the year 1696, something again brought the desire of the Finns on the Delaware for a minister and religious books, into the mind of Charles XI. king of Sweden. Whatever caused it, whether his queen's death or his own death lurking before his eyes for a deadly cancer in his abdomen. Or it may have been the terrible famine that his kingdom now was a victim of, for winter's cold having descended over Sweden and Finland in the midst of summer and the crop of the year had been wiped away. While scores of thousands of his subjects were dying for hunger, the letter of these Finns, once deported from Sweden, in which they describe the abundance and plenty amongst which they were happily living, may have got into the mind of the king again.

The king discussed about the matter with Jesper Svedberg, provost of the Cathedral of Upsala, and gave him to read the colonists' letter. Provost Svedberg, while traveling in Germany, had learned of a property donated by the early Christians for the conversion of the heathen, and was now within the Swedish territory at Stade, in Bremen. He had also learned that the income of the property had been converted into traveling expenses of the nobility, who converted no heathen. It had been therefore proposed that the income should be applied in the convertion of the Jews, but now another opportunity offered, and the provost exclaimed: "In America, most gracious sovereign, where there are many Swedes who now need and desire ministers, bibles, hymn-books, and various other works of devotion, there is now a good opportunity to convert the heathen, yea, to see to it that the children of Sweden do not become heathen as they dwell among them. Thus can those means be used in accordance with the wills of the deceased; otherwise, his Majesty would find it hard to answer to God for the violation of those wills."

Accordingly the matter was left into the hands of Olaus Svebelius, Archbishop of Sweden, and provost Svedberg, who had connection with the department of theology in the University of Upsala, selected two students, Andreas Rudman and Erik Bjork, for the mission. These ministers were Swedes, as Springer in his letter had said that all the Finns understood Swedish, they however came from the neighborhood of the Finnish settlements in Sweden. Besides these two ministers, Jonas Auren from Vermland was sent by the king to make a study of the inhabitants and the country and to return to make a report about the same to the king. Upon the request of the archbishop, the ministers were granted by the king "permission to return after few years, and obtain suitable preferment, as it would otherwise be a great hardship to leave their native country." The grant being signed by Charles on February 22, 1696.

The party of ministers left Sweden in August 1696, and having met some delays in London, travelled by Virginia and Maryland, reaching the Finnish colony at the Elk River in Maryland on the midsummer's day, June 24, 1697, where they were a great surprise. The Elk River Finns immediately dispatched messenger to the congregations on the Delaware, informing of their ministers arrival and the people soon came to conduct their ministers to their destination.

Upon the arrival of the ministers to their congregations, they found the Finns almost worn out of their books. Besides an English Bible and Catechisms, presented by William Penn to their church, the Rev. Bjork says in his letter "we hardly found three books." These had gone from hand to hand so that all the children had been taught to read. The ministers brought with themselves thousand one hundred and ninety volumes of religious books as gifts to the colonists, and five hundred Luther's Catechisms to the Indians, in their own language, that had been translated by the Rev. Johan Campanius, while he was in the colony in 1643 to 1648. The Indian catechisms as well as the Bibles and church books were stamped with the king's initials in golden letters. The Indians were very much pleased for their gifts and liked to hear the books read to them, also engaged Charles Springer to teach their children to read.

The old churches of the Finns were likewise in ruinous condition and outgrown for the increased population, but the congregations had grown rich, so the building of new churches was soon started. On the 28th of May 1698, the corner stone was laid for a new church behind the old fort in Christina, (within the present Wilmington in Delaware), to replace the Crane Hook church, which stood about a mile and a half from Christina and had been built by the Finns in 1667, to replace the old chapel in the fort. The new church of Christina was built of granite, the dimensions inside of the walls being sixty feet in length, thirty feet in breadth and twenty feet in height. The foundation was built six feet thick, the walls three and a half feet up to the windows and above that two feet thick. On the outside of the front wall, abbreviated inscriptions of Latin were fastened in iron letters, which translated reads, "If God be for us, who can be against us. In the reign of William III., by the grace of God, King of England. William Penn being Proprietary. William Markham, Deputy-Governor. The most illustrious King of the Swedes, Charles XI., now of most glorious memory, having sent hither Erik Tobias Bjork of Westmanland, the Pastor of the place." The church was ready for use in the early summer of

1699, and was dedicated on Trinity Sunday, on July 4, 1699, receiving the name Holy Trinity Church. A collection of about two hundred dollars was taken in, on the occasion.

The upper congregation had some difficulty in agreeing about the place for their new church. The people living along the banks of the Schuylkill, wished that the church should be built at Passayunk, where on October 1, 1695, ninety-six acres of land had been bought for that purpose and a parsonage already existed, (at present Point Breeze). Those living in Shackamaxon, Taokaninck and on the Neshaminy Creek, wished the church for their convenience to be built upon the same ground where the Wicaco church then stood. While others, living as far down the River as Marcus Hook and those on the New Jersey side as far down as the Raccoon Creek, who belonged to the Wicaco congregation, wished that the Tinicum church, at which the bones of the early settlers were buried, and for being the first church on the Delaware River, should be honored and kept in repair as long as possible, and afterwards a new church built at the same place.

While the Christina congregation was building a fine church the Philadelphia congregation could not agree about the place where to build. The Rev. Rudman, who was ministering with the Wicaco congregation, finally became disgusted and threatened to leave for Sweden, upon which the congregation left the question entirely to the ministers to settle. After which it was decided to build the church at Wicaco, close by the old church, where also was an old graveyard. The church land at Passayunk was to be kept as the church property forever, but the present minister was to be at liberty to reside in his own place on the Society Hill (at the present intersection of Pine and Front Streets) where he had twelve and a half acres of ground, given to him by his new brother-in-law, Valentine Cock. For the convenience of the people residing below the Schuylkill River, a ferry boat was to be maintained by the congregation for the crossing of that river. Which all was set forth in a document and subscribed in a meeting at the church glebe, in Passayunk, on September 18, 1698.

The building of the church was then started with zeal. The

masons who had finished their work at the church of the Christina congregation came up to Wicaco, the carpenters following. Materials were brought from the old church on the Tinicum Island and within a year the church was nearly completed. Upon the west end a place for a belfry was laid out, until some bells could be obtained. The dimensions of the church inside of the walls were sixty feet in length, thirty feet in breadth, and twenty feet in height. The foundation being of stone, the walls of red brick, every other one glaced black. On July 2, 1700, being the first Sunday after Trinity, the church was dedicated, the ceremony extending over three days. The dedication fiest was attended by numerous assembly, the Finns from far and near arrived to it, besides there were many German Lutherans and English Episcopalians, to whose benefit the dedication address was repeated in English by Pastor Bjork. The three Swedish ministers who officiated in the ceremonies, were robed in surplice and chasuble. The German Theosophic Brotherhood, who in 1694, came to the country and settled in a kind of a cloister at the Wissahickon, and among whose were a number of scholars, assisted in the ceremonies with instrumental music and singing. The dedication was a notable event in the colony. Gloria Dei (God's Glory) was the name given to the church.

The little bell of the Tinicum church was attached to the new church, although no belfry was built before a larger bell could be obtained. The bell has its own history, it was sent from Sweden by the New Sweden Company in 1644, for the Tinicum church that was built by the colonists in 1643. It went through a fire when the church burned down in 1645 and was again rang when a new church was dedicated on September 4, 1646. After the downfall of the Swedish rule on the Delaware, Armegot Printz, remained in the colony for some time to dispose her father's properties. In 1662, she sold the Tinicum Island to a citizen of Holland, J. de la Grange, and with it the church that stood on her father's land. To recover the church bell, the members of the Finnish congregation had to work two days each on the Hollander's farm during the harvest time. As half of the price had not been paid, on account of the death of the buyer, "Miss Printz" came to recover it and was allowed to take possession of the Island. The Finns then demanded a written assurance that she is not going to sell the bell again, which was given on May 24, 1673, Peter Cock and Jonas Nilsson appearing as witnesses. The bell was used in the churches of the Finns for one hundred and sixty-two years, before it was recast larger in 1806, and got the form as it today appears at the church of Gloria Dei. It has the following inscription: "Cast for the Swedish Church in Philadelphia Stiled Gloria Dei. G. Hedderly Fecit 1806 partly from the old Bell dated 1643. I to the church the living call and to the grave do summons all."

The new churches of the Finns were then the landmarks of the country. The Rev. Bjork, in writing about these new churches to Sweden, says that, "we have completed the great work, and built two fine churches, superior to any built in this country particularly that at Christina." He also says that Francis Nicholson, Governor of Maryland, and Blackstone, Governor of Virginia had with their suites visited the churches.

These new substantial edifices for worship, greatly strengthened the morale of the Anti-Quaker party and laid the final check to the conversion of the new immigrants to Quakerism. As we have already made notice of the Quaker schoolmaster, George Keith, started in 1692, a schism in that sect. Then in 1694, after Keith had left for England, there arrived from Germany a company of forty new emigrants, who had united themselves into a mysterious brotherhood. Among these men were a number of Students of Lutheran Theology from the German universities, and their chaplain during the voyage. Heinrich Bernhard Koester, continued in that capacity in their colony at Wissahickon, where they built for themselves a block-house dwelling, surmounted by an observatory, the first one in America. Before their arrival to the country, they had been led to believe of the existence of a German Lutheran Church in Germantown, which was the first settlement of Frankfort Land Company, that was started in 1683, after the company had bought 25,000 acres of land from William

Penn. When the brotherhood arrived to their destination on the Midsummer Day 1694, they found no church in the first German settlement in the new world, but a little log-house, where Quaker meetings were conducted by Francis Daniel Pastorious, the manager of Frankfort Land Company's affairs in the colony. As this learned brotherhood started to keep Lutheran meetings of their own in a private house in Germantown, it drew the Englishmen to the services in such numbers that it necessitated English meetings to be started for them in a private house in Philadelphia and a congregation was organized, which in 1696 commenced the erection of a house for church purposes. The Bishop of London, having been informed of the religious disturbances in the Province, sent in 1698 to Philadelphia the Rev. Thomas Clayton, to take care of the English Churchmen, (as those who were not Quakers were called). On his arrival he was assisted by Koester in gathering members and in the refutation of the doctrines of the Quakers. Thus became the Anglican Church established on the Delaware. At this time the old Finnish congregations, which had weathered all outside influences, and had nearly sixty years' standing on the River, were much strengthened by the arrival of the three highly accomplished ministers from Sweden. The relations between the German Theosophic Brotherhood, the new English Episcopalian congregations and the old, strong and wealthy congregations of the Finns became very intimate. The strength of the Finnish congregations greatly encouraged the others, and towards the close of the year 1698, partly at the suggestion of the Swedish ministers, an emissary was sent by the German Brotherhood, to Europe in order to report the conditions in the Germantown settlement. To this mission Daniel Falckner was selected, and when he returned to the colony in August 1700, he was accompanied by several new theological students, among whom was his brother. Falckner also brought with him consternation to Pastorius, for having been deposed and Falckner producing his commission as the agent of the Frankford Land Company. Pastorius however continued in the office, having the support of the Quaker Council and the controversies finally ended in the failure of the Frankfort Land Company.

After having been less than three years in the country, Pastor Rudman found himself in declining condition for the development of disease of the lungs, and was obliged to request for another minister to replace him. Upon which the Consistory of Upsala, in Sweden, sent the Rev. Andreas Sandel for Rudman's relief. Mr. Sandel arrived to Philadelphia on March 18, 1702, and Rudman was preparing to return to Sweden, having received a charter of promotion, but had been invited by the Lutheran Congregation in New York to become their minister, which invitation Rudman accepted and left Philadelphia for New York in July, 1702. This Lutheran Congregation occupied the old Lutheran Church built by the Finns. The church having had ministers who officiated in the Dutch language, it had made converts among the Dutch Reformed population and many of the Finns having moved to the Delaware River, the members of the congregation at this time were largely Dutch.

Mr. Rudman did not stay long in New York however, his wife was a native of the Delaware River and had her property and inheritance, relatives and friends there, while not a voyage to Sweden could be taken up for Rudman's poor health. In the summer of 1703, they were all prostrated by plague of yellow fever that was then raging in the country, therefore they decided to move back to their home in Philadelphia. Before Rudman departed from the New York congregation, he secured a minister for them in his place. Among the German Theosophical Brotherhood was a student of Lutheran Theology, Justus Falckner, who had arrived to the country in 1700, when his brother Daniel Falckner returned to the colony from a mission to Germany. On October 27, 1703, Rudman wrote to Justus Falckner in the name of the New York congregation, proposing the ministerial position. This became accepted by the candidate, but having not yet been ordained for the office, the ceremony was performed in the Gloria Dei Church of the Finns, in Wicaco, on November 24, 1703.

This ceremony, being the first ordination of a minister in the Western World, has a manifest historical significance. It was a solemn ceremony, enacted in rustic, although in the best circumstances that then existed in the country. The venerable church was yet bare and unfinished, the tower and the side projects had not yet been built. The interior exhibited rough walls and rude benches made of large boards. The unadorned altar on the east end of the church, and the wooden railing, separating its recess from the rest of the church, were in harmony with the primitive surroundings. The temporary earthen floor was undoubtedly covered with clean sand and sprinkled over with chopped fir branches, as this was done by the Finns after an ancient habit even on wooden or stone floors, to produce fragancy into the atmosphere.

The little bell of the old Tinicum church, which had a pathetic history of its own and whose sonorous melodies had during the past fifty-nine years, in the solemn stillness of the Sunday mornings, called the Finnish settlers along the majestic Delaware to the worship, was tolling in this bleak November morning while the Finns from far and near were moving towards Wicaco, on foot, on horse back and in boats along the Delaware. The elderly people were clad in their unpretentious homespuns and the younger generation indulged in the fineries brought from abroad to Philadelphia by merchant adventurers.

The front benches in the church became occupied by the invited guests, the Theosophical Brotherhood, among whom was the Rev. Daniel Falckner, brother of the candidate for ordination. They were partly clad in the habit of the German university students, others in the pilgrim garb of unbleached homespun. The rest of the church was occupied by the members of the congregation, sprinkled with English churchmen and Quaker dissenters. And few Indians who were attracted by the wonderful music of the new organ, added to the picturesqueness of the scene.

The venerable little bell was again rung and while its melodious tones, resounding from the virgin forest on the New Jersey side of the Delaware, were calming to stillness, forthwith burst the little organ in the gallery into a voluntary, Jonas Auren of Vermland being at the keys. The echo of the organ was supplemented by violin, hautboy, trumpets and kettle-drums. Then followed the singing of a processional anthem in Latin, accompanied by the music, and the little procession appeared by the west portal. It was headed by two church wardens, Johan Cock and Andreas Benkson, clad in breeches and shoes with large brass buckles, the habit of gentlemen of the day. They were followed by the candidate, wearing the collegiate gown of the German University, and being accompanied by the Rev. Andreas Sandel, in black clerical robe, as sponsor and acting as consistorial secretary. Lastly came the Rev. Andreas Rudman, acting as suffragan or vice-bishop for the occasion and being robed in a girdled surplice, with chasuble and stole. The suffragan was accompanied by the Rev. Erik Bjork, wearing the black clerial robe.

When the procession reached the chancel rail, the two wardens stood on either side of the railing, while the suffragan and the two ministers entered within the chancel, the suffragan taking position in front of the altar, upon which were placed a crucifix and lighted tapers, and the two assistants ranged themselves on his either side. The anthem being ended, the suffragan opened the services with an invitation to prayer. Then followed the lengthy ceremony of the ordination, according to the Lutheran Liturgy.

A week after the ordination the Rev. Justus Falkner arrived to New York, where he officiated until his death in 1723.

Mr. Rudman, after his return to Philadelphia, ministered in the English church at Oxford and also in Philadelphia. His desire to return to his native land was finally interrupted by his death on September 17, 1708. Being nearly forty years of age and leaving a widow and two daughters. His remains lie beneath the chancel of the Gloria Dei Church in Wicaco.

About the time of the arrival of the three Swedish ministers at the Delaware, there arrived one Peter Schaefer, a native of Turku, Finland. Schaefer had the degree of Master of Arts in the university of his home town and was chased by the church authorities for his Pietist teachings, wherefore he boarded a ship in 1693 and after traveling in several countries in Europe finally arrived through England to the Delaware Colony. In Philadelphia

Magister Schaefer presented himself to Edward Shippen, one of the prominent holders of public offices of the time. He was permitted by Mr. Shippen and his wife Rebecca, to stay in their house as a guest for six weeks, during which time he persisted in living upon bread and water. The people of Finns Point (present Upper and Lower Pennsneck) in New Jersey, desired Schaefer to keep school for their children, which he did for a while. Afterwards he went to preach for the Germans in Germantown, and although the New Jersey Finns desired him to become their minister, Schaefer did not respond to the invitation but resolved to return in the year 1700 to his native town in Finland and finally succumbed in prison at Gefle, Sweden, for his religious opinions.

Before the arrival of the Rev. Sandel at the Delaware, another clergyman, Lars Tollstadius, had come to the colony from Sweden on his own accord, and was accepted by the Rev. Rudman to assist him in the Wicaco church. However, after the arrival of Sandel he was released and was only permitted by the other ministers to teach the catechism for children, for having not been commissioned for minister's office by the Consistory of Upsala, although he had sought for appointment. The Rev. Tollstadius however did not abide with the wishes of the other ministers, but went to the Finnish settlements in the West New Jersey, on their invitation, and preached every Sunday, first at the Raccoon Creek and then at Finns Point. As this territory was divided between the Wicaco and the Christina churches, the ministers of these churches objected so much more, as it diminished not only their congregations, but their income.

The Finns of West New Jersey had aided in the building of the Christina and Wicaco churches, and had been promised by these congregations aid when they wanted to build a church for themselves. The aid was not however forthcoming, as the ministers of those churches did not want the church built. But many of the people had to travel a long distance to get to the churches that already had been built, and besides had to cross the Delaware River in boats, which in winter time was very dangerous, some times even impossible, as the River is packed with floating ice, that is moving fast up and down the River with the tide. The West New Jersey settlers therefore did not abide with the wishes of the "regular" ministers, but commenced to build at the Raccoon Creek a church of their own in 1703, which became finished in the next year. The church was built of hewn logs, in the old Finnish style of architecture. On the second Sunday after Trinity, the church was consecrated by the Rev. Tollstadius, the other ministers failing to attain, although having been invited.

The Finns of West New Jersey, however soon lost their minister, as on the 29th of May 1706, Tollstadius was drowned in crossing the Delaware in a canoe. Before his death, the congregation had found objections against him, for his irregular mode of living.

The Rev. Jonas Auren, whom Charles XI., king of Sweden had sent with the other ministers to the Delaware, in order to make observations and to map the country, after which he was immediately to return to report to the king, was still in the country, as the king died before the arrival of the ministers to their destination. After doing some missionary work among the Indians, Mr. Auren settled in the Finnish colony at Elk River, in Maryland. Before that he had become acquainted with the Keithians in Philadelphia and was now a self confessed Sabbatarian, advocating Saturday as the real Sabbath, for which he was not in favor with the other Swedish ministers. The Finns of West New Jersey invited Mr. Auren to be their minister, after the death of Mr. Tollstadius. but he was not immediately willing to leave his congregation at the Elk River, however sent one Mr. Brunjan to be a lay reader and schoolmaster at the Raccoon congregation. and finally, in the spring of 1707, moved himself there. Although Auren retained his Sabbatarian notion, he was forbidden to urge it upon his new congregation by order of the governor of New York, before whom the Rev. Bjork cited him to appear. However he wrote an almanac in English, calling it "Noah's Dove." in which he advocated the sabbatarian views, this caused Mr. Bjork, minister of Christina congregation, to publish an answer and refutation with the title: "A little olive leaf put into the mouth of that so-called 'Noah's Dove,' and sent home again, to let her master know that the waters are abated from off the face of the ground."

The Rev. Auren presided over the Raccoon Finnish parish until the year 1713, when on the 17th of February he died, leaving a widow, whose maiden name was Lydia Gustafsson and whom he married in 1710, besides two sons.

At this time there was a good supply of ministers, despite Mr. Auren's death. There was Mr. Sandel in Wicaco and Mr. Bjork in Christina, besides the Rev. Andreas Hesselius and the Rev. Abraham Lidenius, who arrived to the country on the 1st of May 1712. Mr. Hesselius was to release Mr. Bjork, who desired to return to his native country, and Lidenius was to assist in each congregation. Mr. Bjork like most of the Swedish ministers, had married from his congregation and had some property to mind about, remained in the colony despite the new ministers, until June 29, 1714, when he left for Sweden with his wife and five children, having before his departure received a commission to a pastorate in Sweden, signed by King Charles XII., in Timurtasch, in Turkey, where the king had entered after the defeat of his Swedish-Finnish army, in the battle of Poltava with the forces of Peter the Great of Russia.

Mr. Lidenius was desired by the Finns of Pennsneck to become their minister, wherefore he settled there on December 5, 1712, and after the death of Auren, he also served the Raccoon congregation. In 1715, the Pennsneck people commenced to build a church of their own, on the middle of the neck, on the highway. The place being known today as Church Landing. The church became finished however only in the spring of 1717, when it was consecrated on the 31st of March, and was called St. George's Church. It was built twenty-four feet square, of hewn logs and weather boarded, as the Finns used to build their log houses.

As the parsonage of Raccoon was not suitably situated for both churches, a farm was bought in 1720, for a new parsonage, in about midway between the churches, which were apart from each other about sixteen miles.

Since 1712, there had been three ministers for the Finns, but on June 25, 1719, Mr. Sandel of the Wicaco Parish left for Sweden, with his wife Maria Dalbo, whom he married in the colony, and two children, after having received a royal commission for the pastorate of Hedemora. It is interesting in this connection to note, that one of their grandsons became an illustrious general, Field Marshal Count Sandels, who during the Finnish War of 1808-9 gallantly led his Finnish Jaegers against the Russian multitudes.

Mr. Sandel was succeeded in the Wicaco Parish by the Rev. Jonas Lidman, who on the first Sunday in Advent was installed to his office. Between the departure of Sandel and the arrival of Lidman, the ministers of Christina and Raccoon parishes attended the Wicaco congregation. With Mr. Lidman arrived another minister, Samuel Hesselius, brother of Andreas Hesselius of the Christina Parish. Mr. Samuel Hesselius was to be assistant minister at Wicaco, until his brother's departure for Sweden. At first it was settled that he should preach for the Finns at Calkeon Hook and at the Neshaminy Creek, but as those Finns at Manatawny had some fifty miles to travel in coming to the Wicaco church, at the Parish meeting in Wicaco, on the 27th of March 1720, they pleaded Mr. Hesselius to move to live at their settlement, which was agreed and Hesselius was to take from there care of Neshaminy and by later decision also of Matzong (Matson's Ford) Finnish settlement.

The place called Manatawny was situated on north side of the Schuylkill River, between its two branches, the Manatawny and Manasisk Creeks. A part of it belonging to the present Montgomery County and the greater part to the Berks County. Some Finns who had sold their farms to the English immigrants, had settled there few years since, and on October 20, 1701, William Penn, before his second and last return to England authorized the Finns to take possessions of 10,000 acres of land there, without being obliged to pay for it anything else than their traditional quit-rent of one bushel of wheat per hundred acres yearly. This parcel of land consisted essentially of the present Amity Township,

Berks County. The place where the Finns had their church, they called Morlatton, and is the present Douglasville. The church was built in 1733, of oak logs, had seats for 120 persons and was provided with iron fireplace. From Morlatton, Mr. Hesselius also ministered new German settlements in the neighborhood, called Falkner's Swamp, which originally was started on land purchased by the Frankfort Land Company.

Pastor Lidman of the Wicaco Parish left for Sweden on the 14th of November 1730, after having received assurances of suitable preferment as his reward of having come to America. The Wicaco congregation thereafter employed as their temporary minister a Swede Johan Eneberg, who had been preaching in the German settlements. For some reasons, known in Sweden, Eneberg was not commissioned to his office and it was only in the beginning of January 1733, that a new commissioned minister, the Rev. Gabriel Falk arrived to Philadelphia, where he and his servant were well received and provided by his congregation, after having lost everything when the ship on which he came over was wrecked in the Delaware Bay. The congregation also provided him with a new parsonage, which was built on the church land at Wicaco. The house was built of brick, two stories high, and had two rooms on each floor, with a convenient kitchen and garret besides. Before this, the ministers had been living in the parsonage at Passayunk or in their own houses.

Pastor Falk became to enjoy the graces of the Wicaco congregation only for few months however. One of the elders of the church fell under his suspicion of having improper relations with his own daughter, and the case having been taken to the court, Falk was condemned to pay five hundred pounds damages for the scandalized man and was driven away from Wicaco. Falk had been expelled from his student nation at the University of Upsala in 1720, likewise for scandalizing.

Thereafter Pastor Falk was preaching to the Finns at Morlatton about ten years, moving in 1735 to live there. From there he also took care of the German congregation of Falkner Swamp between the years of 1735 and 1742, where a log church was built in 1741.

Abraham Lidenius, who had been pastor of the Raccoon-Pennsneck congregation since 1712, departed to Sweden in 1726, and the newly arrived minister, the Rev. Peter Tranberg, who had been sent to release him, was installed in his place on June 30th of the same year. With Tranberg arrived from Sweden the Rev. Andreas Windrufva, as an adjunct pastor, and the two ministers agreed with the approval of the people, to divide the congregation between themselves, so that Tranberg was to preside over Raccoon church and Windrufva take care of the Pennsneck church. The former was to receive as regular salary forty pounds from Raccoon and the latter twenty pounds from Pennsneck, besides a house and provisions and a horse for his service. The arrangement soon however became into termination as Mr. Windrufva died on November 5, 1728, leaving a young widow of the Jaquet family.

The New Jersey congregations again became united under one minister, Mr. Tranberg continuing to preside in both churches.

In October 1723, the Rev. Andreas Hesselius left for Sweden and his brother, the Rev. Samuel Hesselius, pastor of the Finnish congregation of Morlatton succeeded him as minister of the Christina congregation. At the arrival of Samuel Hesselius to Christina, fifty acres of the land of the parsonage was sold for 40 pounds, to buy him a negro woman as servant. There was at this time also in dispute a will that had been made to the benefit of the Church. A childless member of the congregation, Aaron Johansson, had on the 20th of November, 1701, bequeathed all his property to fall to the church after his wife's death, except a part of it was to fall to Pastor Bjork, who was then the minister at Christina. The church wardens in office at that time were appointed executors. The farmer Johansson died in 1707, whereupon the church wardens had the will recorded in proper form. When Provost Bjork left for Sweden, the widow was still living, but she agreed with the church wardens that Bjork be allowed his share in fifty-two acres of land, which Bjork sold before his departure. The remainder was a valuable island in the Christiana Creek, about five miles from Christina. One of the two church

wardens was Edward Robinson, an Irishman, who had by inter-
marriage united himself with the Finnish congregation. Mr.
Robinson adopted the widow, calling her his mother, and got the
widow to change the will for his benefit. In this he was supported
by English Law, which prohibited to will land to any church,
and although the Assembly of the Province had enacted a con-
tradictory act, it did not finally become a law as it was repealed
in England. Likewise the widow's support had to be taken into
consideration. Before Andreas Hesselius left for Sweden, in 1723,
the widow had died and therefore the will went into effect, and
as Robertson insisted of keeping the land, a complaint was made
by the elders of the church to Governor William Keith, who
appointed three Justices of the Peace to examine the affair, and
there the matter remained. The case could not be very well
taken to the court, on account of the English law, unfavorable
to the church. The congregation thought that whatever could
be got from Robinson voluntarily, is best to take, and Robinson
agreed to contribute 15 pounds in all for the will, the homestead
being then valued over 700 pounds. Some members of the congregation notified these transactions to Provost Bjork and Bishop
Svedberg in Sweden, likewise that Samuel Hesselius was using
his time in attaining the English congregations and was neglecting his own church for weeks and the teaching of the children.
Although Samuel Hesselius was not alone guilty for giving much
attention to the English churches, as all the Swedish ministers
from the time of Rudman and Bjork did it for the gifts or regular
salaries that they received for doing it, from the English Society
for Propagation of the Gospel in Foreign Parts. In a letter of
December 11, 1710 to the Society, the Vestry of the English Episcopalian Church of Appoquimininck are describing the great
services that Bjork had been doing to their congregation and
petitioned some reward for him from the Society, saying that
he was receiving from his own congregation only 15 pounds yearly,
although Mr. Bjork during the first years at least received about
100 pounds, besides extra income from all burials, baptisms, marriages, churchings, etc., and had the parish house and a large

glebe land to enjoy. Mr. Bjork left the country with a fortune. On account of the informations against Samuel Hesselius, he was strongly admonished by Provost Bjork and Bishop Svedberg, by letter, of neglect of his congregation and selling and giving up the Bread and Cheese Island, that was willed to the church by Johansson.

Governor Patrick Gordon likewise had received complaint against Robinson, from the old pastors Bjork and Andreas Hesselius. Upon this the governor appointed three Justices of the Peace to investigate. All parties concerned in the matter met on the 6th of September 1729, on the Brandywine Ferry, and Samuel Hesselius was totally acquitted of being guilty to any neglect of duty, or as regarded the sale of land. The Pastor sent over to Bishop Svedberg the decision, also good testimonial from the English clergy of the Province, from the English church in Chester and one from his own parish. Furthermore he decided to return to Sweden and with new testimonials left the country in November 1731. Samuel Hesselius had married in Manatawny, Brita Laikan (Laikainen), who soon died. His second wife Gerdrud Stille died during the voyage to Sweden, and was buried to the ocean. Hesselius arrived to Sweden with four children, and his recommendations from the colony did not help him in recovering the confidence of the church authorities upon him. He received a parish only in 1751, and died two years later.

Before the arrival of the Rev. Gabriel Falk to the Wicaco church in 1733, the congregation was presided over by the Rev. Johan Eneberg, who had come to America about that time and had been preaching first in the German Settlements. As the Christina congregation now became vacant after the departure of Samuel Hesselius, Eneberg came once a month to preach in that church and the Rev. Tranberg from Raccoon likewise attended the Christina congregation. Finally Eneberg moved to Christina, having received a commission as pastor of that congregation from King Frederick of Sweden, given at Stockholm on July 4, 1732. The Christina congregation at this time was preferred by the Swedish ministers, and Eneberg entered upon his duties there at the beginning of 1733.

At this period the Finns along the Brandywine and the Christiana Creeks had become great producers of wheat and all kinds of provisions. These they brought down the creeks to the neck of land formed by the conjunction of the above said creeks, where they had their church, in whose neighborhood merchants had sprung up. Finally there was born an idea of building a town like Philadelphia on the neck, it being much the same as the neck of land between the Schuylkill and Delaware upon which Philadelphia was first laid out. Just as Philadelphia was built a little distance above end of the neck, so was this new town built a short distance above the end of the peninsula. The good, navigable shore on the Christiana Creek and the fact that the old highways met at this section, favored this site for a commercial centre. The land at this section was owned by Andreas Justison or Gustafsson and by the Christina Church. On September 1731, Andreas Justison assigned to his son-in-law, Thomas Willing, an Englishman, a part of his land on the Christiana Creek, and the latter laid his parcel out for a town plot, after the plan of Philadelphia, starting to sell lots for adventurers in his "Willingtown." At 1735, the new town had about twenty houses, but at that time many lots were sold and new building activity ensued so that in the year 1736, the town plan shows thirty four houses. On November 18th of the latter year, the Christina congregation likewise commissioned their church wardens, together with one of the elders, to act for the church as trustees in order to divide the church glebe and lay it out into streets and building lots and then to rent out these lots, to give deeds for the same and to receive the annual rents. They were to do this in their own name, as it was against the English law to a church to engage in any land transactions. The trustees were to keep book and to make account of their transactions to the congregation once a year. The minister of the church was to receive two-thirds of the yearly income of the lots and the remaining one-third was to be used for the maintenance of the church and parsonage. Two town lots were to be left to the parsonage for the use of the minister. An Englishman, Goldsmith E. Followel, a citizen of Willingtown, who was the sales agent for the lots to his Quaker friends, was assigned as the bookkeeper of the corporation, on bond of five hundred pounds.

But the provision, made by the Christina congregation, that the minister was to receive two-thirds of the income of the town lots, was most injurious to the land property of the church, as the ministers, desiring to make out of the land as much as possible, before their return back to Sweden, continually harrassed the trustees, who were obliged to make presents of lots to the ministers to rent out the lots as fast as possible, and to give from their own pockets moneys that had not come in regularly from the rents, wherefore they were forced to sell lots to get reimbursed. When the Rev. John Eneberg left for his native country in 1742, the church property was already much vasted, and before his journey, the trustees were obliged to advance to him one hundred pounds upon unpaid rents, for which they afterwards had to sell lots to pay the sum.

In 1740, the church wall on the north side was found to have bent outwards by the weight of the roof and the settling of the foundation, it was therefore necessary to built two arches for the support of the wall. These arches were built over the doors, and served as vestibules. The bell still was hanging in a walnut tree on the side of the church, but now a little wooden tower was built upon one of these outbuildings and the bell hung in it. The walnut tree was then cut down as the squirrels made it a perpetual home for themselves, on account of the nuts, and building their nests upon the arches injured the roof.

The new down was growing very handsomely, having more than one hundred and twenty houses in 1742. As the Trinity Church was the only one in the place, it became more and more the object of attention. On Christmas day, matins had been celebrated in the church, but as they became too much the curiosity of the new English population of the town, who gathered staring at it and to make fun of it, the celebrations were discontinued. To acquaint the reader to this festivity, we describe how Christmas was celebrated in the peasant homes in Finland during the very recent years. On the Christmas eve the peasant invited his tenants to his home, where in the large, rustic hall of the peasant house a Christmas tree had been set up, and at the blaze of fire in the large fire place, amplified by lit candles of the Christmas tree, a supper was enjoyed, Christmas hymns were sung and holiday stories from the Christmas magazines were read by some student member of the family, who had come home for the holiday season. The evening was pleasantly concluded by the distribution of gifts to the tenant families. These consisted of some products of the farm, as a large loaf of rye bread, which for Christmas was sweetened by fermentation, and a piece of pork or the like. Those tenants who did not keep horses were invited to gather again to the house in the morning, between four and five o'clock, to be taken to the Matins in the church. For the journey to the church, the horses were harnessed luxuriously, and a great number of bells were attached to the harness. Early in the Christmas morning the country-side was then one hum of bells, after intervals superseded by the toll of the church bells, as the people rode to the Matins in sleighs. At the church were rows of stalls for the horses, each peasant having his own stable there. The large windows of the church were full of lit candles, making the edifice a perpetual light tower in the December night of the north. Over the aisles of the church, between intervals, arches had been placed with lit candles. The reflections of the prisms in the chandeliers and of the gilded ornaments of the altar, gave a brilliant aspect to the environment. The services consisted of an organ recital, singing of Christmas hymns, chorus recital and a sermon about the Child of Bethlehem, which by the acquisitions during centuries had developed to the highest pitch of elocution. The congregation, at the dawn of the daylight, marched out of the church at the rythm of the organ and the tolling of the church bells. Then the bell bedecked horses were drawn for comparison, the homeward journey was started, each party to his own direction, and although in other occasion it was against the etiquette to pass another church party on the highway, on the Christmas morning there was a great race, which was talked about with great delight during the rest of the holiday season.

The church of Wicaco had been without a minister since the latter part of the year 1733, having been served by Eneberg from Christina and by Tranberg from Raccoon and Pennsneck, but on the 2nd of November 1737, a minister, the Rev. Johannes Dylander arrived to Philadelphia from Sweden. At this period the position of the Swedish ministers was getting difficult for the reason that great part of their congregations did not understand the Swedish language. The early Finnish colonists, having been mostly born in the Finnish settlements in Sweden, had not fully acquired the Swedish language and had all passed away long since. Their descendants had been acquainted with the Swedish language only by the Swedish ministers and schoolmasters who taught them to read the catechism. At the arrival of Mr. Dylander, the congregation preferred the English language for their church and many had united with the English churches. The Wicaco congregation had only sixty families left on the arrival of the minister, but after Dylander had acquired the English language and was preaching on the Sunday afternoons in that language, he could increase his congregation into one hundred families. He also preached in the Wicaco church during more than a year, early in the morning in the German language, to that nationality, who were without minister. Mr. Dylander was an industrious man and was so well liked, that the English ministers of Philadelphia made a complaint against him because the English had acquired the habit of celebrating their marriages in the Wicaco church. During his time the church went through extensive repairs and a new organ also was installed. The church finances also became improved for the reason that the suburb of Philadelphia, called Society Hill, had stretched itself to the neighborhood of the church, so the church land was divided into city lots and were rented out through the church wardens. The glebe in Passayunk likewise was rented out for pasture land.

Besides taking good care of his congregation Mr. Dylander travelled in the outlying Finnish, German and English settlements, delivering as many as sixteen sermons weekly. This however soon broke his health, he had on account of sickness to give up the German and English services and his entire work was terminated by death on the 2nd day of November 1741, Mr. Dylander left a widow who was the daughter of Peter Cock of Passayunk. He was interred beneath the chancel in the Wicaco church, the funeral being conducted in English by Pastor Tranberg, in presence of a large and cosmopolitan congregation.

Pastor Dylander having died and Pastor Eneberg of Christina church having left for Sweden on August 10, 1741, the Rev. Tranberg of Raccoon and Pennsneck was the only Swedish minister left in America. Mr. Tranberg had requested the Consistory of Upsala to be appointed for the Christina congregation after the departure of the Rev. Eneberg. This had been granted to him and while Mr. Eneberg still was in the country, Tranberg became the minister of the Christina Church, on August 1, 1741. Although the Christina people were pleased to receive a minister, the people of Raccoon and Pennsneck were much displeased for his transfer, especially as they felt that Mr. Tranberg had been well treated and had massed a fortune during his fourteen years with the New Jersey congregations. In a resolution entered into the Raccoon church book the congregation resented the arbitrary manner of the transfer by the Swedish king and bishop, declaring that the congregation alone had to do with the ministers, and that no more ministers to be ordered from Sweden.

The parsonage of the Christina congregation, in the Willington, now becoming to be known as Wilmington, had become antiquated, so Mr. Tranberg decided to build a house of his own, and for this purpose was given a lot, near the old parsonage, by the congregation. The house was built of brick and was then one of the finest in the new town, which at this time had some six hundred inhabitants. The negress of the parsonage, who in 1723, was bought for forty pounds, had likewise become old and contrary, wherefore she was sold in public auction at the slave market, bringing only seven shillings. A cow was the most valuable part of the inventory of the parsonage, that were turned over to Mr. Tranberg.

Like in the Wicaco congregation, here too the Finnish descendants had not had enough opportunity since the coming of the English people to keep up their understanding of the Swedish language, despite the efforts of the Swedish ministers. English had become the language of communication between the old settlers and the English, German and other new immigrants. A large part of the Finnish descendants preferred the English language to the Swedish in their church, besides there were many English non-Quakers in Wilmington who did not have any church at all, therefore, by the desire of the congregation, services were held in the morning in Swedish and in the afternoon in English. Mr. Tranberg also attended several English churches and sometimes also preached in the German church at Lancaster.

The land affairs of the church were the same as during the time of Mr. Eneberg. Some of the ground rent did not come in regularly and others did not come in at all. As the minister's income depended upon what was realized from the church land, the trustees naturally were chased by him to convert the property into money. To satisfy the minister he was given one whole block in Wilmington as his property forever, not however as settlement for the uncollected ground rents, as these were afterwards fully drawn out. In 1745, a new arrangement was invented by which the church land was committed into the hand of two trustees, who were to handle the property as their own and to sell, rent and sue in their own name. For this each of the trustees were required to give a bond of five hundred pounds for the congregation. The property was fairly well managed by these trustees, only some moneys were lost for having been lent out without security, also notes were taken as part payments for lots and when the buyer occasionally failed, the notes became worthless.

The Wicaco congregation notified in a letter of November 16, 1741, to the consistory of Upsala, Sweden, about the death of their minister, the Rev. Dylander, and requested for a new minister. But it was only on October 20, 1743, when a new minister the Rev. Gabriel Naesman arrived to Philadelphia. On the arrival of Mr. Naesman, he found the congregation in extremely bad shape.

There were but few old people yet who could understand Swedish, most of the people had joined to the English churches and to an association established by George Whitefield, who by great elocution attracted the people of every variety of faith, while others were let away by so called Moravian Brethren or Herrnhuters. These Hussite dissenders were known as Moravians from their original abode, and as Herrnhuters from their patron and bishop, Count Nicholas Ludwig von Zinzendorf had given them in 1722 land on his estate in Saxony, where they established their settlement known as Herrnhut (Lord's watch). Their first permanent settlements in Pennsylvania were Bethlehem and Nazareth. In December 1740, Count Zinzendorf arrived to Philadelphia, there being at this time about twenty-five or thirty Moravians in Pennsylvania. A sermon delivered by Count Zinzendorf, on the 10th day of January 1741, in Philadelphia, translated into English and printed by Benjamin Franklin in 1743, is found today in the Helsingfors University library. It had been given by Miss Elsa Cock of Philadelphia, on May 7, 1750 to Professor Kalm of the University of Turku, Finland, on his visit to America. Count Zinzendorf was a great elocutionist, and as the German immigrants, who came in numbers to the country at this time, were poorly provided or without a minister, he made a great success among the Germans.

A Swedish student, Paul Bryzelius, who had joined the Moravian Brethren in Germany, arrived in the first larger Moravian expedition to America, called the "First Sea Congregation," which landed at Philadelphia on June 7, 1742. Mr. Bryzelius, who was assigned to work among the Finns, was in the country before the arrival of Pastor Naesman, and had found an opportune time as there was only one Swedish minister, the Rev. Tranberg, working among the Finns. When Tranberg left the Raccoon and Pennsneck parishes, these were attended about a year by a Swedish student Olof Malander, who came to the country with the Rev. Dylander in 1637, to work as schoolmaster. But there are found complaints against his wife and Malander himself became imprisoned for debts, after which he obtained employment in the printing office of Benjamin Franklin. He joined to the Moravian

Brotherhood, and produced the Moravian catechism in the Swedish language at the Franklin's printing establishment in 1743, having been translated from the German by Bryzelius. In January 1743, Bryzelius was ordained as a Moravian minister, by Bishop David Nitschmann, whereafter he was appointed by Zinzendorf to preach among the Finns at Maurice River, Cohanzie, Pennsneck, Raccoon, Ammasland, Potomock and Calcoen's Hook. As the churches of Raccoon and Pennsneck were without minister, these were open to the Rev. Bryzelius, while the congregation of Wicaco had not accepted his offer to preach. All these had to be met by the Rev. Naesman, on his arrival in October 1743. And more than that, Pastor Naesman was struck to a very vulnerable point, as his rival, Mr. Bryzelius, was the more acceptable to his congregation because he did not accept any salary for his work, but declared that the Moravians would not preach for money. In the Raccoon congregation was found however people who desired to hear the newly arrived minister of Wicaco to preach in their church, and on the third Sunday in Advent 1743, Naesman arrived to officiate there, supplanting Bryzelius who remained as listener. When the service was over, the Naesman party desired the congregation to invite him to preach there once a month, while Bryzelius declared that he is ready to preach them twice a month. This led to a lively argument between the two pastors and their supporters. However Naesman could not attend the Raccoon church every Sunday to keep his flock together and to the Pennsneck church he was not even invited, it had completely fallen to the Moravian sect. The Rev. Tranberg of Wilmington occasionally preached in the Pennsneck church, but he was not so particular about sects, he and his wife are accused of having been sympathizers with the Moravians and Bryzelius was welcomed to their home. The affairs became into culmination in Raccoon, in December 1744, as Bryzelius was to preach in the church. A great number of people had assembled, one party was composed of the supporters of Bryzelius and the other party was there to keep him out of the church, still others had come only to enjoy the fun. As the opposition party had the church-key, which they did not give up, therefore the supporters of Bryzelius broke a window and one of them crept in to open the door from inside. But no service could be held on account of the fight, noise and confusion that ensued. The affair ended that an arbitration court of twenty-five men were agreed upon to gather at Gloucester, New Jersey, before which appeared the Rev. Naesman and the Rev. Bryzelius as spokesmen for their respective party. Mr. Naesman at once overawed his opponent by flourishing a diploma as Master of Arts and also a minister's letter and commission from the Consistory of Upsala. He made complaints and accusations against Bryzelius, who completely disappointed his followers by not making any reply. The Moravian party was fined fifty pounds and prohibited for keeping services in the church.

The Moravian movement among the Finns in western New Jersey, however did not perish to this, and although Bryzelius was recalled from the mission in 1745, there were now other Swedish students of theology at the disposal of the Brotherhood for this mission. The German Lutherans of Lancaster, Pennsylvania, had received upon their application a minister from Sweden. This was the Rev. Lars Nyberg, who arrived to the country in 1744. Mr. Nyberg had been converted to Moravian Brotherhood already in Sweden, although he kept it a secret, but within a year he had fully disposed himself, had married a Moravian sister and brought the congregation in turmoil and became closed out of the church with his party. Although Mr. Nyberg kept in Lancaster until 1748, where he founded a Moravian church, he visited the Finns in New Jersey and supplied them with Swedish missionaries, among which was Abraham Reincke, son of a Stockholm merchant, whom his parents had sent to Germany to study theology and had joined to the Moravians. Mr. Reincke's records show his operation among the New Jersey Finns, starting in the spring of 1745, after the recall of Mr. Bryzelius. The Raccoon and Pennsneck district was suitable for the new Swedish adventurers, who did not know the English language, as the people there were descendants of early Finnish and some Dutch settlers whose children had been taught to read in Swedish by the Swedish schoolmasters that came to the country with the ministers or by themselves as adventurers. As only few English had settled there, there were no English schools nor such a daily need of the English language as in other places along the Delaware. Therefore these were the last Finnish settlements to become Anglinized.

Pastor Naesman had repeatedly urged the Finns at Raccoon to call for a minister from Sweden, but Mr. Reincke, preaching around in the private houses and in the Pennsneck church, kept with the aid of Mr. Nyberg the congregation so scattered, that it was only on November 17, 1745, when a petition was finally mailed. And as things did not work fast in those days, it was on May 25, 1747, when the Rev. Johan Sandin was appointed to the mission as Provost of the Swedish ministers in America. After eighteen weeks journey, Pastor Sandin arrived to Philadelphia overland from New York, on March 29, 1748 and preached his first sermon in the Raccoon church on the following Palm Sunday. But the Pennsneck people held to the Moravians, and although the church had been closed for their preachers in 1746, the Brethren again occupied the pulpit there at the arrival of Provost Sandin. As Mr. Sandin offered his services to them, they accepted his offer only on the condition, that he officiate in the English language. This naturally was hard for a man newly arrived from Sweden, and Pastor Sandin has much complaints to make in his letters to the Consistory of Upsala. He found the conditions here much different than in Sweden. The people could not be prevailed upon here for church discipline and besides there was the general Anglinizing movement going then on among the non-English colonists, a movement in the evolution of nations against which an individual or group of individuals will be out of luck. Provost Sandin's struggle against the great odds however were not long, after having been in the country a little less than six months, he died on September 22, 1748, leaving a widow, m. n. Anna Margareta Sjoman, with a daughter and new-born baby to a strange land.

As the Finnish and the German congregations were hard pressed by the Moravians, some of the members of these congre-

gations worked for a union against these intruders. The Finnish
congregation of Wicaco had received as a member one Peter Kock,
a newly arrived Swedish adventurer, (not belonging to the Peter
Cock family of the early colonists, whose descendants were now
mostly known as Cox), who had engaged in business in Philadelphia. As the descendants of the old Finnish families, who had
built the church, were not taking much active interest in the church
affairs, on account of being Anglinized and not knowing the Swedish language, Mr. Kock became the real leader of the church
affairs. He supported and worked for the union of these old
churches of the Finns and of the German Lutherans, but Pastor
Naesman of Wicaco was against this plan for the reason that
these old Finnish churches had valuable properties in church
buildings and lands, while the German congregations still were
poor. But Mr. Kock, who had large business interests among the
Germans, insisted upon union and finally tried to get Pastor
Naesman out of the way, by writing against him to the Consistory
of Upsala requesting his recall and offering to pay the travelling
expenses of a new minister. On the other hand he tried to force
Mr. Naesman to quit, by holding the rents that came from the
lots owned by the church, that were to pay the salary of the
minister. Mr. Naesman however managed to make his living
by preaching in the outlying settlements.

The Consistory of Upsala, not being able to notice that the
real fault of the troubles was that the Swedish ministers had
grown out of date in America, sent two new ministers for the
Finnish congregations on the Delaware. These were the Rev.
Israel Acrelius and the Rev. Erik Unander, who arrived to Philadelphia on November 6, 1749, bringing a letter from the Consistory of Upsala to Pastor Naesman advising him to prepare for
his return to Sweden, as another minister, to replace him, was
only detained in Sweden on account of falling sick when the other
ministers departed. This was a disappointment to Pastor Naesman,
as he had thought that things would be alright now as his opponent Mr. Kock had lately died.

Pastor Acrelius who had been appointed as provost of the

Swedish ministers in America, likewise brought a recall to Sweden for Pastor Tranberg of Christina, who after Provost Sandin's death had written to the consistory of Upsala, desiring to be promoted to the office of provost, but which did not materialize for he was suspected of Moravian sympathies. Pastor Tranberg did not however live to be disappointed, for he died on a visit to his old congregation in Pennsneck, on November 8, 1748, and his remains were interred beneath the great aisle in the Trinity Church at Wilmington.

The Moravians had made a considerable progress among the Finns in New Jersey. At Raccoon their meetings were held in private houses, but in Piles Grove they built a church of their own, which was dedicated by the Moravian Bishop Spangenberg and the Rev. Lars Nyberg in 1749. The Finnish church at Pennsneck was very much theirs since the death of Pastor Sandin, while at Maurice River they had a meeting house, which was dedicated on December 18, 1746. Meetings were also held at Great and Little Egg Harbor.

The first burial in the Moravian graveyard at Piles Grove church was that of Molly Holstein, wife of Lars Holstein, who died on November 20, 1748, nine days after the birth of a child Mary.

Among the prominent families of the old Finnish colonists, that belonged to the Moravian congregations in New Jersey, were the Holsteins (original name Halttunen, changed to Haltun, Holton and Holstein), the Mullicas, first settlers and founders of the town of Mullica Hill, New Jersey, (original name Mullikka), the Locks, descendants of the Rev. Laurentius Carolus Lokenius, the Rambos, descendants of Peter Rambo, the first emigrant to America from Finland, the Kyns, (original name Yrjana Kyy, changed to Jurriaen Kyyn, Kyn and Keen) and the Senecksens (original name Sinikka).

After the death of the Rev. Sandin in August 1748, and Pastor Tranberg in November of the same year, the Finnish churches had only one Swedish minister, the Rev. Naesman, and his standing badly shaken by the machinations of the Swedish merchant Kock. Fortunately there arrived on September 15, 1748, to Philadelphia Mr. Peter Kalm, Professor of Economics at the University of Turku, Finland. Professor Kalm came to America to discover plants that might be cultivated in the northern countries of Europe. Being a minister's son from the northern Finland and himself an ordained Lutheran Minister, Mr. Kalm used his time in the winter of 1748-49 to preach in the Raccoon church on Sundays. He remained in America until February 16, 1751, during which time he made a systematic study of the vegetation of Pennsylvania, New Jersey, New York and Eastern Canada, and the flora of Sweden and Finland became much enriched by the seeds and plants that Professor Kalm took with him or shipped before his return. During his stay here, Kalm married the widow of Provost Sandin in Raccoon, in February 1750.

Professor Kalm, on his return to Finland, commenced to write an account of his observations during his journey to and in America. This was done in the manner of a diary, and three volumes of it became published between the years of 1753-61, containing observations made until October 2, 1749. It was his plan to continue the work in three more volumes, but he developed some eye trouble and his time was much occupied in the University and in the endeavor to make the American plants successful in his experimenting grounds, besides he had taken up the ministerial duties of a parish near the town of Turku and had the ambition to become a bishop. It was only in 1778, that Kalm was ready with his fourth volume, but in the meantime his publisher in Stockholm, Sweden, had died and the business discontinued, and although Kalm's first volumes, which were written in Swedish, had been translated and published in several languages, he could not find a Swedish publisher, who would have taken up to continue the publication of his work. While negotiations were going on to publish them in the German language in Germany, Kalm died on November 2, 1779, and the rest of his work never became published. The manuscripts became lost, which is regrettable as the published part of his work is the best source in existence for information about manners, customs, social conditions and about the life in general at that period in America. Kalm's manuscripts became the property of the University of Turku in 1826, and it is believed that the manuscripts for the unpublished part of his American travel were destroyed in 1827, when the city of Turku was devastated by fire and with it went into ashes most part of the library and archives of the ancient university. Fortunately Kalm's diary, which had served as the foundation for the printed volumes, and little further, has found its way to the library of the University of Helsingfors. This embraces the time up to January 12, 1750.

A number of books, of which some are the only copies in existence, printed by William Bradford, Benjamin Franklin and Reinier Jansen, collected by Professor Kalm during his visit in America, are today found in the library of the Helsingfors University.

If Kalm, as being a naturalist, had given himself scientific names to the great number of new types of plants and animals that he discovered in Northern Europe and America, instead of modestly leaving it to be done by Carl Linné of Sweden, his name would be known today among the great naturalists of the time. However his name is immortalized by the scientific name Kalmia latifolia of the beautifully blooming Mountain-laurel, that is the chiefest adornment of the forests in America in which Kalm spent two years and a half in studying. This name was the contribution of Linné.

As the Rev. Eric Unander arrived to Philadelphia on November 6, 1749, to become the minister for the Finnish churches of Raccoon and Pennsneck, the services of Mr. Kalm were no longer required there. Mr. Unander also preached for the Finns at Maurice River and on the Timber Creek, during week-days. In June 1751, there arrived another minister, John Abraham Lidenius, to be assistant minister with the New Jersey congregations. Mr. Lidenius was a native of Raccoon, who was taken to Sweden in 1725 with his parents, the Rev. Abraham Lidenius and Maria, daughter of Van Naeman. He alternated with Unander in preaching in the settlements on the east side of the Delaware River, and also went to preach for the Finns in Morlatton at Manatawny. In November 1752, Mr. Lidenius by the desire of the people of Morlatton went to reside with them and in the following month became married there, to the daughter of the village tailor Ringberg. The Finnish church in Morlatton had been served for few years before this by the German Baron Muhlenberg, who was the minister of the German congregation of Falkner Swamp.

The Rev. Olof Parlin who was commissioned by the Consistory of Upsala, together with Acrelius and Unander, on May 29, 1749, for a mission to America, had recovered from his intermittent fever to which he fell at the time that his partners departed for the journey, and arrived to Philadelphia on July 7, 1750. Mr. Parlin replaced the Rev. Naesman in the Wicaco parish, whom the congregation provided with twenty pounds for traveling expenses, besides paying the balance of his salary which amounted to ninety-six pounds and thirteen shillings. But Mr. Naesman did not hurry back to Sweden however, it was only in November 1751, when he left Philadelphia for the West Indies, leaving his wife Margaretta Rambo and a little son David behind him. In the islands of Antigua and St. Eustasia, he was trying his luck in business and also was tutoring and preaching to the new German colonists, finally reaching Amsterdam, Holland, from where he wrote to the Consistory of Upsala informing of his want of means to reach home and likewise had his wife and baby in America. In the meantime letters of the new Swedish ministers in America had made the Consistory aware that Mr. Naesman was not so much to be blamed but the fault was in the people. (The real fault being that but few of the Finnish descendants understood the Swedish language and their parents having been born on the Delaware River, they felt themselves Americans.) The Swedish government therefore provided for Mr. Naesman one thousand five hundred daler in copper coin and an equal sum was deposited in London for his wife and child. While in the uncertainty in waiting his reply from Sweden, Mr. Naesman interested himself in the science of medicine. And after having spent three months in Paris, France, specializing in the department of midwifery, he intended to return to Pennsylvania as a physician, but as he was looking for passage over the ocean in Rouen, a letter from the Archbishop of Sweden was delivered to him, informing that money for his home journey was already in Amsterdam and likewise for his family in London. Mr. Naesman therefore changed his plans and returned to Sweden, where he received one thousand two hundred daler in copper per year for five years, nearly corresponding to the time that he had left his congregation, besides the title of Professor was bestowed upon him, which is the greatest honor in the line of learning in Sweden, furthermore he was appointed to the first class parish of Christianstad.

The Finnish congregations on the Delaware, now had four Swedish ministers, and new spirit had been introduced to the churches. The Moravian movement among the Finns had subsided, the Rev. Nyberg had disappeared from the scene and although the Rev. Bryzelius appear in the Moravian churches at Piles Grove and Maurice River, his spirit is broken. The Rev. Nyberg finally appears in Sweden, regretful and pardoned.

The management of the Wicaco church property was permanently settled upon twelve trustees, who were to elect twelve new trustees in their place from the members of the congregation, after only five of the first twelve survived and the same proceeding was to continue. Two of the trustees were to be annually elected as administrators, who should collect the rent and give an account of the same to the vestry of the congregation. The yearly rents at this time amounted to fifty pounds. A contribution was taken up in the Wicaco congregation and the roof, windows and organ of the church were repaired, also the churchyard and parsonage grounds were fenced in. At the Wilmington church the hymnbooks were rebound, the church was emptied from birds' nests from the inside, the walls and ceiling were whitewashed, the pulpit and chancel around the altar polished, the altar provided with linen, which all had been neglected in late years, and the women of the congregation came together and scoured the floor and pews of the church. New windows also were made to the church and the roof was repaired. The congregation collected fifteen pounds to buy a horse as a gift to their new minister Acrelius. Furthermore, a new parsonage was built in Wilmington, of brick, three stories high, with two rooms upon each floor, while the old parson house was converted into an outbuilding and stable for the new one. The accounts of the management of the church property in Wilmington were audited when a deficiency of about fifty pounds was found and the management rearranged on more equitable basis. The income from money and lots owned by the church at this period exceeded fifty pounds. Besides his salary and extra income the minister had been for his use provided with a considerable area of garden, grain field, forest and meadow land.

In Raccoon the parsonage was repaired and several rooms added to it. The garden was fenced in, and a fine vegetable garden made in front of the house, also a barn was built for the use of the minister. The farm belonging to the parsonage was well fenced, the fields manured and increased by new clearings. The meadow was ditched and cleared up, increasing it to many loads of hay.

But despite all the good will of the Finnish descendants to preserve their forefathers' religion and the edifices of worship built by their ancestors, all went to ruin for the selfish desire of the authorities in Sweden to propagate and preserve the Swedish language in America. The third article of the instructions given by the Consistory of Upsala to Provost Acrelius, to be followed by the Swedish ministers, orders that all teaching in the schools must be done in the Swedish language. At this period the Finns had nearly forgotten the Swedish language, they apologized to Provost Acrelius that they did not understand Swedish, although they did like to. Therefore, while the Wilmington congregation had in 1753 and 1754 as many as 516 members, only 68 of these were communicants. The Philadelphia congregation had 430 members and only 21 communicants. The Raccoon and Pennsneck congregations had 450 members and proportionately little communicants. The people, although they remained as members in their forefathers' churches, went to the English churches for not understanding the Swedish language. The parents likewise sent their children to the English schools to learn a language that was not only useful but necessary for any advancement in the country, where it now was the universal language.

The Rev. John Lidenius of Morlatton, who was a native of the Delaware River settlement, better understood the psychology of the natives, and preached and taught school in the English language, wherefore he was warned in brotherly way of it by Provost Acrelius, and when it did not change his attitude, although he was likewise persuaded to retract by the German ministers, who also were engaged in the hopeless task of fighting the Anglinizing movement among their congregations. The Provost wrote on October 31, 1754, to the Consistory of Upsala, requesting the suspension of the Rev. Lidenius from the Swedish ministerial office. Mr. Lidenius now started to think of the consequences at his probable return to Sweden, he would not have any hope of receiving a minister's office there, in a country where it was so highly valued. He therefore left Morlatton in the spring of 1755, and settled at Amasland, where he preached on three Sundays a month and the rest of the time in Marcus Hook and other places. Mr. Lidenius was welcomed to the society of his ministerial brethren and on May 23, 1755, Provost Acrelius wrote to the Consistory of Upsala, recommending pardon for Lidenius.

But all these had exactly the results against which the Swedish ministers were so eagerly fighting. For the futile efforts of the Swedish government to maintain the Swedish language among the Finns in America, the Finnish descendants even lost their forefathers' religion. The Finnish congregation in Morlatton, together with few English families in Reading, Pennsylvania, agreed to call an English minister for themselves and subscribed to pay to the minister sixty pounds in yearly salary. In 1760, they wrote to London, England, for the Society of Propagation of the Gospel in Foreign Parts, desiring a missionary of the church of England, and proposing to the office Joseph Mathers, who was born in Pennsylvania. An English Episcopal minister Alexander Murray was soon sent for them, and on April 9, 1763, he writes to London about the conditions in his parish. There were then thirty-six families in Morlatton, consisting of 232 souls, whereof 65 were under seven years of age. Most all the people were Finns, of which in 1760 twenty-seven could understand Swedish.

On June 17, 1765, the church wardens and vestrymen of the "Episcopal Congregation at Morlatton, in the County of Berks," wrote to the Society of Propagation of the Gospel in Foreign Parts, at London, "That your petitioners do most heartily concur with their Brethren at Reading in presenting their humble and grateful acknowledgments for the benefit of the Mission appointed them and are sincerely desirous to pursue every measure that may conduce to its establishment, and as they are allowed sixty pounds out of the profit of a lottery for repairing their church, they have engaged to raise one hundred pounds more for forwarding that necessary work and which must cost them considerable more before it is completed. But as it will accommodate themselves so they hope it will also encourage others to unite with them and enable them soon after to provide a glebe and parsonage and a better maintenance for their worthy missionary," etc.

The position of the Swedish missionaries in America was not to be envied at this period. They were fighting against the birth of a new nation that nature had destined to evolve out of different sections of humanity, therefore they were men of hard luck and their letters to the Consistory of Upsala and their annals are full of doleful complaints. The Rev. Acrelius writes about the "downward slide" of his flock that : "Formerly the church people could come some Swedish miles on foot to church; now the young as well as the old, must be upon horseback. Then many a good and honest man rode upon a piece of bear skin; now scarcely any saddle is valued unless it has a saddle-cloth with galloon and fringe. Then servants and girls were seen in church barefooted; now young people will be like persons of quality in their dress; servants are seen with wigs of hair, and the like; girls with hooped skirts, fine-stuff shoes, and other finery. Then respectable families lived in low log-houses, where the chimney was made of sticks covered with clay, now they erect painted houses of stone and brick in the country. Then they used ale and brandy, now wine and punch. Then they lived upon grits and mush, now upon tea, coffee, and chocolate."

In another connection, Pastor Acrelius shows himself to be very fond of luxurious cooking and a great admirer of the noblest of wines. He also wore a wig, which he is said to have placed upon the pulpit while preaching. Where he got these privileges, he fails to explain.

Another minister, the Rev. Erik Nordenlind, who arrived to the country in September 1756, before having been two months in the country wrote the first one of his eight petitions to the Consistory of Upsala asking to be recalled home.

Provost Acrelius left for Sweden on November 9, 1756, after having petitioned to be released three years earlier. The Rev. Parlin of the Wicaco congregation died on December 22, 1757, Mr. Nordenlind continuing with that congregation. The Rev. Unander of the parish of Raccoon and Pennsneck, who had petitioned his archbishop to be permitted to return to Sweden with Mr. Acrelius, was appointed to take the latter's place in the parish of Wilmington, while Mr. Lidenius of Amasland was appointed to the parish of Raccoon and Pennsneck.

Once more the Swedish authorities made a grand assault for the maintenance of the Swedish language in America. On June 12, 1758, the Rev. Doctor Carl Magnus Wrangel, and the Rev. Andreas Borell, were commissioned to go to America, Dr. Wrangel, who was one of the Swedish branch of nobility, of the illustrious Esthonian family of Wrangels, was to be the provost of the Swedish ministers, and his commission for the maintenance of the Swedish language was as drastic as ever. The fifth article of his commission reads:

"For keeping the Swedish language in power, the ministers must take all imaginable care, and not without absolute necessity in their transactions depart of it, less to let their audience occasion to think indifferently and equally unbiased way thereof, if they desire in the future teachers from Sweden. To this end they must also keep the Swedish books in busy and active use, and when the ministers visit in the houses of the members of their congregation, they shall instruct how the Swedish books should be used. And when the old people of the family die, the ministers must ask for the Swedish books found in the family, and not to allow them to come to another hands, but those who use them; otherwise to take them away, and allow no books sold, exchanged, given away, or disposed in any manner whatever, but to the true purpose of the mission."

The authorities in Sweden must have had a wrong illusion of the chances of the Swedish language in America. The Morlatton congregation had already fallen off from the reach of the Swedish missionaries, who at this time were sent uninvited to this country. In the congregations of Philadelphia and Wilmington, there were only a handful of Swedish speaking families of newly arrived Swedes, who had been coming in with the ministers. These had not been able to support missionaries, but the Finns who had built the church had provided the same with lands of which incomes now were derived. In Philadelphia the income from the lands handsomely paid the salary of the minister and the maintenance of the church, while in Wilmington the income was larger at this period than could be well used for these purposes, therefore the Swedish missionaries in these congregations could afford to preach in Swedish for the empty churches. The descendants of the Finns, although still interested in the churches of their forefathers, went to the English churches where they could understand the sermons. In the Finnish churches of New Jersey and especially at Raccoon, the position was somewhat different. There the Finns had not had the opportunity to send their children to English schools, but had their children taught to read by the Swedish schoolmasters, that were brought in by the missionaries. Therefore the Finns in New Jersey retained some understanding in the Swedish language longer than those in Pennsylvania and in the present state of Delaware. The New Jersey parishes were not however so desirable to the Swedish missionaries as were those of Philadelphia and Wilmington, for the reason that the salaries in the former parishes were paid by contribution, as the church lands there did not produce much income as yet. Besides this, the salaries there were liable to be small, as the Finns there, although not numerous, had four churches, a Lutheran church in Raccoon and another in Pennsneck, and a Moravian church in Piles Grove and another at Maurice River.

The Moravian church at Maurice River later was used by the Lutheran congregation, after Paul Bryzelius, the Moravian propagator had finally left the place for having become converted and forgiven, and embraced in the flock of the "right minded shepherds."

The new missionaries, Wrangel and Borell, arrived to Philadelphia in the beginning of April 1759, where Wrangel delivered his installation sermon on the 15th of that month. The Rev. Nordenlind, who had been preaching in the Wicaco church since the death of Parlin in December 1757, was commissioned for the Raccoon and Pennsneck congregations, in place of Lidenius who received his commission for the Wilmington parish. And Unander of Wilmington was recalled to Sweden. However all these arrangements could not be carried on, as the New Jersey congregations did not want Nordenlind, who seemed to have fallen too much away from the holy spirit to the country's distilled spirits. Lidenius was satisfied to remain in Raccoon, for his poverty, to escape moving expenses and because he was liked by the people there, although complaints are made about his great love of liquors. And the Rev. Unander could not immediately start to Sweden on account of his debts. A letter of Dr. Wrangel to the Archbishop of Sweden, on October 13, 1760, partly explains the cause of the poverty of these three ministers. He says: "I am ashamed to mention that the strong drinks of this country have been the greatest ruin for a part of our ministers, who however both here and in the fatherland do not shame to complain for poverty, although their consciousness tells them that a saving in this had freed them from such load."

Dr. Wrangel undoubtedly was right, as at the time Nordenlind was minister in the Wicaco church, the extra incomes, besides regular salary, the use of parsonage and the use of land, according to the Rev. Unander, were 2000 Swedish copper daler. This income came especially from marriages, as the English peoples of Philadelphia had acquired the habit of getting their marriages solemnized in the old Finns' church of Wicaco. Yet poverty seemed to have been the second name of Nordenlind in his letters to the authorities in Sweden.

On June 1, 1759, the Swedish ministers sent a petition to the Consistory of Upsala for Nordenlind, who desired his recall. Upon this, it was sent to him from Sweden on October 10, 1760, but before this Nordenlind was no more. On a visit to the parsonage of Raccoon he fell sick and died on September 30, 1760. His remains were interred in the Wilmington church two days later.

The relations of Dr. Wrangel and the Rev. Unander were not very cordial, as the latter was disappointed of not having been commissioned for the office of Provost, and therefore tried to make every hindrance to Dr. Wrangel. However, for the economic situation of Unander, Dr. Wrangel in conjunction of the other ministers, sent a petition on June 1, 1759, to the Consistory of Upsala, requesting that Unander might stay some time in his parish, although he had been recalled to Sweden.

At this time, the Wilmington congregation was threatened by a loss of some property. In 1749, the church land property was left to two trustees, who were to handle the land as their own, as the English laws forbid a church to own land for its maintenance. One of the trustees, Anders Tranberg, son of the former Pastor Tranberg, died in January 1759, and had one thousand and two hundred pounds of the congregation's money in his care. The congregation could not sue for this in the court and there were some difficulties to get it out. To prevent this in the future, a new charter was drafted to replace the old charter of the year 1699. In the new charter, which was accepted by the government on October 27, 1759, it was provided that the church property was to be left to the care of nine commissioners, who together with the minister were to elect two trustees, to manage together with the minister the property of the congregation.

In case some of the commissioners die, the congregation was to elect a new man in his place.

The relations between Wrangel and Unander grew worse with time, and the former desired the latter's return to Sweden, according to his recall. Finally it went so far that Provost Wrangel appeared in the Wilmington church and notified the congregation of pastor Unander's recall to Sweden, besides making some accusations against the minister, which led to a scene and verbal encounter between the two ministers. Pastor Unander however left the country in the last days of July 1760, and Anders Borell became the minister of the Wilmington parish.

According to the desire of the congregations of Raccoon and Pennsneck, Lidenius stayed there, and the ministers in their letter of June 1, 1759, petitioned the Consistory of Upsala for the acceptance of this arrangement. Soon after the home journey of Unander and the death of Nordenlind, the New Jersey congregations began however to get in trouble for their favorite son. The Rev. Lidenius, for his over mediation with the distilled spirits, could not keep himself out of debts. To pay his creditors, the congregation allowed him to sell from the forest of the church, fifty cords of wood in 1760. Besides the congregation often waited in vain in the church as no minister came to preach. And worse than that, the pastor was imprisoned by the authorities for denouncing God. The affair came in conclusion when Lidenius in the spring of 1761, was committed to the debtors' prison by his creditors. The congregation paid his debts, amounting to two hundred pounds, to get him out of prison, but refused him as their minister any longer. The other Swedish ministers therefore petitioned on August 21, 1761, the Consistory of Upsala for the recall of Lidenius. The people of the congregation had however great hearts and once more Lidenius was given a chance to come back,—but this he could not do. Dr. Wrangel and others accuse his wife for his downfall.

At this time the Herrnhuters sent the Rev. Paul Bryzelius to the Finnish settlements of Western New Jersey, to take advantage of the conditions there. Here he met Dr. Wrangel, who converted him back to the Lutheran Church, in the autumn of 1760. At the German ministers' council, on October 20, 1760, Bryzelius departed from the Moravian Brotherhood to which he had belonged twenty years, and became taken to the Lutheran ministry. At first he preached for the Finns in Morlatton, until he could be given a position in some of the German churches. In 1761 he was installed in a German congregation in New Jersey. He was then over seventy years of age, had a wife and six children, and was in poor circumstances. Later he became English minister, as "chief chaplain" of Nova Scotia Squadron.

As a result of the request for the recall of Lidenius there arrived on May 3, 1762, to Philadelphia the Rev. Johan Wicksell, bringing from the consistory of Upsala the desired recall. Consequently Lidenius started to prepare for the journey, and delivered his farewell sermons in the various churches in New Jersey and in Wilmington during the month of August and September, while Pastor Wicksell was installed to the New Jersey congregations on July 11, 1762. The fathers of the Consistory of Upsala had been prudent so far as to send the traveling money of thirty pounds to the hands of Dr. Wrangel, to be delivered to Lidenius as soon as he was ready for the journey. But they were not far-sighted enough to buy a ticket with the money, as the journey of Mr. Lidenius ended in the nearest place to satisfy the old craving. On May 12, 1763, Lidenius finally was presented with a letter of expulsion from the ministry by Dr. Wrangel, on power given to him by the Consistory of Upsala, in case Lidenius would not obey his recall.

Hereafter Lidenius never again preached in the Churches, but did some preaching in the homes of the members of his old congregations, and acted as teacher of the school at Rapapu, which he is credited of having done well. In the winter of 1768, Lidenius died in poverty and forgotten. His body was buried in the yard of the house where he lived, but still it was his native soil. What is a golden casket and a tomb of splendor in a foreign land compared to one's native earth.

The Rev. Wicksell preached first time in Raccoon on July

18, 1762, and in Pennsneck on July 25th. The wooden churches had grown old, that of Raccoon was almost beyond repair. The windows of the Pennsneck church were broken and the parish house was in bad shape. In the autumn of 1762 the roof of the Pennsneck church was repaired and the other repairings completed during the following year.

Before the arrival of Wicksell, it had been contemplated to build a town about the Raccoon church, by which income could be derived from the church land. The idea was carried in effect in 1765, when a charter for the town of Sveaborg (after the fortress in the harbor of Helsingfors, Finland) was obtained from the governor of New Jersey. The church land was divided into lots and after a few years about ten houses had been built in the new town. The Raccoon congregation built a new parish house in the town, which was ready on March 14, 1765, when Pastor Wicksell moved in, after having rented the old parish house and glebe for twenty pounds a year. The new parish house in Sveaborg was built of pine logs, two stories high, with three rooms on each floor. A stable also belonged to it and a garden of three acres, with one hundred and fifty fruit trees. Besides these, five acres of marsh was improved to pasture land and six acres on the Raccoon Creek, about three miles below the town, were reclaimed by a dike of six feet in height, for the use of the minister.

A new charter for the Raccoon church, to protect the property of the church, was obtained on October 1, 1765, from Governor William Franklin of New Jersey. By this the management of the church affairs were invested upon the minister, two church wardens and upon six or more vestrymen, however not to exceed eleven persons altogether.

At the Maurice River were living some twenty or thirty Finnish families, of which many still understood Swedish. During the time they were embracing the Moravian teaching, they had built a wooden church. Pastor Wicksell preached in the church once a month, on a week-day. When Wicksell returned to Sweden the Finns of Maurice River desired their own minister, for which purpose they had subscribed a salary of between eighty and one hundred pounds. A member of the congregation promised 200 acres of land for parsonage and five acres for the church, church yard and school. However the Revolutionary War cut off all connections with Sweden and nothing came about it.

At Egg Harbor were living about thirty Finnish families, scattered in a large area. Only seldom had any of the Swedish ministers visited there, when Dr. Wrangel visited them in 1764, they had not seen a Swedish minister in twenty years. Of the people there, it is said, that they were not much interested in the minister's visit and "listened to violin rather than a sermon." Dancing and drinking was much in vogue there and the people lived like pagans, says Wrangel. He found there however a family whose all members gathered in a family worship every Sunday. Dr. Wrangel therefore decided to deliver few revival sermons there and says of having plaid great havoc thereby among the people.

The position of the Swedish ministers in America was becoming more and more difficult. Although in the year of 1760, the Finnish congregations had about 3000 members, among these were few who understood Swedish. The reason of these peoples forgetting the Swedish language so soon, despite all the efforts of the Swedish ministers, was that they were not Swedish by their mother tongue, but Finnish. The early Finnish colonists never had become fully acquainted with the Swedish language, as they used the Finnish in their homes, although Swedish was used in communications between the Finns and the Dutch. Practically the only Swedes in the colony were few families of newly arrived adventurers, schoolmasters that had been brought to America by the missionaries and the families of some Swedish ministers, who died here. The Rev. Unander who was in America in 1749-1760, says that he never saw in any Swedish service here more than fifty people and sometimes not more than twelve, it also happened that not one came to the service. However when English was preached, the services were well attended. In 1767, the English services in the Wilmington church were attended, according to the report of the minister of the time, by 200 to 400 persons.

When the Wicaco congregation on January 2, 1758, in a letter notified the Consistory of Upsala of the death of their minister the Rev. Parlin, they expressed their desire that the new minister should be able to hold services in English. To this the consistory replied that: "As the provost and the ministers have and always have had instructions to conduct all their official business not only after Swedish usages but also in the Swedish language, so the Consistory cannot make any changes in it. Furthermore it is required by necessity that if the American Congregations will look towards Sweden and enjoy the care of the Swedish kings, as heretofore it should be their duty to preserve the Swedish language so that their members, the young and old, the masters, children and servants will obtain their knowledge in Christianity in Swedish and in the same language conduct both their private and common worship."

On the arrival of Dr. Wrangel to America in the Spring of 1759, he immediately saw that the instructions given to him by the Consistory of Upsala, in regard to the Swedish language, could not be carried on as strictly as ordered. The Swedish ministers already had been compelled to use English in their transactions with the members of their congregations and also more or less in the church services, during the last fifty years. In the Wicaco congregation a number of the descendants of the Finns in Kingsessing, who did not understand Swedish sermons, were now contemplating the building of another church, where they would not be bothered with the Swedish language.

The lack of knowledge in English forced the Swedish ministers to act within their instructions on their arrival, but after having preached little more than two months, Dr. Wrangel saw the impossibility and wrote to his Consistory in Sweden, that not one-fourth of the members of his congregation understood Swedish sermons. As Dr. Wrangel was a linguist, it was easy to him to acquire the English so far as to read his sermons in that language and the rest of the services were conducted according to and by the use of the church books of the English Episcopal Church, as the Lutheran Church literature were not then found in the English language. On November 3, 1759, Dr. Wrangel wrote to the Consistory of Upsala that: "A minister, who will satisfy his conscience, cannot possibly altogether deny of preaching in English."

The leaders of the Anglican church did not either remain idle, the Finnish descendants were induced to their Church in Chester, by electing them to the offices of their church. Likewise, as the Episcopalian liturgy was followed by the Swedish ministers in their English services, the Lutherans did not see any difference between these two churches. The lack of Lutheran Church literature in the English language and the propagation of the Swedish language in America, were the causes that drove the descendants of the early Finnish colonists on the Delaware away forever from their forefathers' religion.

On August 3, 1761, the Swedish ministers had a meeting in Wicaco, at which the Finnish descendants, members of the Wicaco congregation, who lived in Kingsessing and in that neighborhood, notified the ministers of their decision to build a church in Kingsessing at their own cost, where the services will be held only in the English language. This was done to hold on to the Lutheran religion and to prevent misunderstanding, they desired the Swedish ministers to inform the Swedish Consistory accordingly.

In notifying about this to his superiors in Sweden, Dr. Wrangel begs the Consistory to use its influence before the king, that the new ministers might be prepared to endeavor by the use of English language to hold the people in their forefathers' religion.

In the Wilmington congregation, the conditions were the same as in Wicaco. The southern wall of the church having given out eighteen inches on account of the weight of the roof and a vestibule, thirty feet wide with walls five feet thick, was necessary to support the falling wall. This work involved a greater expense than one-fourth of the income from the church land property reached and therefore a tax had to be levied upon the members. But the vast majority of the members not understanding the Swedish language and therefore having no profit of the services in the church, refused to contribute unless English is used in the church. The Rev. Borell therefore had to ascend to hold English services every other Sunday, against his instructions from Sweden, and in a letter in September 1762, acceptance for this was requested from the Consistory of Upsala, but the letter became lost on the way.

At the old Finns' Point, now known as Pennsneck, none of the Finnish descendants any longer could understand Swedish and refused any expense unless English is preached in their church, to which the Rev. Wicksell did not see any other way but to accede. Only in Raccoon, where the Finnish children were continuously taught by Swedish schoolmasters, many of the people still could understand a Swedish sermon.

To the petitions for English sermons, the Consistory of Upsala reluctantly consented that it may happen in certain time and places, however adding that the Swedish language must be by all possible ways maintained.

After having won the confidence of his congregation, by preaching in English, Dr. Wrangel found the necessity of reorganizing the English school of the Finns in Kingsessing. For the request of the congregation, he drafted instructions for the schoolmaster. These provided that the schoolmaster must be Lutheran in religion and be well learned in the reading and writing of the English language. The instructions are dated November 27, 1761.

In Kingsessing Dr. Wrangel preached during the summer time in a shed and during the winter in the schoolhouse and in the house of an Englishman Coultas, who had got the benches and the pulpit for that purpose. So great was the interest for the new church that four hundred pounds was soon subscribed for its building. On August 2, 1762, Dr. Wrangel laid the corner stone of the Kingsessing church. The members of the congregation made the work themselves, often there were one hnudred men on the job. The Englishman Coultas, who had joined the congregation and had contributed forty pounds to the building fund, was invested with the supervison of the work. In 1763, the church was ready and was dedicated by Dr. Wrangel. It was called St.

James Church. The edifice was intended for an audience of 600 people, was sixty feet long, forty-five feet wide and had also a balcony.

Several new improvements have been added to the old church of Kingsessing. The church stands on Darby Road, between 68th and 69th Streets in Philadelphia. Kingsessing, the old Finnish town is today included in the city of Philadelphia.

About the time the Kingsessing church was built, another church was built by the Finns at Upper Matzong or Upper Merion. Dr. Wrangel used to preach there once a week during week days and few times a year on Sundays. For the additional work, the congregation agreed to pay twenty pounds for an assistant minister and Wrangel from his side agreed to give free board for the assistant, these arrangements were made in a minister's meeting on August 3, 1761, in Wicaco. Accordingly a minister was petitioned for, from Sweden and the king paid the traveling expenses of the first minister, with the hope that congregation afterwards could be able to provide for the same. As the result thereof Johan Haggblad was sent from Sweden as assistant minister for Wrangel.

The Upper Merion church was built in 1763, and was called Christ Church. It stands on the west bank of the Schuylkill, below Norristown and about sixteen miles from the Wicaco church. The first Finnish settlers in this region were Mats Holstein, (original name Halttunen and originating from Halttulapohja, Kankaanpaa, Finland), and Peter Rambo, (descendant of Peter Rambo and his wife Brita Mattson, both born in Vasa, Finland), with their families. Mats (Mathias) Holstein had one thousand acres of land in the neighborhood of what was formerly called Swede's Ford, after him.

The Rev. Johan Haggblad arrived to Philadelphia on September 20, 1763, as Dr. Wrangel's assistant. Wrangel gave him free board and allowed him half of the extra incomes and later pursuaded the congregation to allow sixty pounds yearly salary for Haggblad, that he might be able to board in the country.

In order to keep the Wicaco church and the newly built annex churches at Kingsessing and Upper Merion in the hands of the descendants of the people who built them, and in order to secure their Lutheran faith, these churches were united into a corporation. Although the incorporators were mostly Finns, there being besides Provost Wrangel presumably one Swede, Otto Nisellis, (Hesselius) the incorporated name of these churches was "United Swedish Lutheran Churches." A charter for these churches was granted by Governor John Penn, on September 25, 1765.

Dr. Wrangel also preached once a month for the Finns at Pennypack Creek, but the people being too few there to build a church of their own, they united with the English and German neighbors to an Episcopalian congregation in 1773.

The school at Kingsessing, having been built for sixty students, could not accommodate all applicants, therefore a new school was necessary. In a letter of November 5, 1763, to the Archbishop of Sweden, Dr. Wrangel tells of another new school, to be built when the church is ready, for which purpose eighty pounds already had been subscribed.

At this time Dr. Wrangel made propositions that students from among the congregations should be sent to Sweden to be prepared as Lutheran ministers for their relatives in America. Thus Wrangel had taken the steps that might have saved to the Finnish descendants their Lutheran religion, that their forefathers so zealously had guarded and had built churches and provided for their maintenance that their posterity might not find difficulty in their worship. Dr. Wrangel had common sense to see that the Swedish language at this period was the destructive force within the congregations, that its propagation drove the descendants of the original builders of the churches away and left only a handful of people, the families of few newly arrived adventurers from Sweden, who had not had part in the building of the churches or in providing their maintenance. For this Dr. Wrangel however drew the displeasure of the Consistory of Upsala upon himself, and became the scapegoat of everything that was not to the liking of his superiors in Sweden, or his fellow ministers here.

On May 29, 1763, Pastor Borell of Wilmington and Pastor Wicksell of Raccoon together sent a letter to the Consistory of Upsala, complaining against Dr. Wrangel, and requesting for his recall to Sweden. Besides all their displeasures towards Dr. Wrangel, they had a strong case against him. In December 29, 1762, arrived to America one Nils Hornell, a Lutheran minister from Sweden, who had escaped from the country, accused of murder. This man was accosted by Pastor Borell in Wilmington during five weeks, after which Borell furnished him with recommendations and a petition to Dr. Wrangel, that he should for the sake of Christian charity find some employment to the Rev. Hornell. This Borell did although having received a warning about Hornell from England. As no other employment was available, Dr. Wrangel allowed Hornell to deliver the Swedish sermons in the Wicaco church, and after the true character of Hornell became known, this was used by the other ministers against Provost Wrangel.

As the result of these complaints against Dr. Wrangel, the Consistory of Upsala on March 14, 1764, wrote to Wrangel, requesting him to petition for recall. In consequence hereof Dr. Wrangel received in June 1765, his recall and at the same time was notified that Pastor Borell had been appointed in his place. Dr. Wrangel knowing Pastor Borell's unfitness to the office of provost, decided to remain despite his recall and did not deliver the commission to Pastor Borell. The pastor had lost his confidence in his congregation by the habit of drunkeness and questionable mode of living, wherefore the services in the Wilmington church were no longer attended and the congregation desired to get rid of him. Of these Dr. Wrangel notified the Consistory of Upsala in his letter of October 1, 1765. This was followed by a letter of October 10, 1765, to the Consistory from the united congregations of Wicaco, Kingsessing and Upper Merion, who desired Dr. Wrangel to stay with them. Before any reply had yet arrived for the above letters, Pastor Borell's position had grown worse. On July 13, 1766, before the church council in Wicaco, Pastor Borell was accused by the widow of the Rev. Nordenlind, of things unbecoming to a minister of the church, wherefore the council declared that it would not accept Pastor Borell as their provost. In the meantime Dr. Wrangel had got additional force fighting against him. On September 20, 1763, arrived from Sweden, the Rev. Johan Haggblad, to be assistant for Wrangel. At the same time as Dr. Wrangel was recalled, he was instructed to install Pastor Haggblad as minister of Wicaco, Kingsessing and Upper Merion. Now Haggblad desired Wrangel's departure, that he might receive the office, but the congregations refused to accept him for his indifference and slowness to learn the English language, and in same letter in which the congregations desired to have Dr. Wrangel to stay here, they notified the Consistory of Upsala of their decision as to Pastor Haggblad. This was taken so hard by Haggblad that he fell sick and died on January 15, 1766. His remains were interred in the Wicaco church. All this made it more necessary to Dr. Wrangel to stay here.

The reply of the Consistory of Upsala to Dr. Wrangel, on April 30, 1766, was entirely different than one would have supposed. The Consistory was much displeased of Dr. Wrangel's stay here and upheld its former appointment of Pastor Borell as the provost. After this, Dr. Wrangel could not see other way but to return to Sweden and arranged for his passage. On Sunday, October 12, 1766, he notified his congregations of his leaving them and invited their vestries to a meeting in Wicaco on October 15th. In the meeting of the vestries, it became divulged that Pastor Borell was impossible, but they would not accept Pastor Wicksell of Raccoon either, for his blackmail work against Wrangel and for a scandal in which he had lately become involved in the German church at Cohanzie, where the Swedish ministers also used to preach, as some fifteen Finnish families were united with that church. The vestries wanted Dr. Wrangel to stay here and promised to stand with him for whatever follows. The vestries could not believe that their letter of October 10, 1765, had reached to the Consistory, as no reply had come. (The letter never arrived to the Consistory.) The schoolmaster, students and a large number of the members of the Wicaco congregation petitioned the vestries to pursuade Dr. Wrangel to stay in the country, therefore, after the rest of the members of the congregations had expressed their desire for the same, a new petition on behalf of Dr. Wrangel was sent to the Consistory of Upsala, by the united congregations of Wicaco, Kingsessing and Upper Merion, on November 12, 1766.

Before this, Dr. Baron Heinrich Muhlenberg, head of the German Lutheran Churches in America, had on September 1, 1766, written to the Archbishop of Sweden, in the name of the German ministers, on behalf of Dr. Wrangel. In this letter Dr. Muhlenberg says that Dr. Wrangel was the only Swedish minister here, fit for the mission and that Borell, Wicksell and Haggblad were the most fatal elements for the church.

That Dr. Wrangel really was devoted to his mission, can be judged of the fact that he was teaching the negro slaves in Christianity and says in his letter to the Archbishop of Sweden on October 13, 1760, of having baptized more than twenty of them.

All the petitions and circumstances in favor of Dr. Wrangel did not make any change in the attitude of the authorities in Sweden. They resented the building and chartering the churches without their authorization and maintained that their orders must be obeyed regardless of circumstances. Steps were taken in order to compel Dr. Wrangel to return to Sweden and Borell was upheld as provost. On April 6, 1767, the Consistory commissioned the Rev. Andres Goransson as minister for Wicaco, Kingsessing and Upper Merion and the Rev. Lars Girelius to be pastor extraordinary with the mission. These new ministers arrived to Philadelphia on October 1, 1767, but in the meeting of the vestries of Wicaco, Kingsessing and Upper Merion, soon after their arrival, there were expressions uttered, that if the congregations have addressed letters to the authorities in Sweden, this has been only out of courtesy and must not be abused and understood that the congregations are by no means bound to accept anybody that some Swedish king send to their neck. When Rev. Goransson told the vestries that he will discuss about it with his superior, Provost Borrell, he was informed that the Wicaco church was closed for Borell.

This situation of the affairs affected Goransson, who had insane tendencies, so much that upon the governor's order he had to be placed in the insane asylum, for being so violent that four men could not hold him. Provost Borell, who had been suffering some time for jaundice, died on April 4, 1768, and was interred on the following day in the Wilmington church. Pastor Goransson, who had now somewhat recovered, officiated at the burial. Among the papers of Pastor Borell were found a forged marriage certificate and other documents, indicating of a private life, unbecoming to a minister.

On May 9, 1768, the congregations of Wicaco, Kingsessing and Upper Merion had a meeting for electing members for their vestries. Pastors Goransson and Wicksell being present, were told that the former could not be accepted for his sickness and in regard to the latter, only his permission from the king of England saved him of being handled as disturber of the privileges that were theirs as subjects of the English crown. At this meeting, Dr. Wrangel declared his intention to depart for Sweden, upon which the Rev. Goransson presented a written request for a final answer of the vestries in regard of him being accepted as minister. The answer was "no," and he was offered a free ticket to Sweden.

The Swedish ministers, opposed to Dr. Wrangel, had from the Consistory of Upsala a warrant for legal steps and to petition the Governor of Pennsylvania for the forcible expulsion of Wrangel. These proceedings were not needed however, as Dr. Wrangel, in the beginning of September 1768, left for Sweden, where he was questioned before the Consistory during four days at his arrival. On August 20, 1771, Dr. Wrangel became appointed to the office of chief chaplain of the royal court.

After the departure of Dr. Wrangel from America, the congregations of Wicaco, Kingsessing and Upper Merion would not accept the Rev. Goransson as their minister. The Consistory of Upsala wrote therefore on May 19, 1769, to Proprietary Penn and to his nephew John Penn, Lieutenant-Governor of Pennsylvania, for their interference in the matter.

On May 12, 1770, arrived to Philadelphia the Rev. Nils Collin, as pastor extraordinary, whom the above mentioned congregations invited to be their minister. Some prevailing however probably had taken place from the side of the Proprietary, as soon after the arrival of Collin, the parsonage of Wicaco was opened to Goransson and on July 12, 1770, the vestry voted him a yearly salary of one hundred and twenty pounds. However when the matter was presented for the approval of the congregations, there were utterances that no king or any Consistory of Upsala has right to impose upon them a minister that they do not want.

According to commissions brought from Sweden by Collin, Wicksell of Raccoon became vice-provost and Girelius became the minister of Wilmington church. At this time the Wilmington church was whitewashed and decorated also a stove for heating was installed. From London was brought a new bell, but as the old belfry was found to be inadequate, a new tower was built on the western end of the church. A communion set of silver also was obtained for the church.

The Rev. Collin originally was commissioned to assist Vice-Provost Wicksell in Raccoon and Pennsneck, and held his installation sermon in the Raccoon church on June 3, 1770.

On September 1, 1773, arrived to Philadelphia another Swedish clergyman, the Rev. Carl Johan Luut, as pastor extraordinary. He brought to Vice-Provost Wicksell his already in 1768 desired recall, Goransson was to be the provost and Collin was commissioned as minister at Raccoon and Pennsneck. Other changes soon took place, when on September 22, 1775, king Gustavus III. of Sweden signed the recall of Girelius and Goransson on their earlier request.

In the year of 1771, Daniel Kuhn, a descendant of the early colonists, went to Sweden to study theology in the University of Upsala, upon the long since introduced proposition that the native Americans are best suited to be ministers for the American Lutheran congregations. In September 1775, after having become an ordained Lutheran minister, the Rev. Kuhn wrote to the king of Sweden petitioning for appointment for the American congregations, after having been previously recommended by Dr. Wrangel and by the congregations of Wicaco, Kingsessing and Upper Merion. Kuhn's case had previously caused much discussion in Sweden, the Swedish clergy in America were afraid that a native American would stay in his position and therefore be on the way of the Swedish ministers. Also it was feared that an American born would pay little attention to the orders of the Swedish Consistory and would care little about Swedish commissions once he had got into the congregations. The Consistory of Upsala therefore did not find it advisable to use native Americans for the mission. And the decision of the king on May 3, 1775, was that only native Swedes would be used for the mission. However exception was made in the case of Kuhn, as on September 22, 1775, he received commission as minister for the Wilmington congregation. On the same day the Rev. Mathias Hultgren was commissioned to follow Kuhn to America as pastor extraordinary, and the Rev. Luut, who already was in America, was commissioned as minister of the congregations of Wicaco, Kingsessing and Upper Merion.

Heretofore the Swedish crown had furnished the missionaries to America with traveling expenses, but by the decision of the royal commission for the reformation of the state machinery, on February 13, 1775, these expenses were wiped out. The Rev. Wicksell's opinion about this had been asked and consequently he submitted his opinions on March 6, 1775. Wicksell thought that he could not recommend that the poor people of the home country should expend money on behalf of people who are daily growing richer.

In 1775, began the struggle for the liberty and independence of the United States. This noble campaign, being well known and well understood, does not require to be reviewed in this work. It was natural that the Finnish descendants, some of whose forefathers had arrived to the Delaware country one hundred and thirty-six years before, were the most eager to fight for their native country. They were the first real Americans, as the Englishmen still were Englishman, and the Germans and Dutch were clinging to their languages, while the Finns already had lost all that tied them to their homelands. The Finnish and Swedish languages that they spoke, had become extinct among the Finns long since. What there was left of the Swedish language was among few newly arrived Swedes and the families of the Swedish ministers.

The old and settled area, inhabited by the Finnish descendants, was very much in the midst of the conflicts of the Revolution. The old, venerable bell of the Wicaco church was carried to safety by the American forces. In 1776, there was a naval encounter opposite the Pennsneck church between English and American naval forces. In the Wilmington church were two companies of American forces encamped in 1777. And in 1778, the English troops broke the pews of the Wicaco church to convert the building into a hospital. The Raccoon church was used for a while as barrack by the American forces and the school house was consumed by fire during the occupations.

The Swedish ministers were not quite in sympathy with the new freedom. Goransson in his provost-book had made utterances that might have cost him dearly if the men who were fighting for their country's liberty had happened to put their hands upon them. Collin likewise was arrested on February 4, 1777, by the American troops, upon information of a member of his congregation. In October of the same year, Collin was again arrested as a spy, after the battle of Red Bank, however he succeeded to get free on both occasions. He admits of having been undecided whether to withdraw behind the English lines. The Rev. Luut left the country on March 8, 1778, without having received any recall and the Rev. Mathias Hultgren was waiting in London for a chance to get passage to America, but the Rev. Daniel Kuhn never got back to his native country, he died in London, on October 7, 1776. Finally on October 19, 1779, Hultgren arrived to Philadelphia, having found chance to come over to New York on an English ship. He brought the recall for Goransson and Girelius.

The Wicaco church at this time could not be used for worship on account of damages made when the English troops used it as their hospital. In September 1780, Goransson left for Sweden, but Girelius stayed here until the next year on account of conditions in his family.

After the Revolutionary War, there were no longer Swedish services held in the old churches built by the Finns. Only in the Raccoon church Swedish was preached still about once a month for a while. The new minister, the Rev. Hultgren in writing back to Sweden about the conditions in his congregations says that: "No sane man would come to be minister with these so-called Swedish congregations, if he could have in Sweden the right idea of the conditions among the Swedish descendants, who have no more sympathy towards anything from Sweden than if it was from Turkey."

The Rev. Hultgren did not have apprehension that these "Swedish descendants" were nearer related to the Turks than to the Swedes, and that their ancestors coming from Sweden could not, for their sad experiences, live to their children the illusion of Sweden being the old, sweet homeland, but a place of persecution, massacres and violence.

The Rev. Collin likewise had many times petitioned to be recalled and on November 22, 1782, his recall was signed by the king, while at the same time Girelius was commissioned as provost although he also had already permission to go back to Sweden. Hultgren at the same time was appointed by the king to be minister of the congregations of Wicaco, Kingsessing and Upper Merion.

At this time the Raccoon congregation had started to finally build its long time contemplated new church, for this, one thousand and two hundred pounds had been subscribed and in 1784, the work was started. The new temple was ready in March 1786, and the Rev. Collin, who on account of the building of it had been interested to remain in the country a little longer, says about the new church that: "Those who have seen America, say that it has few of its equal in country places and surpasses all in the State of New Jersey." The church was built of brick, the length being sixty feet, width forty feet and height thirty feet. It had three doors and three balconies, and twenty-seven windows in two rows upon each other. It was built on the ground of the old church.

The Wicaco church and parsonage likewise were repaired soon after the war and services restored in the church.

Since the end of the war, it had been openly discussed about, that native born ministers were more suitable for the congregations, than those sent from Sweden and in July 1784, the Swedish ministers notified the authorities in Sweden about resolution passed by the congregations, upon the king's decision to withdraw the traveling expenses for the Swedish ministers, the congregations being willing, in recognition of favors extended by the Swedish kings, to pay traveling expenses for Swedish ministers who can preach in the English language.

The Rev. Hultgren left America in 1786, after having received his recall to Sweden. After him the vestry of the congregations of Wicaco, Kingsessing and Upper Merion accepted the Rev. Collin to be their minister, with the following resolution: "Whereupon the vestry do agree to receive the Rev. Mr. Collin as their minister; but at the same time reserving to themselves the right of making any new appointment hereafter, as shall be found more useful and beneficial to the said congregations of Wicaco, Kingsessing and Upper Merion. And the wardens of Wicaco church are authorized and required to write to the Archbishop of Upsala, to desire him to thank his majesty of Sweden, in the name of the congregations for his care and attention towards them heretofore and in the present instance. But as the said congregations will be better suited (the Swedish language being extinct) by the appointment of some suitable minister from this side of the water, and as the Rev. Mr. Collin has expressed a desire of returning to his native country shortly; whenever his majesty of Sweden shall think it proper and convenient to grant him his recall, the mission to these congregations will undoubtedly cease."

On account of the above resolution, the wardens of the Wicaco church, R. Keen and John Stille, wrote to Archbishop Mennander of Upsala a letter, dated at Philadelphia, on June 16, 1786, in which it is said that: "The Vestry, always maintaining a due sense of the care and attention of his present Majesty the King of Sweden and his Royal pudension towards these Churches, has agreed to acceive the Rev. Mr. Collin as their Pastor and Rector, reserving to the Congregations a right hereafter of their own appointment of a minister from this side the .water, should they find it not convenient and beneficial to themselves and for the welfare of these churches, so that hereafter it will be entirely unnecessary for any future appointment to take place from Sweden of a minister to serve in these Congregations, unless a request of that kind should be made in due form, which is not very probable, as the Swedish language is almost entirely extinct in Pennsylvania. Therefore whenever it shall please his Gracious Majesty the King of Sweden to recall from these Congregations their present Pastor Collin, the Mission will undoubtedly cease."

Since the removal of Collin to Wicaco, the congregations of Raccoon and Pennsneck have been served by Episcopal rectors. The Raccoon parish is known today as "Trinity Parish," and the town, originally named as "Sveaborg," after the fortress in the harbor of Helsingsfors, Finland, (now Suomenlinna), is known today as Swedesboro.

In the spring of 1791, Girelius left for Sweden, after his departure and ever since the Trinity Church of Wilmington has had rectors of the Protestant Episcopal Church.

The Rev. Collin was, after the departure of Pastor Girelius, compelled for domestic reasons to stay yet in the country and it seems that he was satisfied with his congregations and they with him, as Collin never left America. He worked with his congregations forty years more and died on October 7, 1831, being eighty-six years of age. After the death of the Rev. Collin, the United Congregations of Wicaco, Kingsessing and Upper Merion elected the Rev. Jehu Curtis Clay, an Episcopalian, as their rector. The Rev. Clay was of Finnish descent, belonging to the Holstein family. These churches have been ministered by the Episcopal clergyman ever since.

Thus all the sanctuaries, built by the descendants of the early Finnish colonists in America, had become Episcopal churches.